Praise for
While They Slept

"The result of Harrison's masterful embellishment is a fascinating and comprehensive examination. . . . *While They Slept* does not provide the easy answers we hope to discover in 'just the facts,' but it offers instead the richer and more enduring illumination of 'the story.'"
—*Los Angeles Times Book Review*

"[Kathryn Harrison's] telling brings moral clarity to the dark fate of a family: the daylight gaze of narrative itself as a form of empathy."
—*The New York Times Book Review*

"Harrison does a magnificent job of sorting through the heartbreak of a family tragedy. By adding insights into her own life, she brings us a little closer to understanding the resilience of the human spirit."
—*USA Today*

"[A] lucid, psychologically probing and disturbing new book [and] a morally nuanced story."
—*Time Out New York*

"You can count on Harrison for white-water prose and ferocious candor. . . . Harrison's intense and resonant inquiry affirms the cathartic power of story, and reflects on the miraculous cycle of loss and rebirth."
—*Booklist*

"Harrison is a gifted writer who tells a story beautifully."
—*Deseret Morning News*

ALSO BY KATHRYN HARRISON

FICTION
Envy
The Seal Wife
The Binding Chair
Poison
Exposure
Thicker Than Water

NONFICTION
The Mother Knot
The Road to Santiago
Saint Thérèse of Lisieux
Seeking Rapture
The Kiss

WHILE THEY SLEPT

AN INQUIRY INTO THE MURDER OF A FAMILY

KATHRYN HARRISON

BALLANTINE BOOKS • NEW YORK

While They Slept is a work of nonfiction. Some names and identifying details have been changed.

2009 Ballantine Books Mass Market Edition

Published in the United States by Ballantine Books, an imprint of The Random House Publishing Group, a division of Random House, Inc., New York.

BALLANTINE and colophon are registered trademarks of Random House, Inc.

Originally published in hardcover in the United States by Random House, an imprint of The Random House Publishing Group, a division of Random House, Inc., in 2008.

LIBRARY OF CONGRESS CATALOGING-IN-PUBLICATION DATA
Harrison, Kathryn.
While they slept: an inquiry into the murder of a family / Kathryn Harrison.
p. cm.
ISBN 978-0-345-51660-2
1. Murder—Oregon—Medford—Case studies. 2. Parricide—Oregon—Medford—Case studies. 3. Abusive parents—Oregon—Medford—Case studies. 4. Problem families—Oregon—Medford—Case studies. 5. Gilley, Billy. 6. Gilley, Jody.
I. Title.
HV6542.H37 2008
364.152'30979527—dc22   2007033519

Cover design: Christine Kell
Cover photograph: © MECKY/Getty Images

Printed in the United States of America

www.ballantinebooks.com

9 8 7 6 5 4 3 2 1

For Binky

PRELUDE

At 2:51 on the morning of Friday, April 27, 1984, the communications center for Jackson County, Oregon, took the following emergency call. All such calls are recorded; the excerpt below was transcribed from a recording. At certain points, the communications center operator (911) is speaking with the caller and, on a separate line, with the Oregon State Police (OSP).

MALE: Hello? Hello? The neighbor girl from over on—

911:    Address?

MALE: Eleven thirty-two Rossanley Drive.

911:    Uh-huh.

MALE: The neighbor girl from over on Ross Lane is here, and she, she thinks that her brother has beaten her parents with a baseball bat.

911:    Can I talk to her?

MALE: Uh, well, I don't know if she can talk or not or—

911:    How old is she?

MALE: Uh, fifteen. Sixteen.

911:    Well, could you tell her this here is the Sheriff's Office and see if maybe I can talk with her?

MALE: Yeah, okay. Hang on just a minute.

911:    We got a sixteen-year-old at a neighbor's house says her brother beat her parents with a baseball bat.

OSP: Okay, this is one at the dispatch—

911:    Sir?

GIRL:	Hello?
911:	Hi.
GIRL:	Hi.
911:	Can I help you? What's the matter?
GIRL:	My brother beat my mom and dad and sister to death with a baseball bat.
911:	What's the address?
GIRL:	Fourteen fifty-two Ross Lane.
911:	When did he do this?
GIRL:	Uh, I don't know when he did my mom and dad, but he did my sister about thirty minutes ago.
911:	Were you home?
GIRL:	I was upstairs in the bed. (*Crying*) I . . .
911:	Are you sure they're dead?
GIRL:	I'm pretty sure they are. I didn't look at them. I couldn't.
911:	Okay. What's your name?
GIRL:	Jody Gilley.
911:	Jody Gilley—G-I-L-L-E-Y?
GIRL:	Yes.
911:	Okay, Jody, what's your phone number at home?
GIRL:	Don't call there.
911:	I won't call there.
GIRL:	Seven seven three—
911:	Uh-huh.
GIRL:	Three three oh eight.
911:	Okay. What's your middle initial, Jody?
GIRL:	L.
911:	And what's the phone number there that you're calling from?
GIRL:	Seven seven nine—
911:	Uh-huh—
GIRL:	Three one oh eight.
911:	What's your brother's name?

GIRL: Billy.

911:    How old is he?

GIRL: He's eighteen.

911:    Is his the same last name?

GIRL: Yes.

911:    Just a minute. (*Inaudible; receiver is covered.*) When did he do your parents? Do you know?

GIRL: I don't know. I was just in my bed and my light, my light switch is downstairs and they flipped it on and my brother and sister came up. And he told her to stay there. And then he went down. I didn't, I'd just woken up, I didn't know what . . .

911:    Uh-huh.

GIRL: . . . was going on. Then my sister followed him down and I heard her screaming and I heard a pounding (*crying*).

911:    And did you go down?

GIRL: No. He came up. He had blood all over him and he said they were all dead.

911:    Did he leave?

GIRL: Well, I was afraid and so I just went along with him and he brought me over here, and we, we were over here and he left.

911:    Does he have a car?

GIRL: He's in my dad's Ranchero.

911:    Ranchero. What color?

GIRL: It's blue.

911:    Which way did he go?

GIRL: I think he—he said he was gonna go get a pack of cigarettes and then go home.

911:    Okay. Just a second, Jody. Hang on, okay?

GIRL: Okay.

911:    We got a possible homicide—

OSP: Oh boy.

911:    —at one four five two Ross Lane.

OSP: Ross Lane?

911: Want me to tell you what happened. I have a sixteen-year-old girl on the phone and she said she was up sleeping and her brother and sister came upstairs and her brother's eighteen years old, and he told her sister to stay up there and that he was, something was wrong with the parents, and the sister didn't stay up there, she followed him downstairs, and the girl that I have on the phone heard her screaming, and a couple minutes later the boy came up and he had blood all over him and he said they were all dead—his mom, his dad, and the sister. And he had blood all over him. He took her over to the neighbor's house. She's at one one three two Rossanley right now.

OSP: Eleven thirty-two Rossanley?

911: Uh-huh. She said the brother is in a blue Ranchero and he left and said he was gonna go to the store and then he was gonna go back home.

OSP: Blue Ranchero.

911: And he's eighteen years old. His name is Billy Gilley.

OSP: Billy . . .

911: G-I-L-L-E-Y.

OSP: G-I-L-L-E-Y.

911: Um-huh.

OSP: The parents are downstairs, dead, at this time?

911: Um-huh. And the sister. Do you want us to get Medford Ambulance to go and stand by somewhere close?

OSP: Yeah, you might. Let me get some patrols going.

911: Okay.

OSP: I'm gonna go ahead and have them contact the scene and then I'll send one over to the—

911: Jody?

GIRL: Yeah?

911: Okay, we have State Police on the way. I want you to stay right there and I'm gonna stay on the phone with you. Okay?

GIRL: Okay.

911: Just a second. Your brother lives at home with you?

GIRL: Yes.

911: Okay. Do you know what store he might go to?

GIRL: He'd a probably went to 7-Eleven.

911: (*With receiver covered*) She said he'd probably gonna go to 7-Eleven.
(*With receiver uncovered*) Okay. How long is this been?

GIRL: It . . . it was about five, six minutes. Ten minutes.

911: (*With receiver covered*) He left about five to ten minutes ago. She said he'd probably go to 7-Eleven and then go home. She said he was gonna go home after he went to the store and got some cigarettes.
(*With receiver uncovered*) Okay, Jody?

GIRL: Yeah.

911: Does your brother not like your parents or something?

GIRL: I guess.

911: Do you know why he would do something like this?

GIRL: I don't know. I mean, there's been a lot . . . we have had a lot of, um, family problems, but I never think anything bad enough to actually kill 'em.

911: Okay. Has, has he ever been violent before or anything?

GIRL: Have they?

911:      Has Billy?

GIRL: Billy. Oh, well, yeah, he can be.

911:      Was he on any drugs or has he been drinking?

GIRL: I don't know if he's on drugs or not.

911:      Okay.

GIRL: But there's guns at home and I'm afraid he's gonna come over here.

911:      There are guns at home?

GIRL: Yes. There's two pistol[s] and a rifle.

I LEARN ABOUT THE GILLEY FAMILY MURDERS ten years before I contact Jody. A friend of mine tells me about the case. She doesn't say much, only that Jody's brother killed the rest of their family while they were sleeping; that he did it because he loved Jody and hoped or believed or maybe just wished that afterward the two of them would run away together—to Reno, Nevada, my friend thinks it was. They were going to take the family car, leave their childhood home, and never return.

That's all my friend says, that's all she knows, and for ten years I ponder those few things: the murders, the crazy brother, the failed escape. I forget them sometimes, but never for long, and over time the story of the Gilley family, the little I know about it, resolves into what's more of a picture than an unfolding drama. I never embellish the scene. I don't know how, or I can't. The magnitude of the crime, of a tragedy that belongs to other people, not to me, makes it sacrosanct; it prevents me from taking license with what I've been told. Instead, my preoccupation wears it down to an essence, just as years of handling might erase details from the profile on a coin. I don't have a face for the boy or the girl. I don't see the house or the bodies within, the blood. All I see is the lateness of the hour and the silhouetted heads of two teenagers in a car, leaving the dead behind.

Sometimes I imagine headlights shining into the dark in front of them, but the two beams reveal only blackness. I—they—can't see what's ahead. What I have is just the barest idea, like a single frame taken from a film, of two teenagers—children, really, sixteen, eighteen—driving away into the night. Driving away from what most people consider impossible, an impossibly violent crime. And one that is, of course, not possible to leave behind.

Is the scene sexual? It feels that way. Not overtly, but even if the brother and sister aren't lovers, even if one never touches the other, still, when I linger at this scene, one assembled from fragments of another woman's past— alleged fragments at that, gossip, unsubstantiated—when I linger, I find it has a forbidden, sexual charge. Because my friend used the word *love*? Because she said that's why Jody's brother did it, out of his love for her?

Yes. Because love, murder, and running away together do imply sex. They do suggest an illicit erotic fixation.

We all read these stories, don't we? In the tabloids, on the Internet, in books of "true crime"? Drawn to what we don't understand, to examine lives darker and more desperate than our own. I'm worse than most, I imagine. A bad habit, reading about murder—this is how I explain it to myself—but it starts innocently enough. It's 1986, and my not-yet husband brings home a copy of a magazine, *Startling Detective*. We're graduate students studying creative writing in the Midwest. Practicing being artful, crafting good sentences, refining our ability to parse the human heart and reveal subtleties of emotion. It will amuse me, he thinks, the artlessness of the magazine.

Because there's nothing subtle about *Startling Detective*. It's sordid and pandering, with gruesome photographs. It cultivates voyeurism, unapologetic in its mission to exploit personal tragedy for mass-market entertainment. I'm fascinated, and he buys me more. They're all the same, yet I don't tire of them. In that way, they're like pornography. In other ways, too. They reveal a need I only half understand, one that finds no answer in my waking life.

Although my dreams are often bloody: I happen on the aftermath of a crime, find signs of struggle in a ransacked room. I discover myself in the role of murderer, careless about the clues I've left, sure to be caught and punished. I'm the decapitated victim, dead but somehow conscious, observing how life goes on without me.

By the time the magazine folds, I'm the mother of two young children, living in New York, working hard, without much time for guilty pursuits. Still, I haven't grown out of my taste for pulpy accounts of murder. My husband isn't sure what to make of this—my sustained interest. Whatever it means, it's not something he wants to encourage, so I end up browsing at our local bookstore, flipping through the true crime paperbacks, their covers splashed red and promising "16 Pages of Shocking Photos!" Even when I don't buy a book, I study the photo insert, as predictable, and mesmerizing, as the text. First come the baby pictures, then the graduation pictures, maybe a wedding scene, a mug shot of the killer or, if he wasn't caught, a composite drawing. And of course there are forensic photographs of the dead body, the spilled blood black where it soaked into the carpet or spread across the pavement.

It's an addiction, true crime, easy to satisfy. There's an endless supply of these books, just as there is of murder itself. Reading one on the subway, I make sure strangers can't see its cover and presume my choice of diversion reveals something about me, as it undoubtedly does.

The thing about the car, the two teenagers in the car in the middle of the night, is that it doesn't go anywhere.

The situation is dire and demands flight, but I never see the car moving. I can't. I can't picture it—them—in motion. The headlights shine onto the road. I can make myself see the surface of the asphalt, its texture, a dashed yellow line, but the car won't move.

It can't, because the lives of the people in the car, the life of the girl and the life of the boy, have been stopped. There is all that came before the murders, enough presumably to provoke them, and there is after. And those two parts, before and after, how can they be put back together? They can't, not really. So that night—the night of the murders—is separate, isolated in time. It isn't continuous with the life that came before or what will come after. It's the point of rupture, of division.

I know about this moment in a life. It's something I've thought about: the way some lives have to be begun again.

In my own case, it wasn't murder but a small and usually innocuous transaction between two people. What happened to me took place in public, and no one noticed. Jody knows of this moment in my life and its aftermath. I've written about it, and I imagine my friend mentions this when she goes to Jody on my behalf, to ask if she's willing to talk to me. In my first e-mail to Jody, when I introduce myself to her, I identify what I assume is a connection between us, this sense of having—living—a life divided into a before and after, as part of what drives my curiosity about her and her family, and the history they shared.

My life stopped the week I turned twenty. It stopped when my father, whom I'd seen only twice when I was a child, suddenly reappeared. His absence had defined my girlhood. Around it I'd constructed twenty years of fantasies. I was an unworldly twenty, with little sexual experience, and I'd never escaped, or resolved, my tortured relationship with my mother, whom I loved and distrusted. I was an only child, raised by my mother's elderly parents, because my mother insisted on living alone. I was anorexic, or I was bulimic; when I wasn't one, I was the other. I struggled with depression, although I wasn't sufficiently self-aware to perceive this and had never willingly seen a therapist. To offset despair, I used amphetamines.

My father, not yet forty, was a prepossessing figure, intelligent, handsome, charismatic. He was also arrogant and grandiose, and acknowledged people only insofar as they capitulated to his demands. But I didn't see this. How could I when I refused to admit that my father had any flaws at all? Captive to my childhood fantasies, I believed they'd come true: Here he was at last, the father I'd invented for myself. The one who knew exactly what to say—that he'd loved and missed me from the moment he and my mother separated, so much that it had nearly killed him.

Immediately, and without reservation, with neither the sense nor the means to protect myself from someone who believed he existed outside the laws that bound other mortals, I fell in love with this man, this father whom I had never known. For a week we were both guests in my mother's apartment, and at the end of this week my father kissed me good-bye, not chastely. I understood— part of me did—the future such a kiss anticipated. But I couldn't articulate it for myself, not at twenty. I didn't have words for what I knew, right away, when my father took my head in his hands and pushed his tongue in my mouth. That he had, in that moment, declared me his object, his property. That he'd taken me for himself and would demand my submission to whatever he wanted. That what he wanted would include sex.

* * *

Later, when my father insisted he couldn't share me, that I had to choose between him and my mother, I chose him. When he forced me to choose between him and the grandparents who raised me, I betrayed them as well. When he disapproved of my boyfriend, I let the boyfriend go. Whatever my father asked of me, I did. When I dropped out of school because I couldn't get myself to class, couldn't think straight enough to take notes or exams, my father was not worried but pleased. Perhaps it was an unconscious wish we shared, that I could become the child he'd lost so long before, stripped of all I'd acquired growing up apart from him.

Or maybe that's as romantic as it sounds, a conceit, and it was never about retrieving what had been taken from us. Our anger dovetailed—was that it?—and we found ourselves allied against my mother, intent on wounding her by destroying me.

I've struggled to figure it—myself—out. There isn't any other subject I've examined with such perseverance. No interpretation, however, changes what happened.

I resisted his sexual advances. I did for as long as I could. But by then it was too late. I had no one, only him, and he wore me down.

It took four years to deliver me to the place where I saw that the person I used to call myself was gone. And all of it, all that transpired, was foretold by that first, single kiss in the Los Angeles International Airport. We were alone there, as my mother hadn't accompanied us; she hadn't wanted to see him off. "You'll miss your flight," I said when he didn't react to a second boarding call. Instead of picking up his bag, my father moved a step closer to me and took my head in both his hands. He held me so that I couldn't turn away, and he filled my mouth with his tongue, but he didn't hurt me, not physically. Still, I was immediately disabled, too shocked to push his big body away from mine, too shocked to struggle, or to think, to make the words follow one another inside my head. Around us, people walked, they waved and called out to one another. Airline personnel announced delays and departures. Planes took off and landed, the high-pitched whine of their engines penetrating walls and windows. Inside myself, though, I had fallen silent.

After, when my father withdrew from me and boarded his plane, I didn't move. His flight left, then another took off, and another. Eventually I was alone at the gate, standing where he'd left me, my hand still covering my mouth, the feel of his tongue, its muscular, wet force, still with me.

Now, remembering that girl, I wonder that she didn't think to rinse out her mouth. To do something—anything. Would it have mattered? Perhaps. Not because what her father did could have been washed away, but had she been able to think of taking herself to the women's room and turning on a tap, had she been able to think of anything at all, to respond in any way, then she might have been all right, she might have been strong enough to refuse her father.

Instead, she stood motionless among the travelers, everyone hurrying forward into his or her life. Everyone except for her.

Jody and I exchange e-mails and agree upon a time to meet, 7 P.M., and a restaurant where we can talk. She knows what I want from her: to see into her family's history; to see into her brother and the people he killed; and into her. I want to know how much she has kept of her sixteen-year-old self, to learn enough about her past that I can visualize a person who no longer exists, a girl whose brother beat their family to death with a baseball bat and who wanted, then, to run away with her.

I know that the adult Jody, now thirty-seven, educated at Georgetown University and at ease among the power elite on Capitol Hill, a communications strategist who has worked with such cultural behemoths as the Kennedy Center, the American Film Institute, and Sundance Institute, must have either buried or silenced or lost the girl she was. I know this not because Jody has told me so, but her continued success in the sophisticated world she's chosen for herself must depend on the erasure of her past, the disappearing of the girl she was at sixteen. She can be one or the other Jody, but she cannot be both. I don't see how she can be both.

"I'm trying to understand your story," I write in my first e-mail to Jody. "To get some kind of hold on what happened to you, and how it is that you continued in your life, when that life was violently interrupted and had to be begun again. There must be many of us whose lives have been divided into a before and after, with an accident, a death, a crime, a crisis, some moment or year or relationship that came between and changed everything. I want to see how your life moved forward from that point of division."

If I have an endless appetite for reading about murder, for seeing how yet another young woman's life is ended, I also need to hear—perhaps I need to tell—the other story, the one about the girl that gets away, who goes on to invent another self, another life.

"This is the story of my rebirth," Jody wrote when she was twenty-five, the opening line of her own account of the murders, titled "Death Faces" and submitted as her senior thesis for graduation from Georgetown. It's a project of narrative nonfiction, an ambitious project, I think, brave. Jody sends me a copy a few weeks after our first meeting. *This is the story of my rebirth.* Of course,

I think, she would have to believe this; she would have to believe that she has been reborn. And yet I'm surprised enough that I stop reading, stop right there, before I've begun. Surprised by what? Her honesty? The relationship of her statement—the statement of a stranger—to my own life?

Or maybe it's her perspective—whatever allows her to introduce the story of her family's annihilation as a beginning rather than an end—that strikes me as unusual.

In the years after I broke away from my father, I dreamed often of car accidents or of buildings collapsing. In these dreams, by some miracle or fluke—it's never a function of ability or intelligence—I escape from the wreckage, I run and keep running until I am some distance away. When I reach a place of safety, I begin to inventory my body, which is naked, stripped of clothing. In the dream, I run my hands over my arms and chest, down my flanks and my legs. I touch every part of myself I can reach, counting fingers and toes, the way a mother does a newborn, to see if I'm intact, all there. How much have I managed to take with me? Sometimes I appear to be all right, at first I do, but I'm injured in a place I can't see. Blood leaks from a wound I can't find. Often a leg is gone and this perplexes me. How have I escaped—run away— without it? In a recurrent dream, my face has fallen into small pieces, like those of a jigsaw puzzle, and I gather up all I can and set off to find a surgeon who can put me back together into a person I am able to recognize.

"We've both forsaken the West for the East coast," I write, e-mailing Jody before we meet, "and I wonder if you feel as I do, that the past is another life, in another country, a place you've left forever. The people with whom you and I grew up are gone—dead or permanently separated from us by what came to pass. You've abandoned the landscape, started over. And yet, of course, you remain yourself. You are the girl who was in the house that night with your brother. You and he are your parents' children.

"I remain fascinated by my father," I tell her. "I don't know who he is. I rebuilt myself after he dismantled me. I feel there are parts of myself that he has yet to relinquish or that I have yet to reclaim. Perhaps, in contemplating you and your brother, studying what came before and precipitated the murders and what has happened since in the lives of the two survivors, I can articulate something both of us want to understand. I can't tell you what that something is, not yet. I'd have to write my way toward it."

Later, after I read her thesis, I think: Was this what Jody was doing, at twenty-five, in writing "Death Faces"? Was she trying to understand how she'd survived, or even *that* she'd survived? And what about her brother, Billy? Because the more I know about Jody, the more I want to understand him, as well, a boy of eighteen at the time of the murders. He had to go on, too; he had to have some kind of life after. And of course I want to know what made him do it, what happened in that family before.

I know my history and Jody's are not comparable, that the massacre of her family was catastrophic in a way I can barely begin to imagine. Almost everything she knew was destroyed, lost. The connection between us— a parallel I assume and she confirms—is that both she and I had a previous self who no longer exists. We didn't arrive at our adult selves through the usual transitions, the normal trials. Instead, a rupture occurred, a violence was done to each of us, an act or acts that were outside our ability to avoid or manage or even understand—the kind of thing that wasn't supposed to happen, didn't happen, could not happen. When it did, its effect was like the foundation being torn out from under a house. Everything came apart; what was salvageable had to be reassembled into a new whole. The adult Jody may be rebuilt from pieces of the girl she was before, but she is not that same girl. The original Jody is gone. I know this from my own history. And I know that in terms of my telling the story of her family, the difference between Jody's and my experiences is as important as the intersection. Were Jody's a story of incest (rather than one that may turn out to include incestuous motivations), I couldn't approach her, it, as I can a story of murder, which, unlike incest, remains for me an impossible something, the kind of violent rupture that is final, and that wouldn't, couldn't happen in a family.

There's a part of the analogy I draw between Jody and myself that she rejects even before we meet. "Your brother lives, exiled from you, and from everyone else," I write in my first e-mail to her. "And my father lives, also and necessarily exiled from me. I wonder if your brother and my father are not similar figures, not through their actions but in the way they exist for us: out of reach, the unknowable recipients of our love, anger, confusion, fear, and more."

Jody replies immediately. I'm wrong, she tells me. She doesn't love her brother. She's tried to, but she can't. "It's me who is out of reach and unknowable," she writes, "and I reserve all my anger, confusion, and fear for myself."

* * *

A self who is out of reach and unknowable. I read those words many times before the two of us meet, trying to understand them, her. Is she stating a human truth that applies to all of us, being philosophical in suggesting that no one can ever know him- or herself completely? Or is she acknowledging something peculiar to herself and, by extension, others who have experienced violence, trauma? Are people like us left with parts of our own psyches walled off, removed from our ability to access them? And are those parts alive? Or are they dead? Are they aspects of ourselves that were destroyed by the shock, whatever it was, and interred within us?

I bring the printout of Jody's e-mail with me when I drive to the restaurant we chose for our first meeting, a Japanese place not far from where she lives in Washington, D.C. Parked a few blocks away, I consider her words, propped on the steering wheel. It's 6:45. Having allowed myself time to get lost, I find the restaurant easily and am early, with minutes to fill. I turn the radio on, then off. I read the e-mail, watch traffic move along Connecticut Avenue, the busy thoroughfare that runs through the capital. A fine rain has begun to fall; the street is wet. Long, dazzling reflections of red taillights spill over its dark surface.

Washington is a city I know only through my husband's family, and whenever I visit I stay with my mother-in-law, who lives near Rock Creek Park. Often when I run in the thickly wooded park, I lose my way. I follow its deeper, unpaved paths and my mind wanders, I forget to watch for trail markers. Today, before I shower and dress to meet Jody, I go for a run and get so turned around that I emerge more than a mile from where I intended to exit. It frightens me sometimes, getting lost. I remember stories of women who disappeared, what's left of their bodies found months later in one of the park's many dells or ditches, and I chastise myself for choosing so lonely a place to run. But solitude helps me think, running helps me think, and I like the way the earth absorbs my footfalls, so that I hardly hear myself as I pass among the trees.

Maybe, too, I want the sense of danger, court it the way I used to as a young woman, twenty-five, twenty-six, when I took recklessly long swims at night. Each time, I walked out of the dark water breathless, exhilarated, my legs scraped and stinging where I'd brushed against rocks I hadn't seen. Again I'd escaped. The heaving black ocean with its wraithlike tendrils of eelgrass reaching around my legs, its hunger, never satisfied, for another and another sacrifice, the gnashing and churning of its depths—I'd swum out of it. My old self, the girl I'd been before, waited in the shadows against the cliff, shoved with my towel in a crease between the rocks. Or maybe I'd taken her along, buried within me. In either case I'd proved it again: the dead girl couldn't drag me under, she couldn't slow my speed.

A self who is out of reach and unknowable. We all have such a self, of course, at least one. But for people who are fated to sift through the debris that remains in the wake of a family's disintegration, the ones who can't stop searching for the piece, perhaps very small, that might explain what happened and why, that secret self whom we glimpse but never truly see can take on a sinister cast. She is dangerous, perhaps, or she is wicked. She is guilty of something—why else would she refuse to be known? She is broken and frail, empty to the point of transparence. Because she remains hidden, she invites a measure of dread. Who is this self that consciousness—conscience?—is unable or unwilling to acknowledge?

If any admission by Jody other than this, of a secret,

unknowable self, could have fixed my desire to understand her life and the lives of her parents and siblings, I don't know what it might be.

What follows is a narrative of a family tragedy, my reconstruction of the events that occurred on April 27, 1984, their antecedents, and their still unfolding consequences for Jody, and for her brother, Billy, who remains in prison. Studying the Gilleys required making inquiries into myself as well, attempts to understand how my enduring fascination with the violent end of another woman's family informs the way I regard my own, very different past.

Jody and Billy provided most of the information on which this account is based. With Jody as my guide, I visited the places where the Gilleys lived and where three of them died, and it was through Jody that I contacted her brother, Billy, with whom she does not correspond and whom I've come to know. Jody introduced me to other people who were affected by the Gilley murders; she and her brother allowed me access to documents essential to my re-creating their lives and the lives and deaths of their parents and of their little sister, Becky.

Mine is not the first narrative of the Gilley family but rests upon and responds to others: the case files of social workers; the memories of people I interviewed; the records kept by law enforcement and by the Children's Services Division of Jackson County, Oregon; the ten psychiatric evaluations made of Billy between the ages of thirteen and thirty-five; the transcript of his trial for murder; the reports compiled by two private investigators hired by Billy's appeal attorney; the affidavits collected for his appeal for a retrial; the appellant briefs that argue against claims made by his appeal. Among all the efforts to understand how a child is driven to so extreme and desperate an act as killing his parents and sister, most revealing are the stories, both fiction and non-fiction, that Jody and Billy have written in the years since the murders. Their words are very much a part of this book; their various accounts demonstrate how essential the process of telling and retelling the story of their family has been to their surviving its destruction.

For Jody and for Billy, the work of putting together a coherent narrative from what were often dislocated, fractured memories has been inseparable from—and even, I believe, the same undertaking as—reassembling what remained of themselves, of salvaging what they could of the children they had been before—before he murdered his family, and before she endured the kind of psychic assault most of us will never have to contemplate.

I

BEFORE

He wanted to marry her. Billy Gilley wanted to fuck his sister. He viewed himself as her white knight, and their parents as the oppressors he was going to save them from.

THAD GUYER
in a conversation with the author,
June 22, 2005

When it comes to family, it would seem I suffer from a malediction.

BILLY GILLEY
in a letter to Jody dated
January 1, 2005

ON THE MORNING OF THURSDAY, APRIL 26, 1984, Jody Gilley went to her neighbor Kathy Ackerson's before school. As was her habit, she went out the kitchen door and cut across the field that separated their two homes. Jody and Kathy had gotten to know each other the previous year, on the bus to and from Medford High, where they were now sophomores. They didn't socialize during the school day; Jody hung with a straighter crowd than Kathy, who by her own admission was something of a stoner. As Jody describes it, she and Kathy weren't best friends, but they liked each other and were frequently in each other's homes. "My next-field neighbor," they called each other. It wasn't unusual for Jody to finish getting dressed over at Kathy's.

"Because you wanted to wear something your mother didn't approve of?" I ask Jody.

"No, the dressing-sexy-for-school thing happened much earlier, in fifth or sixth grade. By tenth grade it was all about looking punk. Ratting my hair, applying dark eye makeup, piercing my ears with safety pins. And all of that happened at school, in the girls' bathroom. At Kathy's it was just, you know, getting ready for school together. Me probably using the Mary Kay makeup she had because her mom sold it, whereas my makeup was bottom-drawer Fred Meyer lip gloss and Maybelline. Also, I was curling-iron challenged, and Kathy could get that perfect eighties feather in a way I couldn't."

I nod. Long, auburn, glossy: Jody's hair is the first thing I notice about her. The way she gathers it into one hand and pulls it forward in a thick rope over one shoulder—the image stays with me after our first meeting, I'm not sure why. Perhaps because it's a pretty gesture. Jody herself is pretty, with a heart-shaped face and hazel eyes, not much if any makeup. Dressed in dark pants and a denim jacket, high heels. When she talks, all the emphasis is in her voice. She speaks without using her hands, as I was taught, unsuccessfully, to do.

Nothing about Jody's appearance surprises me— I didn't, after all, have any idea what she looked like— but her physical presence is itself unsettling. The Jody I know is sixteen, a girl in a car with her brother, the two of them motionless. Petrified, as if the murders had been, like the head of a Gorgon, a sight that turned them to stone. For ten years I've known Jody not as a woman but as a character, one among the many in my head, images taken from books and movies, not so much people as ideas of people, whom I expect never to encounter in the flesh.

There was more to getting dressed at Kathy's than looking the way Jody wanted for school. It was easier in the house across the field. Kathy's parents weren't always fighting with each other or screaming at their children. Her mother didn't look for excuses to punish her daughter; she didn't throw things at Kathy or pin her down and blow cigarette smoke in her face just out of meanness. She didn't denigrate her children or act like reading was a waste of time, the way Jody's parents did. The fact that Jody spent so much of her life hidden behind the cover of a book was a source of conflict at home; her family understood her insatiable, nearly compulsive reading for what it was: escape, judgment. Jody would rather be anywhere than there, with them; she was just biding her time until she could walk out the door, old enough that the police wouldn't come after her and bring her back, as they did her brother when he ran away.

Kathy had brothers, but they were younger than Billy, thirteen and fourteen, and they were good kids, normal anyway. They didn't cause the kind of trouble Billy did— didn't get kicked out of Bible camp for smoking in the woods, didn't get arrested for breaking into cars or setting people's living rooms on fire. They didn't sneak into Kathy's room at night to put their hands between her legs.

After they got dressed that day, the girls rode the bus to Medford High, but, as Jody would tell Detective Richard Davis the morning after the murders, they never entered the building. "We went to Games People Play [a video arcade] for a while and then we went over to a guy's house. And we stayed there for a while and then we went to Pappy's and got potatoes and then we walked home."

Jody had skipped school before. According to Kathy Ackerson, interviewed in 1999 by a private investigator, Jody cared about her grades and made straight A's— "B's," Jody corrects—but she was sixteen years old, and it was hard to have to answer to someone every minute of every day. A few unstructured hours, safe from the strife at home and apart from the demands of her teachers, must have presented a significant temptation.

"Mrs. Gilley was very controlling," Kathy explained to the private investigator dispatched by Billy's attorney for appeal. "Jody had to sneak around to do things she wanted to do," things most parents considered harmless. Not only did Jody have "more than her share of household chores . . . the laundry, the dishes, and the cooking," but while Jody worked, her friend remembered, Linda Gilley just "sat around and smoked cigarettes."

The way Kathy saw it, "there was a war going on between Jody and her mother." She "never heard anyone in the Gilley family say 'I love you' . . . never heard either parent, Mr. or Mrs. Gilley, compliment or give positive strokes to any of the kids."

That Thursday, after Kathy came home to discover the school had telephoned to report her absence, she called the Gilleys' house to see if Jody had gotten in trouble, and if so, how much. She knew Jody's brother was beaten severely when he disobeyed or was caught in a lie, and although Jody doesn't remember having been whipped the way Billy was, not by the time she was in high school, anyway, it was Kathy's impression that Jody suffered her share of physical abuse. She remembered bruises, she told the private investigator. Once, she thought she'd seen a cigarette burn.

But when Kathy called the Gilleys' house, she didn't get to speak with her friend. Instead, Jody's mother, Linda, "answered the phone and said that Jody was grounded until she was eighteen and then slammed the phone down." For the rest of the evening the phone was busy—Kathy presumed it had been taken off the hook—and she didn't see Jody again until 1:34 the next morning.

The idea of being grounded for two years wouldn't have struck the teenaged Jody as unlikely. The way things turned out, she was pretty much always in trouble, she tells me. Punishments overlapped; they were subject to her mother's capricious revisions. On any given occasion, whether Jody was actually grounded or not made little difference. If Linda didn't want her daughter to go out, she'd just say Jody hadn't done the dishes the right way, or had forgotten to dust the living room, or to pick up after Becky, or whatever else came to mind—it didn't matter what.

With a few significant exceptions, Jody's memory of the afternoon of April 26 aligns with what her brother recounts for me when I visit him in prison the following fall, and with his sworn statement: the affidavit he prepared in 1996 for his appeal for a retrial. Billy, who had dropped out of school after the ninth grade, was home before Jody returned that day and overheard his mother making plans to trap her daughter in a lie. Having learned from the school's attendance officer that Jody hadn't shown up for class, Linda told the children's father that, as Billy stated in his affidavit, she "was going to pretend not to know about it, so she could catch Jody." Lest Billy try to warn his sister before Linda had a chance to deceive her, Linda "looked straight at [Billy] . . . and told [him] to keep [his] mouth shut."

When Jody came walking up the road, Billy, who had been watching for the arrival of the school bus, went out to meet her. Linda was too quick, however, and passed him, heading toward the mailbox to make a show of looking inside, "as if to check for the mail" she'd already collected. With their mother hovering too close for them to exchange a word in private, Billy "was afraid to say anything."*

"Why didn't you come home on the bus?" Linda asked Jody.

"I got off at Kathy's and walked," Jody told her.

---

*The account Billy gives me in person is nearly identical to that in his affidavit, prepared twelve years after the murders. Unless otherwise attributed, Billy's quoted dialogue is taken directly from his affidavit.

The scene Billy describes played out just as his mother had scripted it. "Oh, really?" Linda asked Jody. "The school called to say you weren't in first or second period."

Jody tells me she was ready with an answer. "Well, you know how they screw up sometimes," she said to her mother. "Because when I'm tardy they've already took the card down to the office."

The three had reached the kitchen door when, Jody told Detective Davis, her brother, who was carrying his base-ball bat, said he'd "like to bump [their parents] off with it . . . pound them in." Billy contends that it was Jody who mentioned physical retribution first, telling him under her breath that she'd "like to smash our mom's face in."

Linda ordered Billy to stay outside, and he did, his af-fidavit continues, "but just for a little bit. When I got to the living room . . . I heard my mom telling Jody that she knew Jody had skipped all day." It was both chil-dren's impression that Linda was delighted to have caught her daughter in a lie on top of truancy. "Drool-ing," Billy says to me of his mother's eagerness to corner Jody, "foaming at the mouth."

Then, as both Billy and Jody remember, Billy asked Jody a question. Was she all right?, he wanted to know. "Why don't you ask mom?" Jody said. "She has all the answers." At this, Jody told Detective Davis, her mother "got mad and slapped me for being cocky."

"I did have a tendency to mouth off," she tells me.

Even though the family wasn't alone—Glenn Riggs, who worked for Bill Sr., was present—Billy says their fa-ther stood up from where he was sitting on the couch, unbuckled his belt, and pulled it out from his pant loops. He started walking toward Jody, "yelling that he was going to beat her ass." That this transpired in front of his father's employee was something Billy found "es-pecially galling," reported the psychiatrist who inter-viewed Billy two months after the murders.

When Jody's father came at her with his belt, she protested that at sixteen she was too old to be thrashed, and Bill backed off, warning his daughter that she'd better not skip school again. Jody promised she wouldn't and asked her parents what her punishment would be, but Linda hadn't decided and sent Jody to her room. Interviewed later, for Billy's pre-sentencing report, Glenn Riggs characterized their interaction as "short-lived and not flagrant." Nonetheless, he was embarrassed to have witnessed the eruption of a domestic conflict, and he got up to go. Bill and Linda walked Riggs out, and Billy took his chance to run upstairs to Jody's room, the baseball bat still in his hand.

"I asked her if she was all right," Billy said, and Jody told him she "hated our mom and dad and wished they were dead." It wasn't fair, she complained, that when Billy used to get into trouble, their parents would let him off with a warning the first time and punish him only if he repeated the offense, whereas they never gave her that second chance.

As both Jody and Billy recall, Billy became extremely agitated at the suggestion that their parents had ever shown him any leniency whatsoever. He reminded Jody that on many occasions their father had taken him out to the barn and whipped him with a hose until his back was covered with welts and that she'd seen the "black and blue marks where [their] father had beat [him] with his fist."

Describing the incident, Billy recalls that he and Jody continued speaking in this vein, comparing the histories of their punishments. It is at this point that their accounts diverge, over the subject of sexual abuse. Speaking with me, Billy doesn't waver even as much as a word from what he stated in his affidavit: Jody told him "the beatings were nothing compared with our dad molesting her," and she knew their father was "going to try it again."

"Why did she think that?" Billy tells me he asked his

sister, alarmed, and she confided in him that she "noticed our dad stares at her while touching his penis.

"I told her that our mom wouldn't let that happen," and Jody said, "Mom didn't care what he did to her, that Mom had it out for her, and if Mom cared then our dad wouldn't still be living there."

Jody, who reported her father's leering at her and his propositioning her, denies her father ever molested her. For Detective Davis she recounted a different, shorter dialogue between her and her brother, one that made no reference to any sexual impropriety on anyone's part. She told the detective that while Billy was talking—ranting, really—she "just sat there, and he [Billy] just said he'd like to get, he'd like to get rid of them."

Detective Davis, who identified himself at Billy's trial as the one who "more or less directed" the investigation of the murders, interviewed Jody immediately after Billy was taken into custody and again ten hours later, pushing her to recall Billy's "exact words as best you can remember," in hopes of establishing that her brother had announced a clear intention to murder their parents that very night.

But years of physical and emotional abuse had created a context from which it was difficult, perhaps impossible, for Jody to tease out an unambiguous threat. Both she and Billy had wished their parents dead. They'd said outright to each other that their parents were horrible, wicked people who deserved to die for the cruelties they'd visited upon their children. In what was a very human response to neglect, battery, and entrapment, each had fantasized aloud about how he or she might go about killing them. Kathy, who remembered Jody studying how to be a secret agent, said that Jody told her "she could make a miniature bomb and fantasized about blowing up her parents." Jody told Detective Davis that Billy had had the idea to "bash their heads in . . . rent a boat and tie rocks to their feet and throw them in a river."

That two teenagers who had endured year after year of "atrocities which society refused to recognize"—these are the words that Jody used in "Death Faces" to describe a childhood in which one after another social worker failed to respond to evidence of abuse—might dream up violent means of avenging their suffering and escaping their tormentors is neither a crime nor a surprise. In fact, none of Jody's answers to Detective Davis's questions suggest she found her brother's comments shocking or even unusual.

"He just said he'd like to get . . . he'd like to get rid of them."

"Did he say 'get rid of them'?" Davis asked her.

"I don't know if he said . . . I don't remember how he said it, but I know he said something like that. But I never listen to him when he talks like that because I've just . . . I don't listen to him a lot of the time. Just, you know, he's talking and I'll just shake my head."

Despite the inconsistencies among the siblings' various reports—Jody's immediate answers to the police, her subsequent answers in court, her affidavit, her personal written accounts, her current memories, Billy's statements to the police, his interviews with forensic psychiatrists, his affidavit, his personal written accounts, and his current memories—it seems that on the afternoon of April 26, 1984, Jody and Billy engaged in what she understood to be a fantasy of revenge and what he believed was her sincere wish that he kill their abusive parents. Had Jody thought her brother was seriously considering murdering their mother and father, she wouldn't have given him what he received as her tacit approval. Had Billy not misinterpreted her silence—her lack of dissent—as support for his at last taking an unbearable situation into his hands, repaying violence with violence, he might not have killed Bill and Linda Gilley and mortally wounded his younger sister that night.

THE STORY OF THE GILLEY FAMILY BEGINS with an ill-advised romance. Linda Louise Higdon was in high school when she fell in love with exactly the wrong boy. At least this was the opinion of her adoptive mother, Betty Glass, whose 1996 affidavit for Billy's appeal bears witness to her disapproval. "Linda started talking about marrying Bill Gilley, Sr., the father of Billy Gilley, Jr., when she was sixteen years old. Before she started talking about marrying Bill I had seen and heard how he treated his own mother. I remember that Bill was an excellent mechanic but that when his mother would ask him to fix something wrong with her car that he would tell her to 'fix it yourself.' . . . I told Linda that any man who talked to his mother the way Bill did, I would not marry him."

The Gilleys, Betty had concluded, were low class, no better than their forebears, who had been among the first significant wave of refugees fleeing Ireland's catastrophic potato famine of 1846 to 1850. Subsistence farmers for generations, inured to hardship and to hunger, to fate's commonplace rearrangement of human agendas, the Gilleys' Irish ancestors settled in the Texas and Oklahoma panhandles. Seemingly tethered to the underclass, they'd struggled to survive even in a new land of promise, and when drought arrived in the 1920s, famine pushed at least a few Gilleys to a more distant frontier. Among those who flooded California's San Joaquin Valley looking for migrant work was Billy and Jody's grandfather, William Gilley, of whom only a souvenir photograph remains. Taken in Paris on the occasion of the city's liberation from

Nazi Gemany—a seal dated 1945 is superimposed on the print—the card is inscribed "To Billie My Only Son, Love Your Dad." The man in the photograph is clean-shaven, handsome, and completely without expression. He appears as if suspended in a state below consciousness, waiting for an animating jolt.

Whatever William Gilley's nature might have been before he was drafted and sent overseas to war, the soldier who came home was an alcoholic and a wife beater. His son, Bill, who was working in the fields by the age of eight—the fastest potato picker ever, in his mother's estimation—took it upon himself to defend his mother and two younger sisters from his father's blows, inviting retribution even as he learned how to be a father from the poor example whose fists he dodged. He wasn't a young man to waste much time thinking, and he had his own quick temper. Probably, he absorbed these lessons in brutality without any awareness of doing so. Later, much later, Bill's mother would reminisce about Bill's promising her he'd "kill the bastard," conveying regret she'd never given her son the chance to make good on his threat. Instead, she threw her violent husband out of the house and set about divorcing him.

William, however, saved her the trouble. While crossing the highway to get to the liquor store on the other side, William was run over by a truck. Having returned home from war with his body intact, he lost both of his legs, belatedly joining the ranks of veterans whose limbs had been sacrificed in a more honorable pursuit. Two stories elaborate on William's eventual death; both are set on the end of a pier. In the one Jody tells me, her grandfather is fishing from his wheelchair when a thief creeps up from behind, lifts his wallet, and pushes him into the water. In the other, Billy's version, William isn't fishing but rolls himself off the end of the pier intentionally, choosing death over the indignity and impotence he'd brought upon himself. In the absence of any evidence, the difference between the two accounts is significant only for what it reveals about the siblings. Jody attributes her grandfather's death to a malignant force outside of his volition. Billy presumes it to have been a suicide: a culminating act of self-destruction; an admission of despair, of defeat. Whether Billy is making a judgment against his father's father and thus his own male inheritance or projecting his self-loathing onto his grandfather, Billy has decided William's death was one he brought upon himself.

Widowed, Bill's mother, Essie, found a man less inclined to hit her when he was drunk, and she married him. According to Billy, the two made a contentious if not physically violent couple—Jody remembers visits to their house as comparatively peaceful—and while Bill's new stepfather didn't beat him, neither did he show him the interest or affection that might have compensated for his own father's lapses. Bill quit school after the tenth grade. He knew how to make a car run and how to dig a spud out of the ground. He may never have considered it: how it was possible to come all the way across an ocean, from the old world to the new, just to go on picking potatoes and drinking yourself to death.

Linda's father, like Bill's, had also drifted west during the thirties, joining the general exodus of the Dust Bowl years and settling in California. When Linda was born, her father, Lonnie Higdon, gave his occupation as "transfer man" for the McCloud River Lumber Company in Mount Shasta, California. Linda's mother, Phyllis Lorraine Tallerico, came from Oakland, a "pure-blooded Italian," Billy calls his grandmother, who remained in northern California all her life. That the surname Phyllis used, Tallerico, was neither her husband's nor her father's suggests she may have had an earlier marriage, which, given she was only twenty-four at Linda's birth, would have to have been brief. As temporary, perhaps, as the one that followed it, to Lonnie. Linda wasn't even a year old when her mother discovered that Lonnie was cheating on her and shot him dead, earning herself the epithet by which she'd be remembered long after people forgot her real name: the Crazy Italian. Found legally insane, Phyllis Tallerico was sent to a state mental institution and remained there for seven years. Upon her release, she moved to San Francisco, where she lived alone, writing letters and sending cards to her little girl, who never received them.

Lonnie's sister, Betty Jo Higdon Glass, had taken her niece, Linda, to raise as her own daughter, without allowing even so remote a contamination as a birthday greeting from her crazy mother. Betty, who had married a widowed school bus driver named David Glass, was unable to conceive a child of her own. Tragic as Linda's circumstances were, Betty received the news of Lonnie's murder and her sister-in-law's imprisonment as an annunciation. Fate, if not God, had circumvented biology and delivered a baby into her arms. An attractive woman, her career as a model noted in a caption under her picture in a small-town paper from northern California, Betty dressed Linda like a doll, favoring her niece over her two stepchildren and encouraging what would become Linda's preoccupation with her appearance, if not exactly vanity. Jealous of this interloper, with whom they shared no blood, David Glass's children never let Linda forget that her real mother was insane and had murdered her father.

Whatever excuse the Glasses gave when they refused to give their daughter permission to marry Bill Gilley, his family understood that they had been judged and

found wanting, and in turn voiced their disapproval of
the teenagers' plan. But young love can draw at least as
much energy from obstacles as from encouragement. On
Thursday, November 28, 1962, Linda wrote to Bill, who
was serving a drunk driving sentence in the San Luis
Obispo county jail, that the dean of girls had called her
stepfather in for a meeting at the high school and told
them both that she was at risk of being expelled if her
grades didn't improve. As Bill was himself a dropout,
the threat was not as great as her parents would have
wished, and rather than waiting to be dismissed, Linda
quit.

All Linda wanted, she wrote the boy she loved, was to
"get out of the house and find a way up there" to be
near him, a plan Betty thwarted by sending Linda to
what was in essence a juvenile detention home for girls
whose parents had run out of patience with their sexual
independence if not outright delinquency. There Linda
would remain, against her will, for two long months,
time enough, her parents must have hoped, to cool her
ardor for Bill Gilley. That Linda had decided to drop out
of school for love of him only confirmed that Bill was a
bad influence on her. But not one whose spell could be
broken by reform school. Linda came home even more
intent on marrying Bill Gilley than she had been when
her parents sent her away. If she'd learned anything
while she was gone, it was to regard her mother and father as enemies to her happiness.

She was nearly seventeen, she reminded her parents.
In little longer than a year, the law would allow her to
marry whomever she pleased, no matter what they or
anyone else thought of him. Betty knew when she was
beaten. She hadn't changed her mind about Bill; she still
thought he was common, ill mannered, and, to use
Billy's word, "bone-lazy"—incapable of keeping a job if
he managed to get one. But given Linda's determination,

which made it impossible to guess where love left off and pigheadedness took over, their continuing to fight about Bill could accomplish nothing but further estrangement between mother and daughter.

On the eve of Valentine's Day, 1963, Bill Gilley and Linda Higdon were married in Las Vegas, Nevada, with the grudging approval of her parents. The groom was six months shy of twenty, the bride still sixteen, a lovely-looking girl, as Jody remembers from photographs of her mother taken around the same time, with big, dark eyes, olive skin, and tumbling masses of black hair. But beauty is no guarantee of happiness, and Bill and Linda's wasn't a match made in heaven, not any more than Betty predicted. The handwriting, if not on the wall, was still there to be read: two problems that would prove insurmountable for the young couple were those they'd spelled out for themselves in the letters they exchanged while Bill was in jail.

The first was alcoholism, which had made it necessary for the couple to communicate by mail while Bill served out a DWI sentence that seems not to have been an occasion for shame or concern. In fact, Jody remembers the incident that led to her father's arrest described as if it had been a cartoon misadventure, in which "silly Daddy had driven off a curve and landed on the roof of a house," an unexpected frolic rather than evidence of a serious problem. Nineteen is young to be enslaved to a disease that typically develops over the course of years, but Bill was the son of an alcoholic, and his mother and stepfather were drinkers as well, who, Billy tells me, encouraged grandchildren as young as eight to sip freely from their glasses. Probably they'd given him a head start.

The second was infidelity. Each of Linda's letters to Bill reveals not only her fundamental insecurity but also doubts about the permanence of Bill's affection for her. Having gotten a haircut, she told Bill how much older it made her look. "You think you'll still love me in short hair?" she asked, betraying a concern that her looks might not be good enough to keep his interest. A first postscript excuses her messy handwriting; a second inquires if Bill would be angry if she were to go to a movie with a friend's brother, for whom she had no romantic feelings—"Tell me if you object, O.K.?"; the last ends with the entreaty, "Let's not fight because I love you and I want us to be happy together forever." The next day, Linda wrote Bill again, addressing him as "Babe," and focusing on an unresolved—and, she seems to suspect already, irresolvable—conflict over his seeing other girls while demanding that she remain faithful to him. "I want to be your wife, but am I going to have a cheating husband?" she demanded.

"Honey, I miss you so much I stay nerves [sic] all the time," Bill replied, and apologized for having hurt her. "Its [sic] that I love you so much." He couldn't make any promises about getting married when he was in jail, where he "can't even think straight," and where, separated from her, he didn't know what was "going on." Resorting to a favorite rhetorical trick of philanderers, he implied Linda was the one who wasn't to be trusted, alluding to a pessimistic account of his prospects from her friend Vicki. "If you don't [love me] tell me so I can quit making plans about us," he concluded, having avoided the issue of his cheating on her and threatening to abandon her if she wouldn't reaffirm her love.

Months before they were married, the pattern for their life together had been set.

ARTICULATE, POISED, THE THIRTY-SEVEN-YEAR-old woman sitting on the couch across from my chair is hard to imagine as having once been the girl who spoke to the emergency operator, the one who said, for example, "He'd a probably went to 7-Eleven." It's in her diction, her impeccable syntax, and especially in her frame of reference. Greek myth, Shakespeare, Dostoyevsky, Dickens, Camus, Sartre: it's a long list that accrues over the months of our continued conversations and correspondence, one whose disproportionate focus on warfare, cruelty—Elie Wiesel—torture, faith, apostasy—Bruno Bettelheim—justice, and moral responsibility bears witness to Jody's struggle to understand the murders her brother committed. Not his motives, she knew those, but the meaning of an act that both defied and demanded explanation.

Eventually I have the opportunity to study Jody's bookshelves and to borrow from them, and I select a few that represent an array of responses—psychological, sociological, legal—to parricide, as well as a sampling of her college texts, passages from which she has underlined with the fervor of discovery. What emerges most palpably in speaking with her, in reading her books and following the paths she took through history, philosophy, and ethics, is the guilt she endured after the murders—guilt for having wished her parents dead, for hating them enough to have fantasized herself about the crime her brother accomplished.

At sixteen, still a child, she was presented with an existential problem that would starkly define much of her life's work, leaving her with questions that were all but impossible to answer. Should she judge herself on the content of her heart, find herself as culpable as her brother because she'd shared his desire for vengeance? And what about sins of omission? Surely they weighed in the balance. Was she responsible for having failed to prevent the murders? For having, in essence, abandoned the scene of the crime long before it occurred, left in spirit if not in body?

A character who arrives in our first conversation and who will continue to inform our dialogue is perhaps an obvious one, Ivan Karamazov, the intensely moral, cerebral, and tormented brother in Fyodor Dostoyevsky's *The Brothers Karamazov*. In Ivan, Jody found a means of analyzing why she felt as she did in the wake of her family's murder. Ivan's logical atheism and his philosophical rejection of any morality that is based on fear of punishment by God—if it's based on fear it cannot be true morality—leads Ivan to espouse a premise he's never tested: there is neither good nor evil; hence, "all is permitted," even the most depraved acts. Because Ivan shares this idea with the brother who goes on to kill their villainous father, Ivan becomes convinced that he is responsible for this murder he didn't commit. Wasn't the murderer simply the "instrument"—the fulfillment—of Ivan's beliefs?

And if Jody hated her mother and father and wished them both dead, if ultimately she benefited from the freedom Billy's murders purchased for her, then wasn't her brother the instrument of her anger and fantasies of vengeance as well as of his own? Perhaps it was her pain and sense of endangerment that galvanized his resolve. Even if she hadn't, as her brother claimed after his arrest, planned or directed the killings, perhaps her rage empowered Billy to take an action he wouldn't have taken for himself alone. The legal system would conclude that Jody was without blame, but the standard to which she held herself, the one that considered the content of her heart before acts she did or did not commit, was less forgiving.

It's a compelling question that Jody frames within an hour of our first meeting, and I understand why I stopped reading *The Brothers Karamazov* when I did, just after college and fully in my father's thrall, and why I must go back to the novel and read it through to the end. Long after I'd forgiven myself for not having been strong enough to turn away from my father, after I no longer felt I was made permanently unclean by incest, I still found it difficult to manage my guilt over the pain our relationship caused my mother, with whom I had been furious for abandoning me. By claiming the exclusive attention of my father, who she made clear was the only man she'd ever loved, I caused my mother great unhappiness, and her misery had satisfied my anger with her. Hadn't my father, then, been the instrument of my rage, my desire for vengeance?

I want to lean forward across the table and tell Jody that no, of course she hadn't participated in her parents' and sister's murders, that emotions are not equivalent to actions, but I can't. The feelings we hold for people are not without power. Jody's brother freed her from tyranny and abuse, from parents who had become her persecutors as well as his, and from whom she'd drawn apart in every way she could. Her brother damaged her, too, of course, and gravely. He orphaned her and subjected her to trauma and notoriety that even her second self can never completely overcome. But the two—his freeing her, his damaging her—don't cancel each other out. They coexist; in tandem they unfold through time. I know this because the damage my enslavement to my father did to me existed alongside the anger I bore toward my mother; the fact that I suffered does not redeem the injury I caused.

* * *

What is it that I want from Jody, from Billy, and from all the other people to whom I speak about the murders? In the beginning—maybe in the end, as well—I just want to get the story straight. I want to know what happened, and the exact order in which everything happened, and I dedicate the better part of a year to this goal, collecting and creating more documents than I have room to store in my study. Binders filled with chronologically arranged correspondence between Jody and me, between Billy and me; notebooks filled with details of our conversations; questions that occurred to me after we spoke; thoughts I scrawled in the dark, awake next to my sleeping husband, on whatever scrap of paper I could find without turning on the light; notes taken during interviews; legal documents; police records—and that's just the directly pertinent material. There's context, as well, information sifted and indexed and highlighted in the hope of discerning the pressures that drove Billy to kill his family as well as aspects of his experience, whether external or internal, that might have loosened the power of taboo, allowing Billy to give himself permission to murder: Demographic analyses of Medford, including its residents' education, ethnicity, and per capita income. Books on the fundamentals of tree work. Jackson County lumber industry reports. Tables comparing the percentage of Oregon's population who hunt and therefore keep shotguns versus those who fish and do not. Graphed statistical correlations between alcoholism and parricide, between child abuse and parricide, sexual abuse and parricide. Opinions of experts in the legal snarls parricide inspires. Mid-nineteenth-century ship passenger lists that include the name Gilley. Civil War casualty lists that include the name Gilley. The top one hundred songs played on the radio in 1982, 1983, and 1984. A list of all the network television shows during those same years. A report ordered from the National Weather Service containing meteorological data collected at the Medford-Ashland airport station during April of 1984.

Can it possibly matter what phase of the moon hung over the murders? I err in the direction of inclusion. "Gilleyalia" is the name I give my crates of files when I e-mail Jody, joking about the glut of information I have pertaining to her, her family, her hometown. Compulsively, I organize information into outlines and, especially, timelines.

Between April 2005 and February 2006, I make five timelines of the Gilley family's history. Each begins, roughly, with the 1963 marriage of Bill and Linda and continues on into the present. Each is bisected, cut in two by a red line running through the night of April 27, 1984. Before. After. The first timeline is about five feet long, made from a roll of white drawing paper. I bring it to an early interview with Jody, so I can record events as we speak of them. Later, when I realize that five feet is too short, I start over, with a ten-foot piece of the same white paper, happy for the opportunity to neatly transcribe what I've had to erase and move while making adjustments to the previous one. I carry this second timeline, rolled in a tube, when I visit Billy in prison, and I work on it in my hotel room, cross-referencing Jody's memories with what Billy tells me. Linda's one uncharacteristic day of heavy drinking; Billy's sneaking into Jody's bedroom; the electrical fire that destroyed Jody's attic bedroom—these and other events are hard to sequence because Jody's and Billy's accounts don't coincide. I move them around enough times that again the paper gets smudged and creased.

The final timeline is transcribed onto oversize, twenty-four-by-thirty-six-inch sheets of quadrille paper, taped together into an unmanageably long accounting of events both momentous and negligible. I think very carefully about how I fill in the dates so that I won't end up having to redo it again. Perhaps I imagine the blue-ruled one-by-one-inch squares will impose order and help make it readable—not *see*able but *read*able, like a narrative.

I can't not make the timelines. Not any more than I could stop myself from reviewing over and over each minute of my father's visit the year I turned twenty: conversations mostly, and gestures, tone of voice. Over and over I replayed every word I could remember. I read and reread the few tentative letters my father and I exchanged in the year before that visit, looking for subtexts I maybe missed. I went over all I could recall of my first twenty years, including what seemed irrelevant—because how could I be certain I'd recognize relevance? And I couldn't take the chance of overlooking the answer, which might be quite simple and not at all what I expected. I was sure that if I could reconstruct everything in the correct sequence then . . . then what? I'd know? I'd understand what happened, and why?

Yes, that is what I thought—what I think. That if I can tell a story without missing significance or misrepresenting the order of events, I can understand what made things turn out as they did.

On the other hand, if I don't assemble the pieces exactly right, then the story will come apart. There won't be an answer.

WHILE BILLY AND JODY WERE TALKING IN JODY'S bedroom that afternoon, or while Billy was talking and Jody wasn't paying much attention, their mother Linda opened the door at the foot of the stairs and told Billy "to get [his] ass downstairs . . . [that] when she was disciplining Jody or Becky [he] shouldn't get involved." It was at this moment, Billy recalls, that he promised his sister everything would be all right, and that Jody told him she was counting on him and not to let her down, statements Jody is sure she never made.

Downstairs, Billy's father poked his finger into his son's chest and told Billy to butt out, and that "if he wants to beat Jody's ass he'll do it." Then Bill told his son to get out of his sight, and Linda threw the bat at Billy and told him "to get [his] crap out of there."

Billy went outside to practice hitting. The only social interaction he had outside of the family was playing on a softball team his father's employee Glenn Riggs had invited him to join. Having quit school, for the past two years Billy had worked full-time for his father, a period during which, Jody stated in her 1999 affidavit, "physical abuse lessened, perhaps, but psychological abuse intensified. For example, Billy was sometimes paid only in cigarettes, which were parceled out individually or, at best, a pack at a time. I perceived this as a way for my parents to keep control over him both financially and psychologically."

As bad as school had been for Billy, who failed most of his classes and got himself into constant trouble, at least it did provide an alternate environment. Most abused children are not vulnerable to their tormentors all day long; they're safe in a classroom; they tag along to a friend's house in the afternoon. Working for his father, Billy endured relentless verbal assaults. He was incompetent, his father told him, worthless. "You kids," his father would say, including Jody and Becky in his taunts, "are so stupid, if I pulled down your pants there'd be shit all over them because you're too dumb to wipe right." As insults go, this one is a triumph of economy, offending so many sensibilities at once. Vulgar and demeaning, it's also infantilizing, suggesting toilet training and its attendant humiliations. It assumes a father's prerogative to subjugate his grown children and to breach—destroy—all boundaries, exposing their nakedness and effectively calling them his chattel. And, of course, it's ugly; it conjures a shame that would have implicated everyone within hearing, especially, and perhaps most painfully, the children's father himself. Nearly forty years old, Bill had yet to arrive at a level of discourse above that of a schoolyard bully.

Although they'd dropped out of high school themselves, Bill and Linda made sure their son understood that they considered Billy's quitting school to be what Jody calls "a momentous personal failure, giving them license to denigrate him even more frequently than before." She recites for me what had become the refrain to Billy's life: "That he was a loser who would only end up in prison. This was something he heard constantly."

It was an opinion Jody shared. She'd been taught by her parents' example to believe her brother would fail at whatever he tried, and Billy had given Jody reasons of her own to distrust and despise him. While the adult Jody recognizes and has formally acknowledged her parents' persecution of her brother, she is not his apologist. One of the challenges I discover in telling the story of the Gilleys is the ambivalence it—Billy—inspires. The harsh treatment he received summons sympathy; it did not—how could it?—make him sympathetic. The wishful alchemy of a novel can burnish a boy with beatings, ennoble and sweeten him into a David Copperfield or a Huck Finn, but Billy's plot is nonfiction, and it didn't thrash him into the shape of a hero.

For three years, from November 1996 through December 1999, Billy pressured Jody both directly and through their respective attorneys to provide him an affidavit, which she did provide, not because she supports her brother's appeal—she believes he is dangerous and should remain in prison—but because she discovered "the tenor of our family life had not been recorded in the original trial." There were six points that Billy asked his sister to corroborate, and he enumerated them in a letter to Jody postmarked November 29, 1996:

(1) father had a drinking problem and slept around
(2) our parents faught wich [*sic*] included him hitting her and her berating him
(3) father hit us kids
(4) mom slapped and berated us
(5) father's sexual comments and advances toward you
(6) my nurturing and protective attitude toward you girls

The first five were accurate, Jody felt, and she was willing to make a statement to that effect. The sixth she considered an outrageous—infuriating—fabrication because it transformed Billy from a sexual predator into her protector, denying experiences that had blighted her childhood. Worse, when she delayed giving him an affidavit, he sent her a threatening letter. "Jody, you know you fucked me in the past! . . . If you help me now I would completely forgive you . . . if you refuse to help me I will still get out, but it may take longer and cost you your freedom."

When Jody received this message, she showed it to the prison, and Billy's letter writing privileges were restricted. He was to have no contact with her. On reviewing the transcript of Billy's murder trial, Jody learned that by answering only those questions she was asked and volunteering no information—as her attorney had instructed her to do—her original testimony had been misleading by virtue of what it omitted. Without the missing information, she believed her brother "could not have been fairly tried or sentenced," and so she provided an affidavit that included the first five of his six points. Although she personally "could not . . . advocate any change in his sentence," or characterize Billy as having been a protective presence during her adolescence, she did "know that saving Becky and I was at least his rationalization, or even his cause" in the murder of their parents.

LAS VEGAS PRESENTED THE NEWLY WEDDED Linda and Bill with limitless distractions from whatever anxieties their courtship had inspired. They didn't need more than a pocket full of quarters to play the slot machines, and they didn't have to pay admission to a show at the Sands or Harrah's to find entertainment. Two teenagers from the backwaters of northern California could find plenty to look at just walking along the Strip. Back home, though, their choices were less attractive. Either the couple freeloaded off one or another set of parents, whose generosity was grudging at best, or they took off on their own to pick up the only kind of work they were qualified to do, which was—aside from Bill's being able to fix cars—unskilled manual labor.

Or, as a welfare caseworker summarized in a 1967 report that tried to make sense of their precarious financial situation by tracking their movements over the previous few years, the Gilleys had become "seasonal migrant workers." In the interview on which the report was based, Linda described a hand-to-mouth existence that required the energy and resilience of youth. Typically, from February through May, she and Bill worked the potato harvest in Klamath Falls, Oregon. From Klamath the couple drove south to Medford and thinned pears. Then came July cherries in Salem—more climbing, reaching, and picking—August beans in Eugene, then back to Medford in September and October to harvest the pears they'd thinned in June. They were traveling through a pretty part of the world, and there were a few variations: there were apples, peaches, and peppermint. But when the work wasn't tiring it was tedious, and there were no bunkhouses or toilets provided for laborers. To buy a night's sleep in town would use up all the money they'd made that day, so they slept in makeshift tents in the orchards, or, if it was too cold or rainy, spent the night in their car. As for bathing, often the only water to be had was what flowed past in a frigid stream.

When he could, Bill worked as a mechanic for a service station or found a position at a lumber mill, but he lost these jobs when he failed to show up on time, or at all. One of the many social workers that had occasion to interview the couple in the five years between 1967 and 1971 wondered if their itinerancy might be explained by the fact that "from time to time they get itchy feet, or Mr. Gilley desires a different kind of work and he quits his previous employment." Wanderlust was a good guess, but the truth was probably less romantic. When Bill didn't show, it was more likely he was hungover after a night of drinking.

The Gilleys can't have found as much privacy as a newly married couple would have wanted, but by October 1964, Linda was pregnant. She was never a woman who enjoyed sex; in fact, years later, Bill would tell Jody and Billy that their mother was frigid and tolerated intercourse only to prove her love, an implicitly incestuous comment in its disregard for parent-child boundaries, but Linda did have dreams of a family, and a home. Perhaps she even assumed that expecting a baby would force her husband to settle down.

Rather than ushering in a new era of stability, the arrival on June 30, 1965, of Billy Frank Jr. made it easier for his parents to get by on next to nothing. No longer a destitute young couple, now the Gilleys were a destitute family and could apply for public assistance, more often than not their only source of income. After a season or two on the road, Billy, an increasingly sickly baby who was often left untended and underclothed in an outdoor playpen, was hospitalized for what a pediatrician at the Eugene Community Hospital diagnosed as "severe status asthmaticus as well as bronchopneumonia," a potentially fatal condition in the absence of bronchodilator therapy. After this and a subsequent hospitalization, Billy's chronic bronchitis receded into upper respiratory infections but never cleared up entirely. Because the coastal fog and smog of California's San Luis Obispo County tended to exacerbate his symptoms, the pediatrician recommended that Billy remain in the drier central regions of Oregon—the so-called banana belt whose climate produced so much fruit—forcing Linda to acknowledge that taking her baby home to Betty was making him sicker. But often Linda saw no choice but to leave Billy with her mother while she was on the road with her husband. Other times, when Linda was fighting with Bill—about his drinking, about his straying, and increasingly about the footloose lifestyle that both resulted from and encouraged these transgressions—she herself moved back in with her parents and her son. In the affidavit she provided for Billy's appeal, Betty Glass stated that shortly after his son was born Bill "ran off with another girl," leaving Linda and the baby for months "without any money or any food" so that the Glasses had to support them. Bill was jealous of his son, Betty thought; she'd heard him complain that Linda "spent all her time with Billy."

When they were together, the couple chased planting, pruning, and harvesting jobs through the seasons, but there was another reason the Gilleys moved back and forth over the state line. Welfare documents show that they attempted to prove simultaneous residency in both California and Oregon—producing a gas bill here, a receipt for a few weeks' rent there—so as to collect public assistance from both states at once. But, as caseworkers were required to investigate their clients' histories, it took only a few phone calls to discover the deceit.

During the summer of 1966, when Billy was a year old, Linda walked out on her husband and took their baby back to Pismo Beach, California, where she lived with her parents and, according to case files, collected "temporary assistance for about three months." As uncomfortable as Linda's relationship with her adoptive mother was, having a child necessarily tightened her bond to Betty. That she depended on Betty for support her husband failed to provide, while being too proud to admit that Betty's suspicions about Bill had been incorrect only insofar as they underestimated his faults, quickly emerged as the existential trap of Linda's life. The longer she remained with Bill, and the more she invested in her hope that everything would turn out all right—answering her fears of struggling as a single mother with the demand of her hard-line Baptist faith that she sacrifice herself to her wedding vows—the less able Linda became to consider, let alone plan, an escape. What she couldn't predict was the extent of the tragedy she was sowing.

Released in May 1967 from a six-month jail sentence for driving without the license he'd lost after a second DWI charge, Bill reunited with Linda, and the family drifted north toward Eugene, Oregon, where, on August 2, Bill landed himself in an entirely new form of confinement. The Gilleys were taking the afternoon off from harvesting beans when Bill, intoxicated perhaps, or just foolhardy, dove headfirst into a shallow lake in one of Eugene's public parks and broke his neck. Conscious but unable to move, he was transported to Sacred Heart Hospital, where he would remain for two and a half months, following an emergency surgery to fuse the shattered vertebrae in his neck and relieve pressure on his crushed spinal cord. Prongs were implanted in his skull to immobilize his head, and he was confined to a Striker Frame bed that held his body sandwiched between two mattresses and turned him, like a roast on a very slow spit, every two hours.

Even a man with unusual reserves of psychic strength would have trouble bearing up under what Bill's doctors described as a condition necessarily characterized by intense emotional distress. Far from being that individual, Bill Gilley was a poorly parented, ill-educated, prematurely alcoholic field hand with a bad temper. Beyond the relentless claustrophobia and discomfort of being stuck in the frame, he had to endure the apprehension of not knowing whether his future would in any way resemble the one he'd imagined before diving into the lake. Billy has few good things to say about his father, but when he speaks of how violently abusive a parent Bill had been, it's with the understanding that Bill had been severely traumatized by the lake accident and his slow recovery, enough to further degrade an already deformed character. For Bill, the final insult added to his injury was that he was a smoker with a two-pack-a-day habit who couldn't even light a match.

As for Linda, she was pregnant again.

JODY REMEMBERS THAT THE ISSUE OF HER punishment for skipping school on April 26 remained unresolved when the family sat down to dinner at six. During the meal, Billy says, "I noticed my dad would stop eating from time to time and just stare at me," making Billy tense and apprehensive, as such an act of intimidation was intended to do. Of course, were Billy actively planning to murder his parents, any silent look that passed between him and his father would have been unnerving.

Jacksonville Elementary, where Jody and Billy's little sister, Becky, went to school, was hosting a program at seven that evening, and Becky was the star of the fifth grade's performance of "Eat It," a spoof of Michael Jackson's "Beat It" released in 1984 by "Weird Al" Yankovic. As was true of most school events, all members of the family were expected to attend, and by six-thirty Jody was finishing up the dishes. At one point she looked up from the kitchen sink and saw that Billy was outside, "hitting a cardboard box with a bat. He would swing it in two fashions," the pre-sentencing investigation of his crime summarized, either as if he were hitting a baseball or by bringing it down on the box from overhead.

As is unsurprising for any young man stripped of authority and brutalized by his father, Billy had long been enamored of weapons and other displays of potency. He practiced martial arts; he used nunchaku, or "numb chucks" (two truncheons connected at their ends by a short chain or rope); he played mumblety-peg and threw darts. Probably he found it tempting to smash whatever might absorb his anger, including cardboard boxes. After the murders, however, much would be made of Billy's batting this particular box, pictures of what might otherwise appear as an unremarkable piece of rubbish introduced as evidence in his trial for murder, along with the bloodied bat itself. When I visit Billy in prison, in November 2005, he tells me emphatically that he was not practicing murder on a box and makes the reasonable observation that hitting a cardboard box wouldn't be much preparation for bludgeoning a person to death. Instead, he says, he was striking the box thoughtlessly, just whacking it around, off the lawn and onto the driveway. Perhaps he used more force than was necessary, but, after all, people often take out frustrations on inanimate objects.

Before the family left for the performance at school, Billy and his mother argued. According to the report made two months after the murders, by Dr. Barry M. Maletzky, the conflict issued from what Billy intended to wear to Becky's open house at school. In the end, he compromised "and wore clothing of which she mildly approved." Billy's affidavit describes a significantly more threatening face-off in which Linda slapped him for interfering with her disciplining of Jody, a transaction that Jody doesn't remember and Billy may have fabricated for the sake of his appeal. "I told my mom she couldn't expect me to stop protecting Jody," Billy says, "that I guessed I was supposed to sit by and let my mother hit Jody and my father rape her." Linda, according to Billy, slapped him again and told him to get in the car and keep his "fucking mouth shut."

Billy's reports of his mother's verbal abuse often include profanities that are hard to imagine coming from the Linda Gilley whom Jody describes, or the one characterized in various social workers' case files. It may be that Billy uses rough language to convey the level of his mother's hostility, but some of the words he attributes to her, *cocksucker,* for example, sound more like vulgarisms typical of a male prison environment than they do the outbursts of an enraged housewife, especially one characterized by both her surviving children as hyperreligious and squeamish about sex.

"In the car going to the play no one spoke," Dr. Maletzky's report continues. "Mr. Gilley [Billy] said this was typical of the family, as whenever anyone mentioned anything in the car an argument ensued." The school program unfolded without incident. Billy and Jody went with their little sister to see some displays that had been set up for visitors. Jody remembers Becky's performance as having been very accomplished for an eleven-year-old—"a fabulous comedic turn"—and that Becky had enjoyed being the center of attention. "She was a popular kid," Jody tells me. "Spirited. Confident. Very outgoing. She had an attractive personality."

"Was she not punished the way you and Billy were?" I ask, wondering how Becky had protected what seems to have been a joyful nature.

"Was she slapped, cuffed, unreasonably screamed at? Sure, but not as frequently," Jody says. "She didn't challenge their authority. She wasn't a teenager yet."

"What about the stories Billy tells, about how your mother infantilized Becky, that she encouraged her to drink from baby bottles, even at eleven years old? That the two of them played a game in which Becky wore her old diapers that your mother had saved, and that they were always pretending she was still a baby?"

Jody shakes her head. "I think he's made it into something bigger than it really was. I don't remember her wearing diapers. The bottle thing, once or twice. But not the diapers. Would Becky have even fit into them at that age? She was a pretty big eleven."

Among the papers Jody shares with me are a few of her sister's homework assignments, including a "Values Summary," in which Becky listed the ten things she held most important:

1) God
2) Mom and Dad
3) bunny [a plush toy with which she would be buried]
4) dog
5) stereo
6) gymnastics
7) people
8) TV
9) school
10) stickers

Becky felt her strengths were her ability to "get along with more than one person at a time," that she could "keep secrets," and that she was "usually nice." "I like to be with people more than [I like to be] alone." It was important to like oneself, she thought, because then you "won't die feeling like a failer [sic]."

The family got home from Jacksonville Elementary by nine-thirty, Jody told the police. She went up to her room to go to bed; the rest of the family remained in the living room to watch TV. According to Billy's affidavit, Becky and their mother argued after Jody went upstairs. Becky wanted to stay up later; Linda said she had to go to bed right then. Becky cried but eventually obeyed, going to her own room on the first floor. As was usually the case, she woke later and got into bed with their mother. Bill was sleeping on the couch, as he had been for the past six months, ever since he had, as Jody stated in her affidavit, "offered me all the money in his pocket if he could fool around with me."

When Jody told her mother what her father had suggested, Linda threw Bill out of their bedroom and out of the house. For two weeks he lived in a motel across the street from the bowling alley, Medford Lanes, which was as long a period of geographic estrangement the couple could afford. After he returned home, his exile from the bedroom was secured by the revelation of a different sexual transgression. One evening in the fall of 1983, a young woman called the Gilleys' house. The family was gathering for dinner when the phone rang and Becky answered it. There was a girl on the line, Becky told her father, a girl who said she was Bill's daughter. "My dad went to the phone," Billy says in his affidavit, "and told the person that he wasn't her father, not to call again, and then hung up. My dad told my mom that it had been a crank call."

When the phone rang again, Linda answered, and Billy heard her ask the caller "how she knew that my dad was her father." Whatever the girl said was enough to convince Linda, who hung up, called Bill a bastard, went into her room, and slammed the door. Hoping that were he to add another misdeed to his father's growing list of transgressions, together all of Bill's sins might reach the critical mass necessary for Linda to go through with the long-threatened divorce, Billy chose his father's most recent disgrace as the ideal context in which to take his mother out to the yard and inform her that when he and his father were on the road, traveling to distant jobs, Billy had witnessed his father engaging in "extramarital affairs." His mother, he said, "thanked me for telling her and promised not to tell my father where she had learned of his infidelity," a promise she kept for less than one minute. Linda went back in through the kitchen door, and immediately Billy heard his father "yell from inside the house that he was going to kill me." Linda came out to warn Billy that his father was getting one of his guns.

Bill sounded angry enough and had threatened to kill his son often enough that Billy wasn't inclined to wait around and see what happened. Before his father came after him he took off across the field and hid himself in a shed behind Kathy Ackerson's house. Sometimes, Billy tells me, after his father had emptied a few rounds into the field for target practice, Bill would sneak up on Billy when he was mowing the lawn or chopping kindling, hold his pistol to Billy's head, and let him feel the release of the trigger, laughing when he saw how it frightened him.

As she had done many times before, Linda went after Billy and tried to make peace between her son and her husband. This time, however, Billy said he'd had more than he could take and refused to return home. Together, he and his mother came up with a plan. The following week, when the family was going to Redding, California, to spend Thanksgiving with friends, Billy wouldn't come back to Oregon with them. Instead, he'd stay in Redding. He had $500 saved, he says, and his mother gave him another $200, as well as $400 in food stamps, and the advice that he live in his car to save money.

While Linda assumed that Billy was going to make a living doing tree work for an old colleague of his father's, Billy tells me his real plan was to get by as a small-time dope dealer. But before he'd been in California long enough to find any employment, legal or not, he totaled his car and found himself without a place to sleep, without transportation, and, suffering the effects of a concussion sustained in the accident, unable to work. All he needed to reprise entirely the hand-to-mouth existence of the father he feared and hated was an anxious, pregnant wife.

Billy tells me that the concussion was severe enough that it left him with headaches, dizzy spells, blackouts, transient muscle tremors, and blurred vision. When these didn't improve and he started running a fever, he was frightened enough to call his mother, who told him to come back to Medford. Sadly, his memory is that he was homesick. "Not for the family," he says quickly, noting my incredulous and perhaps pitying expression, "but I missed the house and the barn. I missed having my animals."

"When Billy came home again," Jody's affidavit states, "my parents were almost gleeful in his failure . . . now he would have no choice but to do everything that they told him to do, in whatever words and tone with which they chose to abuse him. His failure to make it on his own validated all their predictions—that he would never amount to anything, that he'd always be a bum, even that he'd be better off dead."

Eighteen years old, with several hundred dollars remaining to him and the strongest disincentives to return to where he was threatened, ridiculed, and battered, Billy could no longer summon the confidence of the boy he had been at fifteen, the boy who had said, during a 1980 interview with a psychologist hired by Children's Services, that were he on his own he would have no problem fending for himself. The two years he'd spent working for his father, so isolated from his peers that Linda had often forced the extremely resistant Jody to take her big brother along with her when she went out with friends, had stripped Billy of whatever allowed him to believe in his autonomy. Much as Billy wanted to stay away from home and from his brutal father, his sense of self was so impaired that he no longer believed in the possibility of his freedom—not so long as his parents were alive.

THE SNAKE RIVER CORRECTIONAL INSTITUTION, where Billy has spent the last nine of his twenty-one years of imprisonment, is ten miles north of the town of Ontario, just inside Oregon's eastern border. The closest airport is in Boise, Idaho, where, on November 29, 2005, I rent a car and drive west and then north, in all about sixty miles of Interstate 84. It's desolate country, southern Idaho; at least it is at the end of November. Outside of Boise the land is flat and brown, save the occasional stubble of dry yellow cornstalks, and wind catches up loose flakes of fallen snow and spins them along the shoulder of the road. A single billboard with a verse of scripture marks the midpoint of my trip—1 Corinthians 13:7, "Love bears all things, believes all things, hopes all things, endures all things." I try to read the small print to see which church has sponsored the message, but I'm driving too fast and have to keep my eyes on the road.

Maybe it's the barren, plowed ground beyond the billboard, the way each scrape of the harrow is crusted with a line of old snow, that leaches the familiar words of comfort. By the time I arrive in Ontario it's dusk, and after so many miles of brown the lit-up signs of businesses appear riotous with color. I don't need the map lying in the empty passenger seat to find my hotel; the trademark green Holiday Inn logo is visible among the rest, a Staples and a Wal-Mart, a Kmart, an Arby's, a Taco Bell, a Rite Aid, a couple of diners and auto repair shops, Midas, Jiffy Lube. It's a small town, without much to recommend it.

Early the next morning at the correctional institution,

a few minutes before the first visiting period begins, at 8:15, I stand outside the locked double doors waiting for admission. It has snowed heavily all night, slowing travel and, I gather, shortening the usual queue of visitors to a small cluster of mostly women who huddle at the entrance to the prison, talking among themselves about the inadequately plowed roads and predicting who is likely to have been delayed or prevented from coming. Their conversation makes it clear that they know one another, and I move a little to one side, not wanting to intrude while we wait for the guard to open the doors and begin the security clearance. A couple of the women give me friendly looks, perhaps meant to encourage me to explain my unfamiliar presence. The rest ignore me, or they exchange raised eyebrows with one another, inquiring silently if anyone knows who I am.

After handing my driver's license and completed visitor's form to the officer at the security desk, I strip off my gloves, coat, earrings, and watch, and leave these and my purse in one of the lockers provided for visitors. "Don't forget you can't wear a bra with an under wire," Billy wrote me in anticipation of my visit, and for this occasion I've bought a new one, without any metal to set off the prison's hypersensitive detector. I give my boots, snow still melting and dripping from between their treads, to the guard and pass through the arch of a security apparatus so excitable that the woman in line behind me suggests I go to the restroom and wet my hair beforehand, lest static electricity set off the alarm. Once through the detector, I tug my boots back on and wait in a holding room between the security desk and the visiting area. When Billy's name is called, I'm ushered, still under scrutiny, through a set of silently sliding metal doors so thick they inhibit even fantasies of escape.

I haven't seen a photograph of Billy more recent than his mug shot, taken when he was a wiry-looking kid with brown eyes, brown hair, and a sparse mustache. Now he's paunchy and clean-shaven, the angles of his face softened to the point that they're no longer evident. His gray hair is long enough to gather into a ponytail, but he leaves it loose, falling over his collar. His teeth are bad, crooked and stained as if by tobacco—although it's been years since smoking was permitted in prison—and his expression is wary, nervous. Everything about him suggests a blue-collar job, the labor of his hands rather than his brain, everything except his hands, which are small for a man's, and soft. When he offers one in greeting, an awkward formal gesture, I take note of how pink and smooth his skin is. His hand seems freshly scrubbed, not one I picture holding a wrench or a hammer, nor wrapped around the handle of a murder weapon.

At home I've taken my fourteen-year-old son's aluminum baseball bat and lifted it over my head to bring it down as hard as I could on the dirt under our maple tree, trying to imagine what it might be like to hit someone's head with the intention of crushing it, hit it not once but several times and then move on to another victim. Apart from the emotional resistance I have to overcome to accomplish the imagined act, whacking the ground is not a very useful exercise. It produces a less-than-evocative thud and breaks a single ivy vine, but the jolt travels up the bat into my arm, underscoring the resolve necessary for so intimate a murder, much different from firing a gun from a distance. I remember only one line from *In the Belly of the Beast,* a collection of letters from prison, by Jack Henry Abbott. Abbott wrote about how it felt to stab someone to death, the ebbing of his victim's life communicated to him through the blade of his knife. Taking Billy's hand, I remember reading that book when I was eighteen or twenty and accepting Abbott's description as true. It felt true.

Beyond the security gauntlet, the visiting area presents the bland, institutional quality of a hospital or a school, almost disappointing in its lack of crime drama atmosphere. The windows aren't barred; instead their panes are impregnated with wire grids. The pale light reflected by the fresh snow outside gives everything, even our faces, a clean, almost antiseptic look. Only the inmates' blue denim shirts and jeans, stamped with bright orange prison seals, and the numerous guards, visibly enamored of their khaki uniforms, weapons, handcuffs, and other disciplinary accessories, distinguish the big square room as one within a correctional facility. Like highway patrolmen, most of the guards have full mustaches; a few even wear mirrored sunglasses indoors.

My visit with Billy isn't bisected by a pane of unbreakable glass, and we speak without telephone receivers, but we sit where we're told, facing each other across a short round table that leaves our laps exposed, open to view. We may not move our chairs, set too far apart for us to reach forward and touch each other, and we are allowed no physical contact other than the formalities of greeting and leave-taking, which in Billy's and my case is a solemn handshake that grows only a little less awkward as the days pass. I am not permitted to bring anything into the visiting area other than up to $10 in change, which I may not conceal in a purse or pocket. Among what distinguishes me from the usual crowd is the fact that I carry my vending machine quarters in a Ziploc bag. All the other women, most of whose tight pants and big hair make me look like a schoolmarm in my black skirt and cardigan, keep their change in zippered, clear vinyl cosmetic cases. I might not stick out so much if I were wearing jeans, as I would have if visitors were allowed to wear denim. But we can't. If we did we'd blend in with the inmates' prison blues. On my visitor's application I stated "friend" as the relationship I bore to Billy, but the corrections officers regard me with frank curiosity. "You get what you were after?" one asks on the last day I came to the prison, the same one who noted my New York address on the forms. "Long way to come for a visit," he said.

Billy doesn't seem to consider himself a subject of my writing, or if he does, it's a role incidental to others. In relation to the book I tell him I'm working on, the one for which he's consented to be interviewed, he calls himself a "research assistant" or an "advisor on child abuse," or, because of his efforts to locate and access documents and files from various social service agencies, a "private investigator." The files are those he needs for his appeal, but, he rationalizes, since I want to see them he's acting as my private eye.

"If I wasn't acting as your investigator," he writes in the cover letter that accompanies those files he's allowing me to Xerox, "there were a lot of documents I wasn't going to send you, because they talk trash about me. However, I'm not my client, you are."

In return for his help, I've given him a subscription to *TV Guide,* bought him a few books from Amazon, helped him pay for a new pair of glasses, and lent him the money he needs to make multiple color Xeroxes of the illustrated children's books he's written and wants to submit to publishers. In 2006, when Billy loses his prison janitorial job, which pays $25 a month, out of which he must purchase toiletries, stamps, stationery, snacks, anything he wants beyond his uniform and his meals, I make him another small loan that I don't anticipate he'll pay back. I don't think he imagines I expect to be reimbursed. The word *loan* is a means of saving face, that's all. When Billy gets fired by one of the "screws," guards he describes as unjust and eager to exercise their power, he has to wait ninety days before he can put his name on the waiting list for another job. Of necessity, he's thrifty,

lest he find himself unable to pay for essentials like soap
and toothpaste, but it's hard to save when you make $25
a month.

"So?" family and friends ask when I return to my
home in the East. "What was it like?"—*it* being con-
versing with a man who murdered his parents and little
sister, *it* being visiting a man in prison. It's both easier
and harder than I imagined it would be.

Easier, because for each of our six three-hour interviews, Billy is punctual, cooperative, and eager to please.
Beyond his desire to cultivate my generosity, he seems desperate for contact with the world beyond the prison, even
with a stranger who asks difficult questions. I can't bring
myself to inquire outright—it strikes me as both painful
and perhaps shaming to be as abandoned as Billy appears
to be, by both family and friends—but I think I may be
the only visitor that Billy's had in all his years in jail,
the only one other than his attorney or the psychologists
who examined him for his appeal. Not that he spends his
days alone. When he isn't being punished for breaking a
rule—"thrown in the black box," as he calls solitary
confinement—Billy is housed in the general population of
Oregon's largest prison, a three-thousand-bed facility.
The Snake River Correctional Institution was completed
around the time that the state's Ballot Measure 11 established minimum mandatory sentences for sex crimes,
swelling prison populations and raising the ratio of inmates who are sex offenders from, Billy estimates, 20 percent to 60 percent of the men with whom he lives.
Measure 11, Billy tells me, has made life in jail "a lot more
boring than it used to be. Less violent and chaotic, but
more boring."

"Because it's less chaotic?" I ask. "That's what's made
it boring?"

"No, no." He shakes his head, his expression that of a
teacher assisting a surprisingly backward student. "The

problem is, sex offenders are terrible conversationalists. They're morose. They're self-involved, self-pitying. And most of them are pretty ignorant. You can't talk about anything with any of them for even a minute before they're back on how they didn't do anything wrong, they don't deserve to be in jail, and what a raw deal they got."

Billy's judgment, purely contextual, that ranks convicted criminals on the basis of their ability to make interesting conversation, as though he were assembling a salon rather than commenting on life in prison, is unexpectedly funny, and while I don't laugh, I do replay it in my head, amused at Billy's making such a statement without conveying any of the irony that characterizes some of his other observations. I see, too, how it isn't funny at all, how being incarcerated perverts and degrades a man's moral vision, not rehabilitating him but scrambling his priorities. The long hours, with nothing happening, and no end in sight. Billy does make the interviews as easy as they can be, considering their topic, which is, of course, what makes them hard in ways I can't know until I am actually asking him what it was like to murder his mother and father and little sister.

Too, the content of our conversations is made more burdensome by the fact that I can't record them in the moment, as I am not allowed to bring any electronic device or even a pencil and paper into the prison's visiting area. After each three-hour interview, I hurry out to the parking area, get in my rental car, and drive away from the concertina-wired compound. As soon as I can, I pull over by the side of the road and transcribe from memory what Billy has told me, confident that I've retained almost all of his observations because I'm holding myself to an unnatural standard of attentiveness, one that would be insupportable were it to last longer than the few days I have. When I'm not engaged in a dialogue with Billy, or recording the one I've just had, I find myself falling quickly into a state of passive exhaustion. I go back to my room at the Holiday Inn, order room service, watch CNN, stare out my window as snow drifts down from the darkening sky. Tired and unable to sleep, one night I go to Kmart, then to Staples, drawn through their long, wide aisles by the sedative power of endless choices of toothpaste, dog food, ballpoint pens. After hours of slow-motion browsing, the only thing I buy is a dark red damask tablecloth from Kmart. "Martha Stewart Everyday," it says on the package, and all through December I spread it under my grandmother's holiday china, sometimes thoughtlessly, sometimes remembering Billy, and how institutional environments like prisons and hospitals celebrate Christmas, Easter, the Fourth of July: by changing the decorations on the bulletin boards and the color of the Jell-O from food service.

What I'm looking for in Billy, what I'm trying to strain from our conversations, is evidence of his engagement with—or separation from—his past: the boy he was, the boy who killed his family. He's speaking of a crime that is twenty-one years old, around which I assume he's had to create layers of defenses in order to guard his sanity. I exhort myself to remain alert to details and nuances—to whatever might appear through a fleeting, accidental breach in his psychic armor. But little does. I'll have to wait until later, when in the course of our written correspondence he begins to send me his children's stories, fantasies that, once I know the facts of his life with his parents, reveal themselves as autobiographical and hint at what he can't articulate in a formal interview with a stranger.

The officer who trolls past the table separating Billy and me keeps his eyes on our hands and asks every half hour, in the amplified baritone of someone, like a radio announcer, impressed with the sonorous quality of his own voice, "Does anyone need to urinate?" When he asks, Billy smiles sheepishly and looks away or into his lap, embarrassed by this indignity, as he doesn't seem to be by others. He reports without self-consciousness that at the conclusion of each of our visits, inmates are strip-searched, their body cavities examined to determine if any material thing has been passed to them from the free world. I'm not sure how to interpret his offering me this detail, as he doesn't mention it in the tone of outrage he uses when speaking of other violations he's experienced as an inmate. Maybe he imagines it to be a kind of intimacy, my knowing this about him. Or perhaps he regards it as a proof of his commitment to follow through on the promise he made me: he shows up knowing the humiliation to which he'll be subjected on my departure.

Billy speaks of the murders themselves without hesitation, eager to correct whatever misperceptions he fears I may have formed from other sources, especially my conversations with his sister. The violent end of the Gilley family means that little of its material history has survived: no cardboard box of Super 8 movies; no baby shoes or Little League jerseys; no photo albums; no expired passport, its pages stamped with the dates of a lost itinerary; no family Bible with births and deaths recorded on the flyleaf; no medical records; no diaries; no correspondence beneath the lid of an old cigar box. People who preserve such things are people who want to hold on to their past. Apart from the childhood memories of Jody and Billy, no less perishable and inconsistent than those of any other pair of siblings, there's little with which to resurrect their dead. Very little when compared to the self-referential cocoon the typical American family spins around itself. And much of what remains are photocopies, some of these second- or even third-generation, so ghostly as to be unreadable in spots.

From Jody I have a sheaf of local news articles about the murders; the transcript of the trial in which her brother, Billy Frank Gilley, Jr., was found guilty of the aggravated (first degree) murders of his father, Billy Frank Sr., his mother, Linda Louise, and his sister Becky Jean; the pre-sentence investigation into her brother's earlier deviant behaviors; the transcript of her 911 call; two appellant's briefs responding to Billy's petition for a writ of habeas corpus; as well as more personal items: a note written on a paper place mat from a Denny's restaurant; an exchange of three love letters between Bill Sr. and Linda; nine snapshots, no longer in color but reduced to a Xerox machine's smudgy black and white; a single page taken from Billy's baby book and another from Jody's; two of Becky Gilley's homework assignments; a dental record describing a playground accident on October 10, 1982, that resulted in fourteen-year-old Jody's losing an upper incisor, which was replaced; a letter inviting Jody to join Medford Mid-High's debate team and a subsequent communication from the high school suggesting that her SAT scores indicated she was a good candidate for learning a second language; three personal essays written by Jody and published in her college literary magazine; the affidavit, dated December 20, 1999, Jody provided to augment the original trial's transcript; a college creative writing assignment that includes citations from family documents that no longer exist; and a copy of Jody's thesis, "Death Faces."

The three family mementos Billy has managed to save are a proud letter from Linda to her mother telling Betty that Jody had been invited to join the debate team, and two snapshots of his maternal grandparents.

All the other documents Billy keeps are those generated by his appeal, including welfare and Children's Division case files, school records, reports made by a private investigator, thirteen affidavits his attorney has collected to establish mitigating evidence his court-appointed lawyer did not present at his original trial or sentencing, and nine psychiatric evaluations, the first made in July 1978, when he was thirteen, and the last in August 2000. In addition to evidence demonstrating the incompetence of his original lawyer and citations seeking to reveal his home life as typical of parricide cases that (prior to 1984) received verdicts of manslaughter, Billy's appeal presents a third category of evidence: the opinions of the two clinical psychologists who tested Billy after he was sent to prison that Billy suffers organic brain syndrome. "It was quite clear," Dr. Robert Stanulis's affidavit reads, "that Mr. Gilley had a brain injury because he had sustained significant head injuries at the hands of his abusive father."

Dr. Will Levin's report suggests that certain of Billy's cognitive deficits were "associated with multiple head traumas."

Organic brain syndrome causes "varying degrees of confusion, delirium (severe, short-term loss of brain function), agitation, and dementia (long-term, often progressive, loss of brain function)."* In other words, the conclusion at which the two doctors' testimony points is that Billy was mentally incompetent at the time of the murders as a direct result of his having been knocked out by falling tree limbs and by his father's beatings.

"Did Billy ever come home from work with any kind of head injury?" I ask Jody.

"Not that I was aware of. You're referring to his claiming he has brain damage?"

I nod. "He says your dad would drop tree limbs on

---

*As defined by the National Institutes of Health.

him. That he did it intentionally, from overhead, while
Billy was working on the ground."

"It doesn't make sense," Jody says, "because it's the
workers on the ground who are responsible to stay out
from under the boom. To keep their eyes on where it is
and avoid it, because debris does come down. Anyone
with any tree experience knows that."

"So you don't think . . . you think it didn't happen."

"I've worked on site before, I've watched my dad
work. When I did brush—and that is all that Billy did,
cut brush and run the chipper—you do not pick up
brush under the bucket. You wait the ten minutes until
it has moved to the next area, then you cut or drag the
brush to the chipper and run it through. It could be that
my dad didn't try not to hit him, because any rational
person would pay attention to where the boom and
branches were. Besides, wouldn't Billy have come home
bloodied? Wouldn't he have said something at the
time?"

JODY AND I VISIT MEDFORD IN EARLY AUTUMN, when the surrounding foothills range from deep evergreen to the flaxen of dry grasses, the occasional black silhouette of a single live oak imposed on the yellow. It's a landscape of abundance, farmland cut out of the original forest into orchards and pastures. Acres of pears give way to hilly paddocks of goats and sheep, horses and cows. The occasional apiary has a roadside stand selling jars of honey on the honor system: a box nailed to a post with a slot for accepting bills and coins.

In contrast to its environs, Medford itself looks like countless other little cities through which I've driven on road trips across the United States, each an unconscious drift of clutter over an otherwise unoffending landscape: strip malls and mini-marts; an attenuated string of businesses devoted to auto maintenance—Midas, AAMCO, Firestone, and so on—giving way to car lots, used and new; Safeway, Rite Aid, Kmart, Costco; the fast food roster of McDonald's, Burger King, Taco Bell; Chevron, Exxon, Texaco; a movie theater with a busted marquee; an out-of-business bowling alley; and on Medford goes. None of these seems either necessary or unnecessary, and there's a flat, faded, grimy quality to the streets, a sort of sprawl endemic to small town America, as if there will always be enough space to waste more of it. In the 1970s, it was pretty much the same, Jody says, just half the size, and cable TV, PlayStation, and the Internet hadn't yet killed off the bowling alley.

The Gilleys settled in Medford in 1970, on Dyer Road, a short, unpaved track on the outskirts of town. Their house had three small bedrooms, enough so that Linda's mother could come up from California occasionally and help out, as long as Billy and Jody shared a room. Of the time she spent with her daughter, son-in-law, and grand-children, Betty Glass recalled that Bill "was mean to Billy and seemed jealous" of his five-year-old son, that he was a generally abusive parent, and that the two-year-old Jody would kick and scream if her father tried "to touch her or hug her," suggesting a level of terror I don't hear in Jody's accounts of her early childhood. Betty's comment is likely a belated embellishment, in-tended to bolster Billy's appeal by corroborating her grandson's assertion that Bill Sr. had molested his daughters, or Betty may have fallen so under the sway of Billy's version of the past that she didn't remember her own. When subpoenaed by Billy's post-conviction coun-sel, Billy's defense attorney testified that he'd spoken with Betty more than once in the immediate aftermath of the murders and she "never related to me ever any kind of history in terms of abuse."

Whatever Betty did or did not witness, the only material record of her version of what unfolded in the Gilley home is an eight-page affidavit, prepared for Billy's appeal and dated November 12, 1996. Outspoken in her support for her grandson in the months after the murders, when Billy was jailed and awaiting trial, Betty was not, in the opinion of at least one judge, a disinterested witness. She'd always been eager to believe the worst of Bill, and while the form of an affidavit—a sworn statement, stamped and notarized—lends it the appearance of truth, portions of Betty's were rejected as hearsay by at least one judge.

With two small children, bills to pay, and an unemployed wife, Bill Gilley had moved his family into what the Jack-

son County welfare office considered a "suitable"—
modest—home that was "sparsely furnished." They
"were having difficulty getting all the utilities turned
on," the caseworker reported, and Bill still didn't have
the one thing that would alleviate the increasing pressure
he was under: a real job. He worked occasionally as a
mechanic for Nelson's Garage in Phoenix—a tiny town
between Medford and Ashland—and he drew a couple
of weeks' salary here and there from a mint farm in
Grants Pass, about thirty miles northwest of home. Beyond a lack of training and perhaps aptitude, the discipline of regular employment was one Bill had yet to
teach himself. As for Linda—no less influenced by media
than any other American housewife, especially by TV's
glorification of the nuclear family—she would always be
keenly aware of the discrepancy between what she had
and what she thought she should have. While she waited
for what never happened, her family's arrival into the
middle class, she economized by shopping at Salvation
Army and relying on swap meets for furnishings, house-
wares, and clothes. The family owned a used television
set, and Billy reminisces for me about spending happy
hours with his mother, watching old movies and eating
popcorn. Among the memories he recounts, though, this
one is generic, unblemished, and without texture, suggesting to me that it's more wishful than accurate.

"My mom and I were very close when I was little,"
Billy reports, but the same was not true of him and his
father, he tells me. In fact, all the untroubled childhood
memories Billy recounts specifically exclude his father.
When Bill was away from the house, Billy and Linda did
chores together, made meals together, and he "liked to
pick flowers for her and make her things at school." At
the same time, Billy was besotted with his baby sister.
One of the Gilley family's cherished and central myths—
not an untruth but a story told and retold until it

acquired a sanctity that defied anyone's questioning it—was of the young Billy's devotion to Jody.

"I fell in love with Jody the first time I saw her," he tells me. "I used to play with Jody all the time. I'd keep her company, talk to her while she was in her crib." Billy called his sister his own baby and would alert Linda whenever Jody was wet or crying. "Mama," he'd call, "my baby needs changing. Mama, my baby needs her bottle."

Jody has few memories of her first years but concedes that she and Billy were close as young children. They played and bathed together, shared simple chores, and later her mother often spoke of her brother's devotion to her at that age. An indifferent housekeeper, Linda was more inclined to sit on the kitchen floor and draw pictures with her children than mop that floor, or to leave the laundry waiting while she watched TV, but she did keep house after a fashion. She made do, Billy tells me, with his washing the floor, as well as a six-year-old can wash a floor, she tried to brighten up the place with contact paper, and she had dinner for Bill when he came home, the point at which things tended to deteriorate. Linda couldn't resist nagging Bill, about money, mostly, and about his drinking.

"I remember my mom berating my father continually. All the time," Billy says. "My father responded by periodically beating my mother and smashing the furniture."

"Is that what you remember?" I ask Jody.

"My mother gave as good as she got. He'd throw something. She'd throw something."

It was around this time that Billy says he saw his drunk father raping his mother. Frightened by the sound of fighting on the other side of the wall, Billy left his bed and went to his parents' room, where, his affidavit reads, "My mom had a bloody face and she was crying." When Linda noticed Billy in the doorway, she told him to return to his room. He didn't understand what was going on and should leave them alone, she said. Assuming it isn't a fantasy concocted to make his father appear that much more of a brute, this early memory of Billy's is called into question by the process of memory itself. What psychology identifies as "primal scenes" are understood as having been created at least as often as they are witnessed, giving form to a child's apprehensions about sex, which even when consensual may appear as a violent subjugation. Too, all of us have what are called "screen memories" that protect us from what we cannot bear to contemplate. Like dreams, screen memories are assembled by the unconscious from parts that are real— experiences from our waking lives—and others that are imagined. Still, if the rape of his mother that Billy recalls as an adult, independent of any witness, cannot be taken at face value, it is not without significance.

Sandra Renfro, a neighbor of the Gilleys from 1971 to 1974, said (when Billy's post-conviction counsel approached her for an affidavit) that Bill Gilley had a drinking problem and was violent when intoxicated. "Linda did confide in me," Sandra stated, "that the bruises and black eye that I had seen on her on several occasions were from Bill hitting her." She'd also seen Bill hit both his children so hard, she said, that they would "fly across the room." Ironically, given his treatment of them, the sound of his children crying made Bill furious, and whenever one of them did cry he "would yell at Linda and tell her to have the kids 'shut the fuck up.' "

Linda's closest friend, Frances Livingston, stated during an interview with a private detective that Linda refused Bill sex when she was angry with him, and it wouldn't be surprising if Bill, who tended to impulsive and violent behavior whether drunk or sober, bloodied his wife's nose while forcing himself on the woman he considered his by law. If a marriage license made him responsible to pay bills, didn't it also offer compensations?

Whether or not it involved rape, Billy was traumatized by his parents' fighting, especially, he tells me, by those conflicts that erupted at night, after he was sent to bed. By the time he was in first grade he was so frightened of the dark that he had trouble falling asleep and, once asleep, was frequently awakened by nightmares. There was a simple solution, of course, but his father refused it. Bill wasn't going to pay for extra electricity, he said, just because his son was such a coward that he wanted a night light. It seems that Billy, at seven years old, was already subject to a code of manliness that would prove damaging for years to come, and his mother did nothing to protect him. With respect to what was or was not ladylike, Linda would have her say with Jody and later with Becky, but the definition of a man was Bill's to establish.

This prerogative determined the outcome of another incident from Billy's early childhood, one that would become a second, more disturbing memory, with witnesses other than Billy. Summers presented Linda, Bill, and their children the chance to visit Betty and David Glass in Pismo Beach, for a family vacation that didn't cost much. The Glasses lived near the shore, but even in midsummer northern California ocean water can be uncomfortably cold, and the children swam in a pool belonging to their grandparents' neighbors. One afternoon, as Betty recounted in her version of the story, she saw "Bill jumping off the diving board into the eight-foot depth holding Billy tightly. . . . Bill did this until Billy was blue all over his body."

Enraged when he discovered his son in the pool wearing water wings, Bill stripped them off and said, according to Billy, "today was the day I was going to learn to swim." For her affidavit, Betty remembered a more aggressive threat: "You're going to grow up to be a man, not a sissy, even if I have to kill you." Whatever he said, Bill took his son, minus the water wings, onto the diving board and jumped in holding him tight. At the lowest point of their submersion he let go, forcing Billy to make his own way to the surface. The hostility—the malice—of this "lesson" would have frightened a child who could swim. Billy, who could not, was terrified. He broke through the surface sobbing and screaming, which further angered his father and hardened his will. Over and over again, no matter how Billy begged, wept, and struggled to get free, and in spite of Betty's and Linda's pleading, Bill took Billy up onto the diving board and held him so fiercely that even during the minutes Billy was out of the water he felt he couldn't breathe. "Each time he jumped off the diving board he would drag me down under the water," Billy says. "My grandmother yelled at him to stop but he just kept on going. I remember inhaling water and I began to cough and gag . . . and my father just kept on going." Jody, who was five at the time, remembers her father "throwing Billy into the pool and my mother telling him to stop it, and a sense of being very anxious."

Betty had gone inside to fetch Linda, and both women were now trying "to get Bill to stop torturing Billy," as Betty put it. Billy's grandmother's version of the story ends with Linda forcibly removing Billy from the pool and taking him inside. Billy, however, in his affidavit, taken twelve years after he had killed his parents and sister, remembered that his "grandmother threatened to hit [his] father with a board to make him stop."

I don't make the connection until months after Billy tells me the story, but once I do I can't dismiss it: in mistreating his son, Bill re-created the life-threatening incident in which he himself had been the victim. Five years after he'd been pulled, paralyzed, from the lake in Eugene, he forcibly rehearsed Billy's entry into and exit from water, in order to "make him a man." Perhaps the compulsive scenario wasn't, as it seemed to Billy, conceived to punish and terrorize him. It may be that his father had been in the thrall of an inexorable psychic demand that he prove and reprove his own manhood, in the form of his small namesake's ability to save himself from drowning.

Not that this excuses a sadistic transaction whose emotional impact grew only larger as time passed, the memory of it having become, for Billy, an internal monument to his father's cruelty. Nine years after he prepared the account in his affidavit and twenty-one years after the murders, when Billy and I talk about the diving board incident, Billy tells me his grandmother threatened his father with a baseball bat belonging to his grandfather and, further, that this was the same bat with which he later beat his father to death.

Rather than Betty having made so menacing and inflammatory a gesture at her volatile son-in-law, it seems likely to me that Billy's memory is inspired by his wish for a grandmother who was powerful enough to save him—a woman with a weapon she was willing to use. That the weapon would change over time from a nondescript piece of wood to the same bat that ended his father's life speaks not only to the vengeful quality of Billy's rage at having been abused by his father when he was too young to defend himself but also to his need to create a coherent narrative for a life that was severed— rendered incoherent—both by what he had done and by what had been done to him.

In the years after the 1984 murders, both Billy and Jody would continue to be preoccupied by what was, for each, a profoundly important work in their now separate lives: creating a coherent narrative. To preserve himself from psychic disintegration, Billy had to tell himself the story of the murders—their antecedents, accomplishment, and effects—in a way that allowed him to understand and live with himself: a story that made sense to him. And, if his appeal were to succeed, granting him a retrial, the version of the story in his affidavit needed to make sense to other people, too, explaining the murders as a response to brutality. In this context, to *make sense* is a process not only of discovering but also of inventing meaning, creating what was *not* there all along. In terms of narrative's ability to knit and hold a life together, it may not be factually true that Billy murdered his father with the same baseball bat that his grandmother threatened to strike Bill with, but to Billy it makes perfect sense. A legal lie and a narrative truth, it draws a line of causation that connects the murders directly to the abuse he suffered.

Jody, who escaped being murdered, was left with a narrative task as daunting and necessary as her brother's. The law would punish Billy for what he'd done, relieving him of that burden. Jody, however, would have to live with what she failed to do. Even had she not been unconsciously complicit in the murders, still she had to manage the guilt she felt for having failed to anticipate and prevent her brother's killing their family. To this end, she, too, needed to review years of domestic blight in order to understand what provoked her brother's violence. She had to discover how she could go on to have a life that wasn't ultimately overwhelmed by the fact of the murders.

At the beginning of our relationship, I could tell Jody that I was compelled by her story and that I had some sense of why I was. Both of us were people who had endured a moment or a period of psychic violence—Jody's far more dangerous and traumatic than mine—that required us either to reattach the amputated past to the future or to embrace what felt truer, and more possible: the idea that a previous self had perished and a new one had invented herself in the dead girl's place. The more I learned about Jody's life, the more of myself I recognized in Jody. Though I hadn't suffered the kind of abuse or deprivation she had endured as a child, I did have parents who were young and damaged, both of whom had abandoned me. My mother had been cold, withholding, and often cruel; the father I embraced as a savior manipulated me into sex. Like Jody, I used books to enter alternate worlds in which I hid myself. Like her, I'd been a striving student who depended on academic achievement as a means of transcending unhappiness. Like her, I had a need for coherence that was sometimes difficult to achieve and maintain. Before my father entered my life, I wasn't happy or particularly sane, but I understood who and where I was in my own history, as much as a twenty-year-old can. Afterward, nothing made sense; everything I knew about myself and my family fell into a rubble of impressions that I could no longer assemble into a shape I recognized, or any shape at all. I myself had no shape then, but was undone, awaiting reassembly.

I also found at least one strand of myself that connected me to Billy, in whose past I glimpsed an anger similar to my own. Even before the reappearance of my father, I had a history of depression, eating disorders, self-cutting, substance abuse, recklessness, and other destructive behaviors, all of which proceeded from my anger with my parents, the violence of which I turned on myself and my body, at least in part because I'd been instructed by examples different from those given to Billy. A male and therefore biologically more inclined toward aggression, Billy had had a raging and physically abusive father on whom to model his behavior. I was taught that girls didn't express anger and that self-sacrifice was a virtue, a route to sanctification. Although Billy and I had behaved very differently, weren't his actions a manifestation of the same species of unbearable rage I had borne unconsciously for much of my life?

THE EARLIEST RECORDED COMMENTS ON Billy's conduct indicate trouble. His report cards from Phoenix Elementary noted that his work habits were poor. Although he seemed to want to improve, he didn't take pride in his work, nor was he organized, focused, or, in the words of his first grade teacher, able to "make the best of a difficult situation." By second grade his classroom behavior had deteriorated to the point that he was falling into frequent conflicts with classmates, and his teacher, who gave him still lower marks for his work habits than those he'd received in first grade, decided that she couldn't promote a student who was so lacking in confidence and so unable to read, spell, or do the required math; she'd have to hold him back for another year of second grade. As school records demonstrate, the only area in which Billy displayed competence was art, and it was art that elicited the only words of praise that Billy remembers having received in his entire elementary school career.

On January 8, 1973, Becky Jean Gilley was born, and Billy had a second baby sister and felt the same kind of pride in her as he had in Jody, five years earlier. Billy tells me that again he called the new baby his own and showed her off to his friends. He held Becky while she had her bottle and helped his mother to change and watch over her, but the connection he had with her was not nearly so intense as his feelings for Jody. He was older now—eight—and he had other children with whom to play and, increasingly, fight. After school, when he wasn't antagonizing boys on the playground, he drifted down the block from Phoenix Elementary to watch through the big storefront window of a martial arts academy. Fascinated by what he saw there, Billy begged Linda to enroll him in a class, for which she managed to scrape together the money, inspiring a lasting interest in a discipline that offered him a chance to experience what he characterizes for me as "positive male role models who encouraged and praised" him, providing a little psychic insulation against his own father.

After briefly trying out the career of firefighter, Bill had settled into what would become his permanent, and final, employment as a tree trimmer. Neither of Bill Gilley's living children remember why it was that he quit working as a fireman—although Billy surmises that his father had one too many scares and decided the work was too dangerous—but it seems unlikely that a man injured as badly as Bill had been in the diving accident could have managed the physical demands of firefighting. Tree work wasn't much better, in that it required him to strap spurs onto his legs and shimmy up tree trunks while carrying heavy equipment. But Bill was in his early thirties, arthritis had yet to aggravate the chronic discomfort in his neck, and he'd made friends with an established tree surgeon who taught him the basics and guided him into the business. In years to come, Bill would acquire an aerial lift truck (commonly called a cherry picker) to reach and cut trees' higher limbs, and he'd own a chipper, a dump truck, and a couple of pickups and employ as many as six workers. In the beginning, however, he was a modest, one-man operation, and had to get up a tree the hard way.

By the time Billy was in the third grade he was nine years old, able in his father's estimation to work when he wasn't at school. After all, Bill had been in the potato fields by that age, even younger, helping his family to get by. And while Billy couldn't do more than pick up debris on the ground—gathering the smaller limbs, twigs, and foliage that his father dropped from overhead—he could do that. When working for his father, of whom he was frightened, Billy tells me he did what he was told and didn't complain: he was the little man he was expected to be. Out of his father's sight, however, and beyond the reach of his temper, he was fast becoming a child with serious behavior problems.

Frustrated by his inability to do the simple school work that came easily to others, including Jody, who was three years younger, and by his vulnerability to his violent father, Billy was not only disruptive in the classroom but also began picking physical fights on the playground, perhaps to prove or assert what strength he had, perhaps to imitate his father. At home there was no chance of prevailing, but schoolyard scuffles were less unevenly matched. And he was testing other limits as well, determined to thwart authority figures who tried to control him in other contexts. Ten years old, Billy was the leader of what he calls "a shoplifting ring." With the help of an accomplice or two, whose job was to divert the attention of whoever manned the counter of a local mini-mart, Billy stole as many candy bars as he could from the shelves. Back at school he'd then give them to girls in trade for jewelry they made and then sell the jewelry. Sometimes, he tells me, he gave candy to girls in exchange for a look at their underpants or the chance to "feel them up." At least this is how he remembers it. Or is it the way he wants to remember himself? The way he needs to remember himself in order to preserve the notion of his having been a fully male child in defense of his father calling him a sissy?

"In kindergarten I remember charming the girls to kiss me and let me look up their dresses. From then on I was full-time skirt-chaser," Billy writes me from prison.

"If you get a copy of my mug shot from the Medford Police dept., you would see that I had the type of looks that women threw themself [*sic*] at me." In fact, his mug shot is not distinguished by his looks, which are average, but by his glazed eyes and expressionless mouth. In a later photograph, taken at the time of his trial, he's clean-shaven with his hair parted in the middle. His deep-set eyes are shadowed, unreadable, and his smile appears empty, a reflex summoned by the camera. Having spent six months in jail, he looks more substantial, and more relaxed. As for his ability to attract women, for all his posturing, the forty-year-old man I encounter in the Snake River visiting room doesn't come across as sexually knowing.

"When Master sets me free, I'll drop the weight, color my hair, and date older women," he confides in the same letter, and I wonder if he intends this aside as a compliment to me, five years his senior. In any case, he affects a confidence lacking in his prison compositions, which include a handful of romantic poems about his fantasy wife. One, written in 1995, speaks of "never knowing love"; another of the same vintage describes the anguish of never experiencing a lover's touch. I ask Jody if Billy was a virgin when he went to jail, but she doesn't know. He had a girlfriend the summer before the murders, when he was seventeen, but Jody didn't spend much time with the two of them.

A lack of experience might explain Billy's attempt to compensate for the deficit by sexualizing his early memories, a process no more conscious than arming himself with the baseball bat his grandmother allegedly brandished, and therefore one that produces an unreliable memory that can't be challenged. Of a little Mexican girl in their neighborhood, Billy tells me that in the course of playing house with him and Jody the girl taught Jody to French kiss, and that Jody in turn taught

Billy, and that brother and sister continued to practice this new kind of kissing, a scenario I suspect is false even before Jody denies any such experiments.

Whatever the genesis of his maladjustment, whether or not it was inspired by his having witnessed his father mistreating his mother in the bedroom, Billy was already on his way to becoming the brother who would sexually violate the sister he loved. Billy was lonely; he wanted intimacy; his understanding of how to treat girls was modeled on his parents. Clearly the children's father was a malignant influence, but Linda had her hang-ups, as well. Betty seems to have done her best to instill in her adoptive daughter a puritanical control of sexual desire. Perhaps in order to correct for tendencies she feared Linda had inherited from a mother who had been sent to jail for committing a crime of passion, she'd wielded the idea of a severe and punishing God with regrettable success.

Stories Billy and Jody tell suggest Linda was not willing to acknowledge that her children were—like all children—sexual beings. In the determination to quash any urge before it had a chance to manifest itself, she often found cause for concern where none existed. Jody remembers an afternoon when she was eight, Becky three. The two girls were hiding in bed, playing when they were supposed to be napping. Jody had taken a toy camera under the blanket; when she pushed its shutter-release button and peered through the viewfinder it showed her a series of pictures that she shared with her little sister. Linda, having heard giggling coming from their bedroom, jumped to the unfounded conclusion that the girls had hidden themselves under the covers not because they were horsing around rather than sleeping but to conceal mutual sexual exploration. She pulled both girls out from under the bedclothes and accused Jody of instigating—or failing to prevent—a game of touching each other's genitals. Becky was too young to understand how she was supposed to have misbehaved, but Jody was frightened by the wildness of her mother's accusation, and by her behavior. Linda shook both girls violently and screamed at them in a way Jody remembers as unhinged—not so much underscoring her point as succumbing to hysteria. On an earlier occasion, when Billy and Jody were so young that they bathed together, Linda caught Billy—in complete innocence, Jody says—flashing Jody from behind his towel and slapped both of them so furiously that the impact of her hand on their wet skin launched flurries of bubbles into the air around them. Perhaps by insisting on incestuous motives where there were none Linda inspired the very feelings she was attempting to eradicate.

Just as discipline in the Gilley household was male-to-male, female-to-female, so was the transmission of sexual mores. Billy was his father's to educate; the girls were Linda's problem. By the time Jody had developed breasts and secondary body hair, her mother had told her very clearly that she was never, ever to allow anyone to touch certain parts of her body between her neck and her thighs. To make herself clear, she pointed out those parts on Jody herself. Wearing an expression that betrays an embarrassment and revulsion that is twenty-five years old, Jody demonstrates her mother's lesson by putting her own hands first on her breasts and then over her crotch, showing me how Linda had touched her.

"Like the 'dirty pillows' scene in *Carrie*?" I ask, alluding to the movie (made from the Stephen King novel of the same name) in which a mother's pathologically creepy and repressive attitude toward sexuality—*dirty pillows* is her way of alluding to breasts—pushes her teenage daughter to madness and the story to a supernatural apocalypse.

"Exactly!" Jody says, and she laughs with me. "That was exactly it."

A psychosexual melodrama driven by adolescent lust and anguish, *Carrie* is an easy movie to laugh about, but its place among pop culture classics rests on the heroine's response to her mother's paranoia and abuse, to the intolerable psychological pressure her mother exerts on her. When Carrie finally snaps, the audience is equally relieved and horrified by what results, recognizing that all of the destruction proceeds from her mother's unnatural lack of sympathy, of basic human feeling. It's this, as much as the phrase *dirty pillows,* that makes Jody and me laugh: the black joke of a mother whose persecution of her child precipitates so violent an ending.

"HE SHOULD HAVE GONE TO MACLAREN," JODY says. "If he had, well . . ." She falls silent. *If.*

Conceived as a social experiment in the 1920s, the Mac-Laren School for Boys, in Woodburn, Oregon, was a vocational training school for juveniles whose delinquency was considered to have resulted from factors over which they had no control: environment and heredity. By the 1950s, MacLaren had become a working farm that not only produced most of its own food but also provided its surplus to other institutions. In this, its most exemplary period, husband-and-wife teams served as house parents and worked the farm along with the 180 boys in their care. In 1977, however, a class action lawsuit was filed against the school, "alleging cruelty to students, unfair disciplinary actions, no due process and citing other issues,"* such as overcrowding to the point that boys were sleeping on the floor. The suit was settled in 1979 and a number of changes resulted, but MacLaren remained a forbidding and terrible place in the public imagination, a name invoked to frighten children into obedience.

On Tuesday, May 20, 1980, Billy, his mother and father, and a caseworker from Children's Services Division appeared before a circuit judge in Jackson County's Juvenile Division for a dispositional hearing to decide where to place Billy, who was fifteen years old and, after a series

---

Oregon Blue Book, "Oregon Youth Authority: Agency History," written 1997 (http://bluebook.state.or.us/state/executive/Youth_Authority/youth_authority_history.htm, accessed October 15, 2007).

of minor thefts, had recently run away from home. There were two choices: to leave him in the custody of his parents, contingent on their getting help for him and continuing to attend the parenting classes they had been instructed to take, or to send him to MacLaren. At the hearing, the Children's Services caseworker offered this assessment of her client: "I believe that Billy is a very troubled young man. Billy is withdrawn and impulsive. It appears that Billy responds to others in whichever way will give him the most attention. He refuses to divulge his memories of his past. I believe this is because he does not want to deal with his emotions. Psychological tests indicate that Billy is a very sensitive person and easily hurt. I believe that Billy is suppressing much hurt and/or anger. He has also found that as long as he attracts attention by doing either responsible or irresponsible acts, he never has time to deal with his inner thoughts and feelings."

Children's Services recommended that the court make a decision based on their caseworker's report, on Billy's "attitude" in court, and on his behavior for the past few days, while he had been living at home with his parents. Presumably in terror of a whipping, Billy had managed to behave very well for five days, but even if he had not, Linda didn't want her son to be sent to MacLaren. She was happy to use the idea of a punitive reform school as a means of controlling him, but Jody believes her mother never had any sincere intention to have Billy sent away, beyond her own control. "Once again," Jody says, her mother's "desire for him to be okay" required Linda to deny how disturbed her son really was, and as usual, her first concern was how the family, especially she herself, might appear to others.

"It was a solemn moment," Jody says of the conversation she had with her mother about Billy, adding that she suspects her mother's uncharacteristic invitation to her to share her thoughts about the possibility of her brother going to reform school was prompted by a social worker's suggestion that the decision involve the whole family, taking each member's perspective into account. "She asked me to join her in her bedroom and she sat down on the bed. I was lying on my side, head cupped in hand, and she told me that they were thinking about sending Billy away to MacLaren, the long-threatened destination. What did I think she should do? I was unequivocal—he should go. Nothing they were doing or saying was changing anything. He kept getting worse and worse."

"Worse and worse" referred, of course, to Billy's growing juvenile record and the domestic discord that resulted from his behavior, but there was another reason Jody wanted her brother out of the house. "I don't remember how old I was when it started, or when it went from something I thought I might be imagining to something I suspected, to something I knew."

It was Billy's creeping into Jody's bedroom late at night, while she was sleeping, with the purpose of molesting her, and even if it was not yet a violation of which she was consciously aware, it would have had the power to intensify Jody's sense that her brother was dangerous, and that she in particular needed protection from him. On several occasions, Jody remembers waking abruptly and feeling "odd, unsettled." Aware that something had disturbed her sleep, she couldn't guess what, exactly, it had been, until one night when she sat up and saw Billy standing by her bed in the dark. "Why are you here?" she asked him. He gave her the unconvincing excuse that he was looking for a pillow, and she sent him away.

Suspicious, and resourceful, Jody set a trap for her brother. She chose her moment carefully. The two of them were sitting in the backseat of the car, waiting for their parents to finish saying good-bye to friends and drive them all home. It was late, and Jody pretended to doze off. After a few minutes, their parents still inside the house, Jody felt her brother's hand steal between her legs. Quickly, she closed her knees and caught his hand between her thighs. As before, Billy had a ready, less-than-credible excuse. He'd been falling asleep, too, he told her, and his hand had fallen inadvertently into her crotch.

Twenty-five years later, Billy's explanation is the same. "I never touched Jody intentionally," he says when I ask him why his sister remains convinced that he did. "We were always left in the car like that, our parents with their friends, Frances and her husband, or whoever, all of them drinking. It took forever for them to get Becky from where she was sleeping and come out and take us home, so we were always falling asleep back there."

"What about when Jody woke up and saw you in her bedroom?" I press.

"If Jody saw someone in her room—if there was someone coming in and touching her, it wasn't me."

"Who would it have been, then?"

"Our father, that's who. He molested both of them, both my sisters. He used to watch Jody sunbathing and he'd have his hand on himself, he'd be, you know, touching himself, touching his penis. I even saw him with Becky on his lap, when she was nine, ten. He'd be massaging her privates, and she let him. She did because he'd give her some change."

Jody shakes her head when I report this explanation.

"You don't think it's at all possible?" I ask her.

"No. Absolutely not."

"He did make sexual overtures," I say, referring to her father.

"Yes, but that was later. And it was different—he didn't touch me."

I consider the idea that Jody may have repressed memories of being molested by her father, but I do so out of a commitment to think carefully and thoroughly about her family history. The Jody I encounter in conversation strikes me as an unusually stalwart and self-disciplined individual. I know that she has dedicated a great deal of time and energy to understanding what unfolded among the members of her troubled family, and has, in her own words, "been pretty open with all the horrors that are normally repressed out of shame and fear." I can imagine Jody refusing to engage with threatening memories, reacting to them cerebrally and sidestepping their impact on her feelings, but not denying them.

If Billy was sexually aroused by his sisters, which he tells me was not the case, displacing his attraction onto his father would allow him to simultaneously keep and disown incestuous feelings. But another motivation for his insisting that his father molested his sisters may be legal. In service to his appeal, Billy has made a study of parricide cases and from them learned what typically provokes a child to violently assault a parent. Physical abuse, a parent's alcoholism, the failure of social services to rescue the child, authorities thwarting the child's attempts to run away, escalating tensions in the months leading up to the murder: the Gilley family exhibited most of the known catalysts for parricide. But if Billy could claim a complete list of predisposing factors, wouldn't his case be that much stronger? In this lies the temptation for Billy to present his father as a sexual predator, providing himself with a noble provocation for murder—he was desperate to protect his sisters from sexual abuse—as he did in his 1996 affidavit, but not when speaking with either of the psychiatrists who examined him twelve years before, in the months after the murders. It would have been a lie based in the truth, as Bill had, during the last year of his life, made inappropriate gestures as well as comments toward Jody, looking at her in a way she describes as "leering" when she sunbathed on the roof of the barn in her bikini, but still a fabrication.

Whenever it was that Jody did at last confirm her

suspicions about Billy—and she can't give me the year—
she went to her mother and told Linda what her brother
had done and was met with disbelief, which she tells me
she received as "an ultimate betrayal. At that moment I
lost any remaining respect [for my parents] or feeling
that I was their child." During the hours-long lecture inspired by Jody's accusation, Linda said to Billy, in
essence, that what was disgusting about her older daughter's claim wasn't that Billy had done it—she didn't believe he had—but that he was so degenerate a person that
his own sister could believe such a thing about him.

"Anyway," Jody says, "beyond the abuse, there were
ample non-abuse reasons why sending Billy away seemed
like the right response to his transgressions. Not that his
punishment at home wasn't ten times worse, but in my
view he was the source of most of the family strife at that
point. There were almost daily calls from school about
fights, smoking, et cetera, or we had to deal with police,
or counselors. And all those yelling marathons—even the
ones that weren't directed at me affected me, all of us."

The judge released Billy to his parents. As only three
weeks remained in the school year, and as he was failing
his classes to the point that, in his caseworker's words,
"his only purpose for attending school would be social
in nature," the court followed her recommendation that
he remain at home for the duration of the term.

A week after the hearing, Billy was arrested for bur-
glary in the first degree and arson in the first degree.

Andrew,* Josh,* and Dwight Martin* were, Billy tells
me, "a family of firebugs" who would and did set fire to

---

*All names followed by asterisks have been changed.

anything. They were bad kids, conniving and destructive, and Billy was with them when they broke into 2792 Old Stage Road, a home belonging to people the Gilleys knew. They rummaged around, stole a calculator, set fire to a bag of garbage, and left. Nervous in the wake of their trespass, the Martins decided to ditch the calculator, but Billy said no, he'd keep it, and the boys parted company.

Two days later, the four met up again and, as a petition filed on June 13, 1980, states, "did then and there unlawfully and recklessly damage a grass-covered area, the property of Jackson County, by fire." When the police arrested the Martins, who, Billy says, were always the first to be investigated when the crime was arson, Dwight ratted on Billy, claiming he'd instigated the break-in and had the stolen calculator. On June 5, the police came to the Gilleys', found Billy in possession of the calculator, arrested him, and took him back to juvenile detention.

"Why did you keep the calculator?" I ask Billy. "Did you really want it?"

"No. I dunno. I guess I just never like to throw stuff away," he says and he shrugs, giving me a sheepish smile.

Certainly Billy was impulsive and he had poor judgment. He was confused, angry, despairing. But this was the first time he'd been involved in an act of deliberate destruction, destruction for its own sake. Perhaps he was, as he says, just a lookout for the Martins—the state came to a different conclusion—but even the lookout is a participant, and burning the home of another family, a happier, more prosperous family, was a new expression of anger, of a kind that so easily gets out of control.

Burning things is exciting. It's beautiful and complete. A form of magic, a transformation.

Afterward, there's nothing left.

"MR. GILLEY," DR. MALETZKY REPRISED FROM his interview with Billy two months after the murders, "had a feeling he 'had to do it'" that night. He "felt defensive of Jody, recognized that he and Jody were teamed together in this family against his father, mother, and younger sister," Becky, whom Billy described to the psychiatrist as "almost the same person" as their mother, giving examples of how Becky always sided with Linda against him. "He lay in bed summoning the courage to act. He said at this point that he understood he had a 'covenant' with Jody to take their parents' lives, though Jody denies any such arrangement."

A subsequent psychiatric evaluation, made by a Dr. David Kirkpatrick, also at the behest of Billy's court-appointed attorney, includes a provoking nightmare that Billy did not share with Dr. Maletzky. On the night of the murders, Billy "dreamed a recurrent dream about his mother and father being vampires and devouring the children." When he woke, after an hour or so of sleep, he was "sweaty" and experiencing dissociation. "In a sort of dream with no physical sensation, no emotions, or sensations, he attacked and clubbed his father with a baseball bat." Whether this prelude of a disorienting nightmare represents a genuine discrepancy between Billy's two accounts—one two months, the other six months, after the murders—a difference between the two doctors' reports of his comments, or Billy's conscious, or unconscious, agenda to provide his crimes an extra dollop of mitigation in the form of his parents' tormenting him even as he slept, can neither be known nor proved one way or another.

"I know his perspective," Jody writes me in an e-mail dated March 21, 2005, before our first meeting. "His rationales are heartfelt and delusional. His pain real and imagined. Much like all of us. Sometimes I see in myself my brother's delusions and my carefully arranged reality becomes less tidy, and so I put that introspection back into the box"—a mental compartment Jody sometimes calls her "iron box," suggesting the inviolable strength she demands of it. But Billy's and Jody's "delusions" are as different as the needs that inspire them. Billy's narratives rationalize his actions, adding layers of causation, reasons for murders he considers justified. Jody's follow an opposite impulse, toward empiricism; she pares away whatever she fears might obscure the truth. If Billy's retrospective includes emotions or psychological nuances that may not have characterized the original experience, Jody removes feelings or thoughts she might actually have had in the moment, worried she may have added them unconsciously after the fact.

"Between 12:30 and 1:00 AM," Dr. Maletzky reported, "Mr. Gilley arose, took his baseball bat, which he had kept with him in his room (he said this was not unusual) and went downstairs." (His room was, in fact, on the same floor as his parents'; it was Jody who had the attic bedroom.) Having erroneously assumed that he could kill his father by striking him on the head just once, "like on TV," Billy "found himself hitting his father repeatedly," because Bill "did not die instantly but moaned and breathed loudly and moved his hand partially to deflect the blows." Then, Billy told Dr. Maletzky, he "stopped abruptly, 'ran like crazy' into his mother's room, put the light on, and beat her approximately five times on the head with the baseball bat. He said that he was not aware at the time he was beating her that Becky was sleeping next to her" (on a waterbed that may have absorbed and diffused some of the force of the blows, explaining Becky's failure to wake). When he realized that Becky was stirring, he grabbed her "so she wouldn't see what he had done, and took her upstairs to Jody's room."

"No," Billy tells me when we talk. "Becky woke up in her own bedroom, on account of all the noise, and then wandered out into the living room."

"She said she wanted to sleep with Mom," his affidavit explains, in contrast to the report he'd given ten years earlier, to Dr. Maletzky, and when Becky became insistent the only thing Billy could think to do was send her upstairs to Jody, so he told Becky that Jody wanted to talk to her, and before she could resist he picked her up and ran up the stairs with her. "Stay here," Billy said to Becky, and he put her down in their sister's room.

"What is it?" Jody asked, turning her face away from the sudden glare of the overhead light. He seemed nervous, and he was speaking loudly, almost yelling at Becky, but these were afterthoughts. In the moment they didn't really register or seem significant.

"I'm a heavy sleeper," she answered the district attorney's prompt at the trial, "and I was real disoriented and not fully awake."

"How did Becky appear to you?" the DA asked.

"She appeared the same. She was disoriented as though she had just woken up."

"Keep Becky up here," Billy told Jody. "Keep her with you." Then he went back downstairs, moving quickly, skipping some treads, and closed her door, which was at the foot of the staircase.

"What do you want?" Becky asked Jody, who remembers that her sister was awake only enough to be annoyed at having been woken. She did not seem alert, as she would have if she'd gotten herself up and already engaged in a conflict with their brother. "Billy said you—"

"I don't want anything," Jody said. "I was asleep."

"I'm going down to Mom," Becky told her. "I'm not staying up here."

JODY LET HER GO. HALF ASLEEP, SHE DIDN'T try to figure out what was happening. Did she ask Becky to turn off the light when she went back downstairs? She doesn't remember. Like so much of what preceded her sister's screams, the light, or the dark, was obliterated by those screams.

She remembers what followed the screams, remembers clearly, although she never did manage to describe it to anyone's satisfaction, the series of noises she was asked about over and over again. How long? How loud? How many? Did they come from the foot of the stairs? From the living room? Your parents' bedroom?

How could the terrorized sixteen-year-old explain to detectives that when this kind of thing happens it's like one of those old home movies that melt and break when the projector has been running long enough to get hot? Damaged frames have to be cut out, the film spliced back together with tape. You can still follow it, afterward, but there are pieces missing.

Whatever happened before the screams—maybe nothing, maybe just the empty frames of sleep—after them Jody sat up in bed, the covers fell from her shoulders into her lap. She heard a noise, and then she heard it again, several times, but it wasn't—it seemed to her that it couldn't have been—real. Or if it was, it couldn't have been what she thought it was: the sound of someone— Billy—hitting Becky very hard, hard enough to stop her from screaming. If it was happening, Jody remembers telling herself, it was happening in a book. Becky was in the book, and Jody was, too. They all were, she told herself, the whole family. Wasn't that how she got through most of her life anyway, by being in a book?

Billy tells me he remembers waiting by the side of the woodstove, trying to come up with a way to keep Becky out of their mother's bedroom, but when she came back downstairs she was intractable, "a brat the way she usually was," he tells me. He blocked her way physically, and she pummeled him and tried to barrel her way through his arms. Although Billy's reports of hitting Becky (and, possibly, his memories of it) are not in agreement with one another, most follow the basic steps of his panicking, picking up the bat from where he'd left it on the floor, and hitting her on the head once with the intent of knocking her unconscious and, he explains to me, failing to take into account the fragility of the skull of an eleven-year-old relative to an adult's. After he hit her, he says, Becky fell, striking her head on the corner of the coffee table before hitting the floor. Only one account, Dr. Maletzky's, based on the interview that followed most closely on the murders, suggests that Billy hit Becky more than twice—"approximately five times," with the initial purpose of "protect[ing] her against seeing the 'mess' " in their mother's room, but escalating in a frenzy of panic until he assumed he had killed her.

Dr. Mario Campagna, the neurosurgeon who testified at Billy's trial for murder, described Becky's injuries as follows: There was a severe laceration behind the right ear from which brain matter extruded and a smaller one on her forehead, near the hairline, that was also leaking brain matter. X-rays revealed that her skull had been shattered in what is commonly called an "eggshell-type fracture where there are fifteen or twenty of them throughout all the skull." It was Dr. Campagna's opinion that Becky had probably been hit twice, hard. It was unlikely, he said, that her head's striking a table as she fell caused either of her injuries.

"So if you hit Becky only once, and you'd already killed your parents, what was all the pounding Jody heard?" I ask Billy.

"The noise of the bat hitting the arm of the couch where my father was lying. After . . . after Becky . . . I went back to where my father was and I started screaming that it was all his fault Becky was dead, and he was . . . he was dead, but I was hitting him anyway, trying to, but the couch—it's one of those where the arms are made of wood, it doesn't have . . . it's not padded or what do you call it? Upholstered? Anyway, the bat kept glancing off the wood."

It isn't until after I speak with Billy in person that I read his affidavit, a copy of which he mails to me, and the explanation is the same: as soon as Billy realized how gravely he'd injured Becky, he says, "I picked up the bat and ran into the living room and stood next to my father. I told him that this was all his fault. I remember I started hitting him and screaming 'I hate you' over and over."

"It's important," Detective Davis said to Jody on the day of the killings, "that you tell me exactly what you heard. Screaming was the first thing you heard when Becky went downstairs?"

"Yeah. She screamed like 'Stop' or 'Ouch' and then I started hearing this pounding."

"You heard the screaming and then a pounding noise. Can you recall whether it was one pound or two?"

"It was a whole bunch."

This was the moment, Jody says, that she knew Billy had killed the rest of the family. "But I was afraid," she told Detective Davis. "I couldn't say anything or do anything because I knew if I did he would hit, kill me, too."

THE PICTURE I'VE LONG CARRIED IN MY mind, of two teenagers in a car that won't move, doesn't fade or change as I learn the fuller story of who the Gilleys were before the night of the murders. That image remains, but I form others as well, and when I think of Jody it's as a little girl playing on Dyer Road, where she lived until she was eight.

In October 2005, when Jody and I visit Medford, we discover that her first home is being rehabbed, turned into a paint store. Still, it's a marginal neighborhood. Lots stand empty, overgrown with weeds and brambles, and a couple of stray dogs nose among the windblown rubbish that has come to rest in a shallow ditch beside what's not so much a road as a long dirt driveway accessing a few homes. When Jody and I visit Dyer Road, we walk together past the same unkempt trees—scrub oak—she used to play among.

Looking up at their twisted boughs, Jody tells me about an alternative world she created as a child, one populated by families of ghosts who lived in the trees near her home. Accompanying her brother to or from the school bus stop, she'd greet them by name as she passed their respective dwellings. I like this picture I have of her, calling out to her ghosts, playing outside rather than reading in her room, and when she tells me her mother used to look out the window and see her sitting on the back fence chattering away to someone no one else could see, I like that, too. Unlike most of the impressions I form of Jody's childhood, the scene seems carefree. At first it does.

But time passes, and I find myself returning to our walk along Dyer Road. I examine the single photograph I have of the road and the trees—one Jody took with her cell phone—and as I consider Jody's ghosts in the context of all I've come to know of her family, increasingly they strike me as sad. Though testimony to her imaginative nature, still they are ghosts, and ghosts are dead. Ghosts are those who have died and yet persist in our fantasies. Doesn't this make them different from other imaginary companions? Might not Jody, as young as six or seven when she created them, have already begun at that age to mourn what, *whom*, she'd lost—aspects of herself, all the Jodys she might have been were it not for the destructive environment into which she was born? Couldn't the part of her mind that dreamt, whether sleeping or waking, have preserved the memory of other Jodys, girls who never had a chance to come to life and whose outlines lingered, just out of reach?

After all, it was only by being dead—deadened—that the sixteen-year-old Jody would manage to navigate the night of the murders, not responding emotionally but thinking, thinking wildly, trying to arrive at a strategy for escape, and for saving herself and what was left of Becky. Jody herself observes that her ability to survive the murder of her family depended at least in part on defenses she'd created long before to protect herself from her parents' cruelty. Billy may have taken refuge in television and comic book heroes, vented his anger and misery at school, but Jody amputated her feelings. She separated her rational, thinking self from the emotional suffering selves, the parts of her that were frightened, angry, grieving.

"CONING MONEY," BILLY SAYS WHEN I ASK how his family afforded the 1976 move from Dyer Road to Ross Lane, eight years before the murders. "That whole place was bought with coning money." He shakes his head and laughs, a noise of contempt.

The house on Ross Lane was bigger than the one on Dyer Road. It had a fireplace and an upstairs and, located in a rural area on the outskirts of Medford, the property included a seventeen-stable barn, a paddock, and three smaller outbuildings.

"But what is coning, exactly?" I ask Billy. "What's involved?"

Billy explains that seed cones, essential to reforestation efforts, are harvested from mid-August through September, when the cones of evergreen trees are mature but haven't yet opened to disperse the seeds they hold, and before hunting season fills the woods with gunfire. Collectors climb the trees using spurs and rake the branches to release the green cones, which are gathered into burlap sacks. At the time, Billy estimates, each sack was worth about $50; coners paid by the sack needed to fill twenty to earn $1,000. But before 1981 (when the Reagan administration cut funds to an array of state and local programs) the federal Bureau of Land Management handed out lucrative coning contracts to tree workers who put in successful bids, paying them for an entire season's worth of work, valued at far more money than even the most energetic worker could earn independently. Among them was Bill Gilley, who made as much as $30,000 each summer from 1974 to 1980, a significant, ultimately crucial supplement to his income.

From the time he was nine, Billy tells me, he went con-ing with his father, working on the ground to collect and pack cones into sacks. With the windfall of each gov-ernment contract, Bill expanded his business, bought equipment, and hired extra hands for the big jobs he landed. In the fall of 1976, feeling flush in the wake of a few fat summers, he and Linda pulled together the down payment on the new place and were confident they could manage the mortgage. For a family with a history of homelessness and vagrancy that had carried them from county to county and from one welfare office to the next, the move represented a sea change. The Gilleys were no longer renting a tiny house on a dirt track; they were landed. Not only did each child have his or her own room, the house included two full bathrooms, a laundry room, a dining room, and a patio. "The fields that surrounded us on all sides seemed like ours," Jody wrote in college, "regardless of who really owned them," and the four acres the family did own was enough that they could keep livestock: goats, chickens. As Jody describes it in "Death Faces," "the house seemed large, and a symbol of my father's middle class prosperity, and our dreams of becoming 'rich kids.'"

When the Gilleys moved into their new home, a small cinder block structure adjacent to the patio, an out-building they'd end up using as a pantry, was filled with junk. Among what had been left behind by the previous owners were a number of unlabeled amber-colored pharmacy bottles holding pills and capsules. Unidenti-fied, perhaps expired, the drugs were worthless if not harmful, but to Billy they represented a potential form of currency: a means of commanding attention from his new schoolmates. The December move had required the older children to transfer to a new school, and Billy tells me he found switching schools traumatic. Although *destabilized* is not the word he uses, he seems to have been knocked even further off balance than he had been before, struggling under the double burden of an abusive home life and an educational system that, having failed to identify his learning disabilities, was also failing to teach him. He removed all the little die-cast cars from his Hot Wheels carrying case and outfitted it with the bottles of pills. Now he had the perfect prop for presenting himself as a drug dealer. He made the mistake of showing the case to Jody, who was shocked and even frightened by what struck her as dangerous rather than exciting or enviable. Determined to get the case away from her brother and hide it before she went to her mother to tell on him—before he took the opportunity to hide it himself—she got only as far as relocating the evidence before Billy discovered her betrayal and became enraged.

Whatever had been true in the past, the incident with the Hot Wheels case would mark the beginning of a new era between Jody and her brother. When Billy learned that Jody had stolen his drug kit, an object essential to his fantasy of becoming a figure of respect among his classmates, he chased her around the house to prevent her from telling on him and, in order to terrorize her into returning the Hot Wheels case, physically assaulted her in a new and horrible way. He forced her to the floor, got a hand inside her underpants, and tried to thrust his fingers inside her vagina—"all his fingers," Jody explains, "like a spatula." He wouldn't let her go, or take his hand away, until he got her to promise to return the case and not to tell on him. If she told, he threatened her, he'd do it again.

I ask Billy about the incident, and he denies having ever attacked, much less molested, Jody. He denies this incident specifically and believes—or says he believes, or has convinced himself—that there was never any break in the love he felt for his sister. Even periods of estrangement from Jody couldn't weaken the bond he had with the girl he loved absolutely, he tells me, from the day she was born.

As far as Jody is concerned, this is one of several instances in which her brother serves the conceit of a spiritual alignment that remains intact no matter what violation is visited on it. Sadly, it seems that Billy's attempt to preserve what he imagined might provide him standing in the school yard caused him to lose what hadn't been a fantasy and what couldn't be replaced: his sister's trust and affection. From this point forward, Jody tells me, her relationship with her brother would be defined by suspicion, fear, even loathing. She had sympathy for the torment he endured, or sometimes she did, but she didn't want him anywhere near her.

There was no way, of course, for Jody to have perceived the importance to her brother of the Hot Wheels case and its contents, no way for her to understand the kind of chronic anxiety he experienced. She was a good student and kept out of trouble, largely avoiding the beatings Billy took. Her confidence increased immediately upon the family's move to Ross Lane, which she took as evidence they'd come up in the world. At that moment, in third grade, Jody Gilley was happier than she would be for many more years, and the only thing wrong with her life, she tells me, was the increasingly disturbed and threatening presence of her brother.

IN MEDFORD, JODY GUIDES ME THROUGH HER childhood in chronological order: middle school before high school, Dyer Road before Ross Lane. The house on Ross Lane is a clapboard structure painted white, with crisp, dark green trim. The present owner, whom I've tried without success to contact, isn't home to let us inside, so we walk around the periphery of the house while Jody explains the layout within, identifying which window belonged to whose bedroom. The contrast between the blood-soaked fantasies inspired by the house's history and the well-kempt exterior before us is disorienting. I ask Jody how it feels to be this close to her past, her "before" life, and she lifts her shoulders in a shrug of what looks like bewilderment.

As long as we remain focused on physical details—the ways in which the property is different, the ways in which it remains the same as it was—it's easy for the two of us to converse. In answer to my questions, Jody points out where Billy stood when whacking the cardboard box, where it was that her father stored his tree service equipment, the location of the plum tree, now twenty years older and larger, that wasn't tall enough in 1984 to allow her to climb from her bedroom window into its branches, the route across the field to Kathy Ackerson's, and so on. But when I ask about the emotional experience of returning to this place, she shakes her head and looks at me blankly, without affect. It's as if her face has lost its animating force, whatever it is that gives expression to her eyes, her mouth. Usually she's a particularly alert-looking individual, attuned to her environment; her eyes and expression quicken to stimulus. Here she seems stunned, as if by a blow or a drug.

I know that this trip is exhausting for Jody—how could it be otherwise?—but when I refer to it as a "forced march" over difficult terrain, she corrects me. As Jody explained to me months earlier, when she feels overwhelmed by what happened in her family, she measures her loss, individual and personal, against the sweeping tragedies of history, the Holocaust, the Civil War carnage at Antietam, the endless crises on the African continent. Doesn't the fact that people survived such epic horrors diminish the significance of her own suffering? "A forced march," she tells me, "is Napoleon's army retreating from Moscow, starving and barefoot."

I remain in Medford a day longer than Jody and come back to Ross Lane alone. Standing in what used to be the Gilleys' front yard, I turn slowly in a circle, willing myself to remember what I see: two white posts marking the entrance to the unpaved driveway; a dormer window over the front porch and another over the kitchen; sun striking the side door's cement steps; the barn with its steeply pitched roof, on which Jody sunbathed, the empty horse paddock; the dense shadows cast by the walnut trees. As far as I know, this is the first place I've visited where blood has been shed and not subsequently memorialized, and it teaches me how intense is the urge to mark where a violent death occurred, to be cautioned as much as informed by a monument, even one as simple as the wood cross friends or family place by the side of a road, bearing witness to a fatal crash. We want to know where to step carefully.

It's quiet on Ross Lane; only two cars pass in the hour I spend there alone. Overhead, the sky is deeply blue and spread with cumulus, clouds with distinct and evocative outlines, hurrying past. I sit, elbows on knees, where Billy, Jody, and Becky must have sat countless times, on the sunny cement step outside the kitchen door, the one through which Jody and Billy left the house on the night he killed the rest of their family. Looking out from Jody's old doorstep, I find myself returning, as I have several times in the past twenty-four hours, to her rejection of my "forced march" analogy. I try out her strategy of dwarfing a private loss by holding it up to a tragedy of huge proportion. And it's true, no private anguish can compare. If inclusion in a history book is the measure of human agony, then the exercise provides a kind of perspective. But I wonder: even an army's pain is experienced one soldier at a time.

IN THE FALL OF 1977, BILLY ENTERED SIXTH grade and was at last tested for the learning disabilities that were evident five years earlier, when he first tried and failed to read. Only with respect to vocabulary, listening skills, and applied math was he above average for his grade level. His reading and other language skills were poor, as was his ability to concentrate effectively. While his vision wasn't impaired, his oculomotor patterns—the pointing and focusing of his eyes—tested as inadequate, as did his visual space perception, which included the awareness of depth. Subsequent tests would reveal that Billy's eyes didn't work together as they should, but for the time being he was given the blanket diagnosis of dyslexia and shunted into remedial classes, which didn't help as he was not in fact dyslexic.

"That must have been frustrating," I comment when we talk about this. Billy looks at me and shakes his head slowly. He's eating the second in a package of two Reese's Peanut Butter Cups, taking small, even bites and using the ruffled brown paper that held the candy to convey it to his mouth without getting his fingers sticky. When he finishes, he folds the brown paper neatly into the shiny orange wrapper and places it on the table next to the can of Mountain Dew he asked me to buy him. At the beginning of each interview I ask if I can get him something from the vending machines he's not allowed to operate, and each time he requests either one or two packets of Reese's cups with a Mountain Dew or Snapple. The fact that I pay for these small things he would otherwise have to purchase with a day's worth of menial prison work makes them something to savor, but I don't think this is what inspires his careful, polite handling of the candy, the way he opens each wrapper without tearing it. Nor does it seem to be one of the countless small rituals on which inmates spend their seemingly limitless supply of time and attention—or it isn't only that. Like his speech, all of Billy's movements are measured, so controlled as to appear almost leisurely.

"Not really," he says, having taken sufficient time to consider the idea of his having been frustrated by remedial language assignments he couldn't do. "See, I'd already given up. The teacher kept telling me I wasn't trying when I was. I *was* trying. I just couldn't do what she told me to. So I gave up. I mean, what was the point?" He raises his eyebrows and holds up his empty hands. The adult Billy, who slowly taught himself to compensate for his visual deficit and began, in prison, to read, seems to have made peace with his disastrous school career. Too, having accomplished academic feats that once seemed impossible, Billy takes evident pride in his belated success, forwarding me his college transcript from Chemeketa Community College in Salem, Oregon, through which he took classes and earned an associate's degree in 1993, while in prison.

"Three point two seven," he reminds me more than once during my visit, referring to his B+ average.

But when he was in the sixth and seventh grades, Billy was clearly an unhappy child. "Nervous," reads one school health record, "frequent headaches and stomachaches." "Emotional disturbance, undue restlessness and shyness," comments another. Not only did school fail to provide Billy the kind of positive reinforcement it gave Jody and later Becky, but his poor classroom performance and his tendency to get into trouble made his home life worse than it might have been had he been a source of pride. Always concerned first with what

outsiders might think of her and her family, Linda focused on the public aspect of Billy's failure and was determined to reform her son, an ongoing project to which
she and Bill brought a lot of energy and little insight, ad-
ministering whippings reflexively without ever seeming
to consider that they weren't accomplishing what was
perhaps never more than the nominal goal of disciplining
their son. Jody and Billy both describe parents who took
sadistic pleasure in punishing their children, and whose
viciousness was enabled by the fact that Linda gave in-
structions for Bill to carry out. With such a system in
place, neither parent had to take full responsibility for
what was excessive, often brutal retaliation for minor,
even trumped-up infractions. Linda was "only" saying
that punishment was required; Bill was "only" doing
what his wife said he had to do. Her religious rationales
and his having been fathered by a battering alcoholic
were the Gilleys' particular recipe for child abuse.

Linda was brought up by churchgoers, her mother
alert to manifestations of the Crazy Italian that needed
to be prayed or punished away, but it was Linda's frustration with her husband that intensified her commitment to rigid Baptist doctrine. Trapped in an unhappy
marriage to a man who, she suspected, drank surreptitiously and cheated on her, Linda would be satisfied, I
imagine, more by a punitive than a forgiving God. Fun-
damentalism excused her from the effort of working out
her own answers to questions of right and wrong, and it
reassured Linda that her long-suffering fidelity would be
rewarded even as Bill's sins earned him a far worse
comeuppance than any she could give him. It was a se-
ductive enough idea that she became an unusually intol-
erant and self-righteous young woman, religious in a
way her parents had never been.

After trying out a few different churches before finding what Jody calls "the right brand of fire and brim-

stone," the Gilleys joined Harvest Baptist Temple, whose membership was large enough that Linda could preserve her anonymity, as Jody says she preferred to do. While most churchgoers enjoy the social embrace of a congregation, Linda wanted only two things of Harvest Baptist: that the doctrine projected from its pulpit reward her martyrdom and that the church bolster the rigid control she wanted over her children's behavior, especially by dampening the emergence of their sexuality. But Jody and Billy saw too much of their mother's hypocrisy to join her in the faith she misrepresented. The idea that sex was a means of procreation not pleasure was one Linda could model as well as preach, but she didn't exemplify Christian tolerance, let alone love.

With a larger house and three outbuildings at their disposal, the strained family had the means to stay out of one another's way and, presumably, avoid a measure of conflict. Always what Billy calls "a hoarder," Linda had her own detached garage in which to keep all the things she couldn't part with.

"Like what?" I ask him.

"Anything. Didn't matter what. Busted toys and old magazines and boxes of papers and who knows what else. She couldn't throw anything away."

Bill had the second garage for his toolshed, and he kept heavier equipment in the barn where, Billy tells me, he also hid his liquor. In contrast to Jody, Billy highlights his father's drinking and misses few opportunities to bring it up, but Jody tells me Linda made sure Bill was usually abstinent—a "mean, mean-spirited, dry drunk who didn't need alcohol to be horrid," Jody calls him. The fact that Bill had an uncontrollable temper whether drunk or sober left him, and his family, without the means to excuse his violence as a result of impaired faculties. Still, both children remember the move to Ross Lane as the point at which Linda forbade Bill to drink in the house, with the result that he did stop in his family's presence, perhaps misleading Jody as to the extent of her father's addiction. On the night of the murders, when Jody at last found a chance to call 911, the dispatcher asked if her mother had been drinking that night, and Jody answered no, that her mother didn't drink alcohol except maybe "she'll have a drink once a year at New Year's or something."

"Okay," the dispatcher said.

"My dad doesn't drink, either," Jody told the dispatcher, who hadn't asked if he did.

"Your dad doesn't drink?" the dispatcher asked.

"No."

It may be, as Jody tells me, that she anticipated the dispatcher's next question, but the fact that her assertion wasn't elicited by a question suggests to me that it was the kind of protest that points up the very thing it denies. Fifteen years later, when she was thirty-one and preparing her affidavit, Jody said, without qualifying the statement, "I believe that my father was an alcoholic."

A close reading of the 911 transcripts reveals a subsequent misunderstanding on Jody's part that bears witness to the Gilleys' home life. When the dispatcher asks her if Billy "has ever been violent before," she answers, "Have they?" reflexively applying the concept of violence to her parents before her brother. Only when the dispatcher clarifies, "Has Billy?" does she answer the question she asked.

What we know, what we know privately but refuse to admit to others, what we know but can't bear to contemplate, what we know in our hearts but not in our brains: all of these exist at once within us, whether we are children or adults. Eight years old when the Gilleys moved to Ross Lane, Jody was beginning to perceive more than she was able to accept and could identify much that was wrong with her family—the ongoing verbal and sometimes physical abuse between her parents, their violent treatment of her and Billy but not Becky, Linda's hypocritical religiosity and her panicked response to sexuality—but it would be many years before she allowed herself to see an underlying catalyst for many of these problems: her father's alcoholism.

Whether or not Bill drank surreptitiously in the barn, the structure's relative privacy and its distance from the house made it an ideal place for him to beat his son. The house on Dyer Road was small, sometimes claustrophobic, but on Ross Lane Linda could make her decision that a punishment was required from inside the house while Bill carried it out remotely, allowing Linda to blind herself to the viciousness of what Bill could claim she demanded. This wasn't an original means of enabling cruelty, of course. Few despots bear witness to the tortures by which they maintain control, and even though what Jody would later call "atrocities" were those of a single troubled family rather than a corrupt social order, it was a college course on the literature of the Holocaust that gave Jody the language she needed to speak about what her parents had done to her and her brother, abuse that went beyond corporal punishment and that she believes was meant to break their spirits and cripple them emotionally so that they would never be able to escape.

In contrast to the incidental cuffs and slaps across the face that both Linda and Bill applied reflexively whenever their children talked back or annoyed them in some way, a real whipping was, Jody says, "threatened, then announced, and only after a period of intensifying dread, administered." But first came "hours and hours of lecturing," marathon harangues during which Billy rarely spoke. Only once does Jody remember her brother breaking his silence, by putting his hands over his ears and emitting a long, awful, and unnerving squeal, like a trapped animal that had abruptly arrived at consciousness to find itself facing immediate slaughter, a noise that perhaps surprised Billy as much as it did the rest of the family. As Billy knew, nothing he could say would prevent or lessen what was to come; defending himself might even provoke an extra lick or two. In the barn, whippings evolved from what they had been inside the house—fifteen to thirty lashes with a leather belt on bared skin—to a more formal procedure, for which *flogging* seems the more accurate term.

"My father whipped me at least once a month," Billy says in his affidavit. "I would get a whipping for not cleaning my room, or for doing my chores wrong, or getting in trouble at school, running in the house, or forgetting to feed the chickens. He almost always tied my wrists to a wall pole or a tractor tire to keep me from moving around."

It hadn't taken many beatings for Billy to figure out that a glancing blow did less damage than a direct one. Earlier punishments, back on Dyer Road, had taught him that if he flinched or writhed inadvertently, the belt didn't make solid contact when it hit his moving legs or buttocks and hurt him less. With the benefit of this experience, Billy no longer remained in place, bent over his bed with his pants off. Instead, he tells me, he'd drop to the ground and "roll around the way you're supposed to do if your clothes are on fire." Predictably, this further enraged his father and made him that much more vindictive. When the whippings were removed to the barn,

Bill welcomed this new privacy as an opportunity to tie his son, standing, to a stationary object, so that he could be sure his target stayed put.

"How did he do that?" I ask Billy, remembering a conversation with Jody in which she wondered aloud if her brother submitted to their father meekly, if he offered his wrists to be tied. But Billy misconstrues my meaning.

"With tree line," he says. "You know, the nylon ropes we used for climbing."

"No, I mean, did you . . ." I leave the question unfinished, feeling that to insist on an answer would be to participate in a past punishment by reawakening the humiliation of it. Besides, if Billy walked out to the barn where his father was waiting for him, why wouldn't he stand still when tied? Jody's question, I decide, isn't literal so much as a mark of her inability to imagine offering her body up for abuse. Her essence remained unbroken and defended, hidden deep within herself, one of the coping mechanisms that would allow her to navigate the night of the murders.

Out in the barn, Bill settled on a garden hose rather than his belt, and as Billy was standing rather than bending over a bed, his back took most of the blows, which raised long welts that left bruises after the swelling diminished.

"Although the beatings were severe," Jody says in her affidavit, "I noticed after a while that Billy endured them with stoicism." But if stoicism is defined by silence and a lack of affect, what looked like stoicism might have been something else entirely: shock, dissociation, Billy's attempt to protect his psyche as he couldn't his flesh.

"I was never taken out to the barn and was almost

never the exclusive recipient of a beating," Jody says, "which for me usually began with my selecting a switch from the hedge, stripping it of the painful knobs, vacillating between the stingy, skinny branch versus the qualitatively different pain of the thicker ones." If there wasn't a good switch, a belt or hanger sufficed. But, Jody says, none of them hurt as much as did Linda's "withholding love and affection, and demeaning my intellectual curiosity."

"Do you think your desire to learn made your mother feel ashamed?" I ask her, imagining Jody's bookishness could have provoked Linda to regret having dropped out of school.

"No. I think it was that my intelligence was a barrier between me and the rest of the family."

"Because you had different interests and wouldn't partake of the family culture of watching *Theatre of Blood,* and all the other horror movies, et cetera?"

"Yes, that. But more because she knew I understood that things were not as they were supposed to be—that the image she worked so hard to cultivate, of the ideal happy family, was a sham."

Bill was physically violent; he could be crude; he had a bad temper. But both Jody and Billy see their mother's part in the familial abuse as equally damaging, perhaps even more for its insidious quality. If they were a pair of criminals—or if they were a pair of criminals of a different kind—it might be said that Linda was the brains and Bill the brawn of their operation. It was Linda who spent more time with the children, Linda who kept track of their transgressions and sentenced them accordingly, who doled out restrictive punishments, like groundings, and who made the dreaded "wait until your father comes home" announcements of beatings to come. "Her [Linda's] vicious dog," Billy describes his father for me. Too, as it was Linda who controlled the household finances, it was she who could, if she wanted, "parcel out favors" like an extra hot shower, when the limit she set was two per week. Because she prepared dinner, Linda could force Jody and Billy to eat what they hated. Most unforgivable of all, it was Linda's pride and narcissism, her refusal to let anyone see just how disastrous was her domestic situation, that prevented her from allowing her children to save themselves, and the rest of the family, from the annihilation that was, at that point, still preventable.

I ASK THAD GUYER, THE LEGAL AID ATTORNEY who became Jody's guardian after she was orphaned, if he believes that Billy had what I characterize as "a romantic fixation" on his sister and intended to run away with Jody after killing their parents. The two of us are speaking in the bar of the Hilton hotel on Sixteenth and K streets in Washington, D.C. It's a conversation Thad has agreed to have at Jody's behest, divulging information he would withhold had she not given her permission. Even so, I could have skipped my trip to RadioShack for a compact tape recorder: he won't speak if I turn it on, he tells me.

After I get used to the abrasive energy of his delivery, it's my sense that Thad's gruffness is diagnostic: he wants to know if he can intimidate me, if I have the mettle required to tell the story of what happened to Jody's family. "Yes!" he exclaims in answer to my question about Billy wanting to run away with Jody. The tenor of his voice is that which accompanies a hand striking the top of a table. "Yes! He wanted to marry her. Billy Gilley wanted to fuck his sister. He viewed himself as her white knight, and their parents as the oppressors he was going to save them from."

"What about Becky?" I ask.

"Becky was an impediment."

"So he believed he could do this thing, that it was possible for the two of them to run away together?"

"Billy is paranoid. He is delusional."

"How smart do you think he is? How intelligent?"

"Billy's a person of maximum average intelligence,"

Thad says, by which I think he means that he believes him to have no more than average intelligence, although the statement's clipped, clinical quality makes it sound even less generous than that. "He has street smarts. He started out normal. There's no organic brain problem." Although he doesn't say so, I suspect Thad believes my perceptions are clouded by liberal sentiment, a haze he intends to burn off with cynicism.

"You're referring to the appeal he's making, the statement from the doctor who claims he has—" *brain damage from being hit so often by his father,* I'm about to say when Thad cuts me off.

"He doesn't."

"I know the documents I've read—the ones collected by Billy's attorney for his appeal—are crafted to convince people of his innocence, but all the same, they corroborate Jody's experience of their parents as abusive."

"Which documents?"

"Well, Henry Linebaugh's affidavit, for one. Linebaugh was the tree surgeon who knew Bill and testified that he was pretty brutal to Billy."

The affidavit describes summer days so hot, Linebaugh said, "you couldn't even breathe up on the trees," with Billy left literally out on a limb, without water, for hours. Linebaugh's memory was that he found the teenage Billy alone and injured on a number of occasions, bleeding enough to require bandaging, with no first aid kit on the site, no other worker to administer it.

"If my dad actually saw whatever it was," Billy says when I ask about his getting hurt, "he'd sorta sneer and ask, 'You don't need a Band-Aid, do you?' in this real sarcastic way." Billy leans forward over the table between us to show me a scar on his wrist. "It's from a chain saw," he explains, and he tells me he got it when working alongside an untrained hire who cut a branch improperly so that it broke and hit the still-running saw, which in turn hit Billy's wrist. "It was bleeding enough to, you know, spurt a little, and the guy, he says I should maybe go to the hospital for stitches, but my dad takes a look, and, you know, it's the same thing, 'You don't *need* to go to the hospital, do you?' So I say no." Billy shrugs. "I took a break, kept the hand up over my head for ten minutes, and tied a rag around my wrist. Then it was back to work."

Hot weather was bad enough; winter posed worse dangers. "A bully," to use Linebaugh's word, Bill forced his son to climb high into the "dense, cold, freezing fog," on limbs that Billy says "were iced over, so I couldn't get even one cleat into it, couldn't get any purchase at all." One very cold day, Linebaugh found Billy stuck "forty feet up in a tree without any protective equipment . . . not even a hard hat . . . his rope snagged fifteen feet below him, in what was an egregious violation of OSHA* guidelines." Basic safety regulations insist that whenever one worker is high in a tree, another remain on the ground below, managing the climber's lines so they don't snag and trap him in the tree. Because tree workers often have to wriggle through tight places, Billy explains, they can't carry the bulky coils of rope they need, but must pull it up after them. Still, the rope can snag, requiring a ground man to help free it. Linebaugh said that the sixteen-year-old Billy "was terrified in the tree with his knees knocking in the freezing fog where his hands were blue." He freed the rope and allowed Billy to descend. The rope was badly worn, "exhibiting signs of being cut by chainsaws."

Linebaugh asked Billy where his father was, but Billy, he said, "was so cold that he couldn't talk because his

---

*Occupational Safety and Health Administration.

teeth were chattering so fast." When he warmed up enough to say something, he told Linebaugh his dad had been gone for "two or three hours."

"Where was he?" I ask Billy.

"I dunno. Sometimes he'd of been inside, having a cup of coffee, gabbing with the client. Or if he was hungover he might of been parked somewhere, sleeping in the cab of his truck."

"Bill seemed to resent and despise his son," Linebaugh said. "Bill constantly put down his son as slow-witted and stupid. I remember when Bill would call to Billy and Billy didn't respond [because he hadn't heard his father over the noise of the chipper], Bill would punch his son in the head and yell 'Hey Stupid!' to get his attention. The force in [sic] which Bill hit Billy seemed hard enough to knock him unconscious, but Billy acted like it was just a normal part of his job. It appeared to me that in his father's mind it was.

"I kept expecting to hear one day that Billy got killed while working for his father," Linebaugh concluded his affidavit. "When I heard that Billy had killed his father, it didn't surprise me at all. I remember thinking it was self-defense."

Thad shrugs off the idea that Billy may have suffered brain damage at the hands of his father. His response to Billy's appeal aligns with Jody's; both believe Billy has created what Jody calls "a mythic scenario that fits the typical parricide case."

"Predisposition to abuse is cyclical," Thad says dismissively.

"Meaning that—"

"Meaning that it cycles through generations."

"That fathers who were beaten tend to beat their kids?"

"Yes."

"But you don't believe Billy suffered from anything

akin to battered wife syndrome, that he perceived himself to be in a perpetual state of—" *danger*? I'm about to
ask before he cuts me off.

"Absolutely not. Those murders were plotted, announced, and executed." Thad voices what he understands to have been implicit in Billy's comments and
actions on the afternoon of the murder: "I'm going to
kill them. Here's how I'm going to kill them. I'm going
to do it tonight."

"And Jody didn't respond because she didn't take him
seriously, she'd heard it before. And he wasn't that
specif—"

"Not just that, he's a sociopath. Billy never freaked
out over what he'd done. He was absolutely cold-
blooded. Nothing like his sister. Jody was immediately
recognizable as a . . . a diamond in the rough. These
families do that, throw off a diamond." *These families.*
The words are patronizing. They make Thad sound like
an elitist, but perhaps his is the perspective that comes
from having worked for so many years with people who
live on the edges of society, impoverished and undered-
ucated. Listening to him speak about Jody, it's easy to
picture him as the Pygmalion Jody suggests he was in
"Death Faces," Jody in the role of Galatea.

Galatea, I remember, was a statue, Pygmalion the king
of Cyprus who carved her from ivory and then, seeing
her perfection, fell in love. In answer to his prayers,
Aphrodite brought Galatea to life. When I come to the
end of my first reading of "Death Faces," I look up the
tale in Ovid's *Metamorphoses,* struck by the fact that
the story Jody chose to illustrate her second life, the one
that began after the murders, confirms what I imagined
to have been their effect. I couldn't picture her as living,
animate. I turned her into a statue; I sat her next to Billy
in a car that wouldn't move. In telling the story of her
life, Jody also characterized herself as a girl who had

been frozen—rendered lifeless—by what she had witnessed. And of course Galatea is a very particular statue, one that is reborn as flesh and blood, imbued with spirit.

"Jody's quality is based in literacy," Thad says. "She is a product of reading. Of her imagination. Billy was illiterate. Into head-banging, heavy metal, nihilistic rock—"

This time I interrupt. "But he had learning disabilities. He couldn't help being illiterate."

Thad leans forward, speaking emphatically, bearing down on me. "Billy Gilley was *informed* by nihilistic, destructive music. Jody may have listened to it, but she was *entertained* by it. And she had many other sources of information. The prevailing reality for Jody was reading. Her bedroom, it was a separate world from the rest of that house, which was filled up with comic books. She had books everywhere in that room. It was overwhelming to see, actually."

"What music did Billy listen to?" I ask Jody, and I tell her about Thad's judgment of its impact on her brother.

"AC/DC and the like. But he also liked the Cars and Blondie," she adds, mentioning two bands I, too, liked as a teenager, saying she's "loath to pin any causality" on her brother's taste in music.

"Acid rock, yeah, some heavy metal, AC/DC," Billy says, "but I listened indiscriminately to rock, I listened to all of it."

I tell Thad, whose expression is one of manufactured patience, a message to me that he's not so much listening as temporarily indulging my misperception, that Billy is no longer the person he used to be, that he's taught himself to read in prison, earned his GED, and associate's degree. I tell him Billy draws a lot, as well, and sends me the illustrated stories he writes.

"You know the first piece of Billy's art I saw?" Thad says. "A heart with a knife in it, dripping blood."

"The letter from jail?" I ask.

He nods. "Nice, huh?" he says.

I have a photocopy of the drawing Thad recalls. It's at the top of a letter Billy sent to Jody from jail, five weeks after the murders, and it isn't a heart but something more ominous, more personal. Through the loop of the cursive uppercase *J* of his sister's name, a loop shaped like the left half of a valentine heart, a short dagger is drawn to appear as if plunged into the initial. Below her name, a small puddle has accumulated from what drips from the hole stabbed in the *J,* as if it were blood from a pierced organ. Thad remembers it as a heart because that's the impression the drawing leaves.

"Yeah," Billy says when I ask him about the drawing, "I was angry. I'd been there, alone in jail, for what, a hundred and fifty days?" (The letter's June 1 postmark indicates it had actually been thirty-five days since his arrest.) "I was angry with her for betraying me. For telling them all of it was me, was all my idea."

SHE WAS AFRAID—SO AFRAID SHE COULDN'T move—and she did nothing. She tells me she remembers knowing what she knew, and telling herself it was happening in a book. How many books had she read in which terrible things happened, the situation appeared hopeless, the heroine doomed, when somehow, against all odds, she was saved? Now, Jody told herself, she was a character in a book, she was the girl for whom things looked bad—very bad—but turned out all right. In the end, they always did turn out.

Trolling through flea markets, Linda would buy the occasional dollar box of used toys or books for her children, and when Jody, twelve or thirteen, found a collection of battered Harlequin romances, Linda bought them for her, inadvertently providing passport into a realm in which Jody would spend much of her adolescence.

"Had she known what was in them"—the pre- or extramarital touching and kissing of which her mother disapproved—"she'd never have allowed me to read them," Jody tells me, smiling, the idea of having gotten away with even so small, so innocent, an infraction still giving her pleasure. But Linda didn't read much aside from the comic books she collected, and Jody did—she read whatever she could get her hands on.

How did she escape? Jody asked herself. *Did the heroine jump out the window?* She tells me she tried to figure out if she could jump out of her window and not hurt herself, not break a leg or sprain an ankle. If she could jump from the second floor and run across the field, across the field to Kathy's, where there was a telephone, a telephone and a door that locked, locked him, Billy, out, then—

But she didn't—couldn't—move. She was transfixed, able to think but stuck there, inside her head, asking herself what to do. What would a character in a book do when she suspected her brother had killed her parents and her sister? When she thought that was what had happened, even though it couldn't be true. Because that kind of screaming was— It wasn't— Jody couldn't think of anything that could make Becky scream like that, except—

"What did he say exactly?" Detective Davis asked her. His tape recorder was running. Before he began the interview he said what time it was, and what day, and he said his name, Richard Davis, and hers, Jody Gilley, and after he said her name he spelled it out for the machine. G-I-L-L-E-Y.

What had Billy said when the two of them were talking alone in her room?

"He said something about how unfair they were, and how he'd like to get even," Jody told him. "When I, when I told him that they were, had been, more lenient with him. And he got real upset and started yelling and saying how he wanted revenge."

"Was it 'bump them off'? Was it 'pound them with the bat'? Which was the phrase he used?"

"I can't remember. It's just, I never really paid attention."

"What other statements had he made? Aggressive statements like this toward your parents?"

"Well. He's talked about it. About different, different ways of doing it. . . . But I never thought—I never thought he was really serious. I thought he was just, you know, ha ha."

"Just idle talk?"

"Yeah. I mean he wasn't acting, you know, like—"

Tie rocks to their feet and throw them into a river. Put ground-up glass in their food. Take the brake pads off their father's truck's wheels. Throw a hair dryer into her bath. Bash their heads in. It was pretending, or it was joking, ugly but not dangerous, because who could be crazy enough to take it seriously? They were just letting off steam, getting back at them—trying to—that's what she thought they were doing. Imagining what it would be like: freedom, the cessation of taunts and blows and meaningless, undeserved cruelties. Of being slapped across the face in front of friends, or grounded for no reason. Of being locked out of her own room so she couldn't run upstairs, turn her radio on, and escape into a book. *Bash their heads in.*

The aluminum baseball bat. He'd been swinging it around in the yard that afternoon. She'd watched him hitting the box with his bat. On impact, the box skidded from the scrubby grass onto the bare dirt of the drive-way. She hadn't thought anything of it. She'd gone back to the dishes.

A clunking, a pounding, she said in court, when the DA asked her. *Thudding:* that was the word Jody used ten years after the fact, in "Death Faces," struggling to write about what happened that night, to articulate and thereby possess, control, manage even a little bit of what couldn't be managed—process it, in the jargon of therapy. *Clonking* was in the transcript of the police interview. She thought there had been two distinct sets of them, she told the detective, two sets of noises. Two immediately after Becky screamed, two thuds to stop the screaming, and then another four or five, but those had sounded farther away.

"It's important that you remember exactly," Detective Davis said of the pounding noises. "Did Becky continue to scream?"

"She only screamed for a little while." Just a few screams, three perhaps, then they stopped; there was a silence before the pounding continued.

Jody couldn't decide how much danger she was in. But it seemed likely that if Billy killed Becky as well as their mother and father, he'd kill her, too. She couldn't move. She wanted to, but she couldn't. She knew that if the character in the book was alive, it was because she had gotten out of bed, and Jody hadn't gotten out of bed, she was just sitting and staring, listening, and a heroine would be doing something. Before her brother came back upstairs, a heroine would have escaped. Out the window—because there were only two ways out of her room, down the stairs that Becky went down, or out the window. So it had to be the window. And it had to be before Billy came back upstairs, because if he saw her going out the window, he would chase her. He was wiry and strong and he wouldn't break his leg. He'd hit the ground running and catch her.

And then there were the guns, her father's three guns. He could be loading one. A pistol, or the rifle. They were down there, in the bedroom closet. Everyone in the family knew where they were. Except maybe Becky. But Billy knew; Jody was sure he'd know where to look. With a gun, he wouldn't even have to jump. He could shoot her from the window.

Which was why it was important for her to get up, get dressed, and go. Jump. Run.

Except that if she moved, it might make Billy angry, and then she wouldn't be able to talk him out of killing her, *bashing her head in*. Billy hit Becky because Becky didn't do what he told her to. But Jody wasn't doing anything, anything that might make him angry. There was something she hadn't done, though. She hadn't kept Becky upstairs. Would he kill her for not keeping Becky upstairs?

"When Billy reappeared with the blood all over his chest," the DA said in the courtroom, "did he say anything to you?"

"He said that he was sorry for killing Becky, and he kept asking me if I thought he was crazy, and he kept trying to impress me with the fact that he wasn't crazy, and he says, 'We're free now,' and he said it was like *Friday the 13th*, to see the killer's view of what he was doing, that that was what it was like and that it was more messy than he thought it would be."

"He was shaking," she told Detective Davis, "and you could tell he was really not well and he's . . . he's talking 'oh we're free now' and all this stuff and I was just in total shock. I didn't know what to do . . . he was breathing hard, kinda jagged more than hard."

Billy had come upstairs empty-handed, and he was wearing nothing but a pair of tan boxer shorts, and there was blood spattered over his bare chest and arms.

"The first thing he said was about Becky," Jody tells me, "that he was sorry he killed her and that we were free. And over and over he said he wasn't crazy."

"I just acted like, you know, it was everyday, so what. It was nothin' out of the ordinary," she told Davis.

Because, Jody tells me, she knew she had to agree with him. Not make him mad. If she didn't make him mad, she might have a minute, a minute to think, to plan, because Billy was pacing around and he was breathing funny—panting—but he wasn't doing anything to her, and he didn't have anything to hurt her with except for his hands, which were bloody. "Do you think I'm crazy?" Jody tells me her brother kept asking her. "Because I'm not."

"No," she reassured him. "I don't think you're crazy."

She was still sitting up in bed, wearing a sweatshirt and underpants, the blankets over her legs. They should go, Billy said. They should get out of there.

"I'm going downstairs to check Mom's purse," he told her.

Jody nodded. He went downstairs and she got out of bed. She pulled on her pants and waited for him to come back up.

"Here," he said when he did. "I'm giving you a hundred. There was three. Three hundred. I'm giving you one hundred." He held the money out to her. "Here," he said. "Take it. We're leaving. We're going." She took it. "Okay," he said when she didn't move. "Come on."

Downstairs, Becky's body lay in the shadows. At first, Jody didn't see her. All she heard was a snoring noise coming from the couch where her father was sleeping, as he had been every night for months. For a moment she thought he wasn't dead but asleep. It wasn't blood on Billy, it was ketchup, and the whole thing was a joke, a horrible, stupid, sick joke. She couldn't wait to tell her mother what Billy had tried to pull this time. Yes, Billy was crazy, really crazy, and now they'd have to admit it, they'd have to do something about it. Except—

—it wasn't a trick. She'd only thought it was; for a second she did. But that was before she really listened to the noises from the couch, like snoring but not snoring. Wetter. Bubbly. Air moving through coagulating blood in her father's throat. So it wasn't a trick he was playing, and it really was blood all over him. Billy was running water in the bathroom sink, rubbing at his arms and chest with a wet washrag. He pulled off the stained shorts and pulled on a pair of jeans.

"He . . . he's not . . ." Jody gestured toward the couch. "He's . . . I can hear him."

Billy was pulling a shirt over his head. "That's just nerves or something," he said. "It isn't breathing." He walked around where Becky was on the floor. "Come on," he said. There were three ways out of the house, three doors, but to get to any of them you had to walk past where Becky was. And now that Jody could see Becky, she heard her as well. Becky was alive; she was moaning.

"Billy—" Jody said, and stopped herself. If she told him Becky wasn't dead, he might hit her again, hit her until she was quiet.

"What?"

She didn't answer. He jerked his head toward the kitchen door, and she went out after him.

JULY 14, 1978. OCTOBER 9, 1979. APRIL 15, June 23, July 16, August 5, September 17, and October 23, 1980.

In little over two years, Billy was evaluated eight times: by a psychologist, a social worker, a clinical psychologist, a physician specializing in developmental disabilities, a psychiatrist, another clinical psychologist, another psychologist, and a team of educational specialists. What exactly was wrong with him?

The first battery of tests had been made at the behest of Westside School to discover reasons for Billy's poor academic performance and for his "poor social relations with peers." The tests administered included an intelligence scale as well as one developed to rate behavior. The psychologist who made the report, Michael Knapp, conducted parent and teacher interviews, as well.

Linda, who had preserved a fantasy of an entirely different domestic life than the one she inadvertently created and had kept detailed baby books for all three children, noting the dates of their first words and steps and other milestones, described her son as a child who had been developmentally precocious during his first years. Billy said his first words at six months, "his first sentence shortly after one year." The only problems his mother reported having with him at home, at the time, were that he didn't take enough responsibility for a boy his age and that he argued with and teased his younger sisters, complaints that would seem universal among parents of adolescents.

"During testing Billy was very cooperative, but was extremely quiet, hardly speaking at all," the psychologist reported. "He gave very brief answers . . . and seemed very tense and rigid. He did not offer any information about himself or his interests spontaneously." His intelligence was found to be average, although "the fact that Billy was very verbally reticent may have spuriously lowered his verbal IQ score." Knapp found evidence of poor short-term memory and concentration, perhaps the result of his feeling anxious and stressed, but did not find support for an earlier diagnosis of poor hand-eye coordination, "locating and tracking" problems, or dyslexia.

Knapp's diagnosis was that Billy's "extreme learning problems in reading and spelling" were "associated with a behavioral disorder, and previously poor classroom survival skills." Essentially, he was failing to pay attention to the teacher. Had the harshly critical voices of his parents resulted in his ignoring all adults in authority? Linda's responses to the "Problem Behavior Identification Checklist" indicated "proneness to emotional upset, social aggression, and unethical behavior." All of this added up to a blanket diagnosis of "behavior disorder." Although given the treatment he received from his parents, it seems natural that Billy was angry, uncooperative, tense, hypersensitive, and, as he'd been "often noted to comment . . . unhappy" because "no one understood or liked him." That Linda had to take a test to help determine what was wrong with a child whom she had witnessed endure a decade's worth of routine brutality and who seemed subsequently to suffer feelings of low self-esteem, hostility, and unhappiness is testimony to how far from reality her own compulsions and misperceptions had taken her. Rather than whipping the devil out of their son, at Linda's instruction Bill seems to have whipped him further and further in.

Knapp recommended that Billy have one-on-one remedial help to bring him up to the appropriate grade level, a level he found him capable of attaining, and that he be referred "to the Mental Health School Consultation Team," who could assess the situation and design a program to help with Billy's "acting-out" in school. With respect to his behavior at home, Knapp suggested family counseling that would include Linda and Bill, perhaps in the form of a "home intervention program." None of these recommendations was followed.

On April 3, 1979, Billy, thirteen years old, "was observed by a witness shoplifting two packs of cigarettes." Billy ran from the store and was apprehended, and appeared with his parents on April 19 at the county courthouse's Juvenile Division for a "warning interview." Six weeks later he and another boy were caught entering an unlocked car from which they removed a pack of cigarettes, precipitating a second warning interview on June 19. In both cases Billy was stealing to support a habit he wasn't old enough to satisfy legally, a behavior he'd watched his parents model from the time he could focus his eyes on them.

As a juvenile offender, Billy was referred to the Children's Services Division. On October 9, he and his parents met together and individually with a psychologist, Carol Wood,* who did her best to discover what was troubling him. Billy tells me that once he was out of his parents' hearing, he spoke frankly of his father's drinking, of the whippings, the verbal abuse, and the violent altercations of his parents. Whether naïve, inadequately trained, or simply lacking the common sense her job demanded, Carol Wood repeated what Billy told her to his parents, suggesting that they were, in Billy's words, "crazy and unfit." Already on the defensive, having been put in the compromising position of being forcibly interviewed by a CSD caseworker, Bill and Linda, particularly Linda, were furious, both with Carol Wood and with their son. They denied everything Billy said and demanded to speak with him in private.

"My parents came to me and were very angry. They asked me if I had said the things about the whippings, the drinking, the beating, the slapping, the yelling, and fighting to Carol Wood. I remember that it was like a checklist that my parents went through with me. I was afraid and I told my parents, 'No.' "

Having intimidated Billy into retracting his accusations, and more damaging, into saying he'd lied, thereby establishing himself as dishonest to authorities he would have to deal with in the future, his parents, Billy says, threatened CSD with a lawsuit based on Wood's wrongfully accusing them of being unfit. In response, CSD fired Wood and destroyed the report, inserting a note into the case files. Wood's evaluation, the note explained, "contains errors of fact and interpretation, and should be disregarded in its entirety," a directive that was easy to follow, as the report was gone. Shaken by his parents' ability to reach beyond the family home and into a county agency whose purpose, he'd been told, was to protect and support children, Billy decided that it was safer to assume no one was on his side.

"From my brother's stories," Jody said in her 1999 affidavit, "I learned that reporting parental abuse would only lead to more of the same." Her one attempt to initiate some kind of intervention was discouraging enough that she didn't risk trying to get help again. At some point during the eighth grade, Jody went to Adam Murphy,* the guidance counselor at McLoughlin Junior High, to try "to find out how to report imminent abuse of herself" to Children's Services. During an argument, Linda had picked up a wooden clog—the closest thing at hand—and hurled it at Jody, frightening her and leaving a bruise on her arm. But the bruise didn't impress the counselor as evidence of genuine physical abuse, and he showed Jody photographs of what that might look like: children who had been battered or burned to the point of life-threatening injury. If something like that were to happen, then she should contact Children's Services, Murphy told her, and he gave her a card with the number of a help line to call were she in real danger.

On December 21, 1979, Linda caught Billy smoking in the unfinished half of the attic, and she and Bill took their son downtown and turned him in themselves for what his juvenile record describes as "Reckless Endangerment," in that smoking in the crawl space represented a fire hazard. Even had Linda's psychic investment in the season been less intense, it seems peculiarly vindictive for the Gilleys to have marched Billy into jail a few days before Christmas, especially for his satisfying an addiction for which they were more responsible than he. They left him there, in juvenile detention, for three days, relenting on Christmas Eve lest his absence reveal what a farce Linda's Christmas pageant really was. The more unattainable her fantasy of a happy, prosperous family gathered round a festive tree seemed, the more fiercely she clung to it. Even though money was always tight, Linda made sure there were a lot of presents under the plastic tree, mostly junk, Jody says. "Nobody ever got anything they wanted, ever. It was almost like she tried to pick out what you didn't want."

"Like what?" I ask.

"Like giving me a plastic action figure of the Creature from the Black Lagoon when she knew I hated that kind of thing." Jody shrugs, but under the shrug there's a palpable irritation and bewilderment—hurt—that lingers decades after the fact. On the surface, wrapped in holiday paper, Christmas looked as Linda thought it should.

Under that flimsy disguise, her gifts were thoughtless, without meaning, or they were outright barbs.

With a referral from the Jackson County Children's Services Division, Linda took Billy to a specialist in developmental disabilities. Based on Linda's observation that "there had been significant changes in Billy's behavior during the past two years," and the corroborating evidence of his record, Billy was tested for chemical abnormalities that can contribute to a behavior disorder. "The tests," reported Dr. Lynn Anderson, "indicate a derangement of glucose and calcium metabolism which can significantly affect behavior: causing such problems as mood swings, violent behavior, learning disabilities, and poor concentration." She strongly advised that all sugar be eliminated from Billy's diet and that he not use illicit drugs. If Linda heeded the advice about sugar, she did so only halfheartedly and temporarily.

"I don't know," Jody says. "Does switching him to Diet Coke add up to making a sincere effort?"

And there's no reason to imagine Billy might have curtailed his smoking pot, which, as he describes it, offered him one of the few respites from the conflict at home.

"If I could be alone, up a tree, stoned, that was really nice. Peaceful."

"You didn't do tree work while you were stoned, did you?"

"Sure."

"Wasn't that dangerous?"

"Nah. It just made everything, you know, look better."

Among all the reports made on Billy from July 1978 to October 1980—all paid for by Jackson County's public school system or Children's Services Division—the starkest, most pessimistic, and, as time would prove, most accurate set of impressions were those recorded on August 5, 1980, by Dr. Frederick E. Fried. Based on his examination of Billy, his review of earlier clinical findings, and Billy's performance on the MMPI,* Billy was, Dr. Fried found, "superficially genial but easily angered or irritated and prone to act impulsively." Although he was bright, he was "unable to profit from experience in the sense that other people do. It is as though, notwithstanding his intelligence, he is unable to anticipate the consequences of his behavior, to predict the responses which will be elicited from others, or to learn those anticipatory anxieties which operate to deter most people from committing anti-social behavior." In short, as evidenced by his history of impaired attention, inability to follow rules, truancy, poor tolerance for frustration, dishonesty, vandalism, theft, and running away, Billy had a conduct disorder, the usual childhood precursor of sociopathy.

Today it's understood that impulsiveness, the tendency to act without thinking, is associated with a host of chronic and debilitating behaviors: alcoholism, drug abuse, smoking, eating disorders, attention deficit disorders, aggression, personality disorders, as well as suicide. Current research into the brain coupled with psychological studies indicate that heredity can predispose a person to impulsivity, as can "emotionally disorienting early experiences."† Together the two can conspire to disable rational response systems. In other words, there are times when impulsive people literally can't think straight. A gene called MAOA, which regulates the activity of serotonin in the brain, has a high-risk variant common to men. Those with the variant

---

*Minnesota Multiphasic Personality Inventory, a standard instrument for psychological profiling.
†Benedict Carey, "Living on Impulse," *The New York Times,* April 4, 2006.

have deficits in the prefrontal area of the brain that shapes responses, as well as in parts of the brain that control emotion. "These deficits in emotional regulation set people up for strong emotional reactions early in life and make them more vulnerable to trauma."* To complete the vicious circle that would appear to describe Billy's situation, "the deficit in cognitive, inhibitory function creates a propensity to act on those emotions later in life."[†]

Assuming Billy's impulsiveness was in part genetic, inherited from an impulsive father, who drank, smoked, and couldn't control his temper, then Billy's biological makeup would have made him particularly vulnerable to that same volatile father, who traumatized him routinely and provided unlimited "emotionally disorienting early experiences." A generation earlier, Billy's paternal grandfather, William Gilley, who beat and traumatized his son, Bill, lost his legs when, suddenly intent on getting to a liquor store, he ran across a highway in front of a truck. Probably the pattern did not originate with him.

Dr. Fried pointed out that "parental rejection" and "inconsistent management with harsh discipline" were factors that predisposed children to develop conduct disorders, often diagnosed among children institutionalized early or bounced from one foster home to another, kids whose experience had been so fractured they had little sense they were safe, let alone loved. Were Billy to remain with his parents, he would require long-term counseling and would have to be held under strict probation, Dr. Fried thought. Even so, he wasn't convinced Billy would improve at home and concluded his report with the comment, "Billy may have to be eventually referred to an institutional setting in order to provide him

*Carey, "Living on Impulse."
†Ibid.

with the structure necessary to function." Unfortunately, it wouldn't be until he was in prison that Billy
had a chance to test the acuity of Dr. Fried's vision.

Until then, he was trapped at home with parents who,
despite their determination to keep him in line, were incapable of fostering an environment that supported
their intentions. Linda had a sharp tongue, and she used
it, Billy believes, not only to provoke his father into
beating him, but also to tempt Bill to threaten her physically. She taunted Bill; she insulted him; implicitly, she
dared her husband to hit her, and sometimes he did. The
way Billy describes it, this wasn't so much masochism
on Linda's part as it was her seeking moral superiority
over Bill. Whenever he hit her—if she could make him
hit her—he provided material proof of his being so depraved as to beat his wife, the badge of a bruise pro-
claiming Linda the innocent victim. But as often as not
he turned on Billy.

"Part of the problem was that my dad felt like I took
sides with her, against him, because I stepped in sometimes when he was gonna hit her. It wasn't that I took
her side, or that I thought she was right," he tells me,
"just that I wanted to stop him from hitting her. So he
got this idea that she and I were against him. Also," he
says, turning his hands up and delivering the statement
without betraying any awareness of the irony of its coming from a man who beat his mother and sister to death,
"you're not supposed to . . . you don't hit women."

One such altercation, in which Linda had been, in
Jody's words, "screaming and spitting angry," and
threatening divorce, ended with Bill's stalking out to the
barn alone, with his shotgun. Just as Linda's saying she
was going to leave Bill was a dramatic gesture from a
woman who, Jody says, "didn't have the force of will to
ever go through with leaving, or to be alone and have to
start over," so, Jody believes, was her father acting out

when he threatened suicide in response. Bill may have had no real intent to kill himself, but he did manage to scare his wife, who didn't have the courage to follow him and sent her children out to the barn in her stead. "Make sure your dad isn't doing anything stupid," she told them.

"When he took the gun outside she became quietly nervous," Jody says. There was "something in her eyes, the way she sent us out there. She wondered had she pushed him too far."

I hear Jody's description, more detailed and active than her brother's, after Billy has told me about his father's threats to kill himself. In fact, I e-mail her about the incident in one of a series of follow-ups to my visit with her brother, assuming she'll confirm my guess that she doesn't remember any such event, that it's one of the places where her and Billy's autobiographies diverge. But I'm wrong.

"As the girl who was sent to the barn to 'talk him out of it' I do indeed remember my father sitting on an upside-down grease can (about the height of a stool, a foot or so in diameter) with the shotgun across his lap, staring at the ground, looking up as we came in" to stop him. While she doesn't disagree that her brother was with her, Billy is not present in her memory of the event.

"How old were you?" I ask Jody.

"Old enough to know that being sent to talk a desperate man with a gun out of doing something stupid was perhaps not in our best interest."

Billy recalls two threats of suicide. Each time, he says, his father left his mother a note, "sat on the ground in the barn, and put the barrel of the rifle in his mouth until my mother agreed to forgive him."

The discrepancy between the siblings' memories of the one threat they both saw may proceed from fact: Billy may have entered the barn first and seen his father in a different posture, one Bill abandoned before Jody entered. But presuming they witnessed the same scene, the difference between what they remember seeing may result from their individual interpretations of the seriousness of their father's intent: Jody feeling it was manipulative, Billy taking it at face value.

Does Billy consider the suicide threat a more significant transaction between their parents than Jody? While Jody never brings it up on her own, her brother alludes to it several times during my visit, and he includes it in his affidavit, the purpose of which is to reveal a domestic life that drove Billy to murder his parents. A further contrast is that Jody gives herself an active role in the drama that unfolded, while Billy never places himself within the scene. He is an observer, what he describes a single image, a photograph rather than a film, a picture of his father with the barrel of a shotgun in his mouth.

Even if we can't know exactly what happened in the barn, Jody's and Billy's accounts, juxtaposed, are useful for the differences they reveal between the siblings: their personalities, their roles within their family, their understanding of themselves. Jody was analytical and cool under pressure. Far from being a helpless witness to disaster, she saw herself as representing a potential solution. Billy felt the import of a situation rather than assessing it rationally. Perhaps he'd been told he couldn't think straight enough times that he believed this to be true. He inhabited a stark and sinister emotional landscape and expected the most damaging outcome to a given situation. Always in trouble, often blamed for what was not his fault, he could do nothing but watch as tragedy unfolded.

"As we exited the house that night," Jody stated in her affidavit, Billy "told me of his plan for both of us to take our parents' car and the money from my mother's purse and drive away to a new life far away. He seemed surrealistically unaware of the full nature and consequences of his actions."

"We're going to Reno," Billy says to Jody in "Death Faces," a creative rendering of the past that gave Jody the freedom to write what she imagined, ten years after the murders, were her brother's thoughts and feelings at the time. In "Death Faces," Billy's plan is "to leave the house with Jody and Becky . . . but never to escape punishment." After dropping Becky off "with family friends," he and Jody "would drive into the night toward the great southwest desert lands . . . [and] a day or a week later," he would surrender himself to the police.

Eager to discover some of what informed the sixteen-year-old Jody's vision of the world, I buy myself a box of fifteen Harlequin romances that would have been published back when she was reading them—between 1970 and 1980—on eBay, for three dollars, and soon learn the formula: A young and inexperienced (i.e., virginal) heroine arrives by chance or intent in a remote land, whose geography and customs are peculiar to her. Often she has been orphaned or raised in such poverty that she must find respectable work, as a governess or a teacher. Or she may be a student, an artist. Because the novel is told from the heroine's point of view, she shares those details of her new environment she finds remarkable. By the end of the first chapter, sometimes by the end of the first page, she's encountered a man who is older and more worldly (i.e., sexually experienced) than she, and is surprised by how powerfully he interests or provokes her. Determined to resist his advances, she can't deny her desire for him. The plot moves briskly through the necessary complications and misunderstandings between the couple, and by the end love has conquered all. The heroine's vigorous emotional workout has left her intact, still a virgin; her hero, therefore, still a gentleman.

But I'm sure it wasn't love that captured the teenage Jody's interest. If it had been, she would have grown bored much more quickly than she did. A discerning consumer of entertainment, the adult Jody's taste in literature runs to Primo Levi and Camus, not authors of the kind of books I imagine following an addiction to cheesy romances. Because she tells me she used to hide them "like a bottle of booze" inside other, larger books, I expect her to confirm my assumption that she turned to Harlequins for their repetitive, narcotic quality, like favorite bedtime stories told over and over, comforting by virtue of being so familiar, so I'm surprised when Jody describes them as "learning tools."

"I wanted them for all the information I could get out of them!" she says, exclaiming what she considers self-evident.

"Like what?" I press, skeptical.

"Like the Bosporus being the name of the strait between Europe and Asia," she gives as her first example. "What it means to have high tea in London, England" is the second.

As Jody's awareness of her family as ignorant and uncultured grew, so did her determination to transcend her origins, to escape becoming like the parents she had begun to despise—for their cruelty, first, but their disinterest in learning cost them her respect as well. If where she'd arrived in the world had denied Jody access to knowledge other girls might have, middle-class girls from good families, she'd find a way to compensate. Harlequins contained the kind of information Jody might have chosen to get from an encyclopedia, if she'd had one at home, and, she points out, they showed her "how 'normal' people behaved and treated each other."

Later, when I think about what strikes me as her unusually resolute nature, I wonder if there wasn't another, more important impression Jody may have taken away from all those scores of Harlequin romances, one that's perhaps so familiar a part of her internal landscape that she doesn't see it. My guess is that it wasn't the heroine's romantic destiny that Jody needed to rehearse over and over, but all the rest of her story. It was managing without the help of a mother and father, without their money or their blessings. It was being brave, and optimistic, and plucky. It was having your own code of ethics that no one but you could corrupt. It was having and keeping integrity and self-respect. And again and again and again, it was landing on your feet in an unfamiliar place and learning, quickly, to thrive there.

THE EARLY HOURS OF APRIL 27, 1984, WERE unusually cold for spring. National Weather Service records indicate that the temperature dipped below freezing, to 30°F, and that the night sky was overcast, the moon waning, only two days from being entirely shadowed by the earth's orbit. A country road, Ross Lane was unlit and deserted.

"Did Billy actually suggest going to Reno?" I ask Jody.

"No."

"So where were you going?"

"I don't know. Nowhere. The plan was just to go out, leave the house."

"And do what?"

"I don't know. I was just going along with him, trying to not make him angry." Trying to figure out how she could summon an ambulance for Becky without precipitating more violence.

"Was there a fantasy of a new life together? The freedom he talked about when he came upstairs to your room? Or were the two of you silent? Is it possible you didn't say anything?"

Jody shakes her head, frowning. "I don't know. Maybe." I nod as I take notes. Later, rereading them, I think of the picture I've carried in my head for so long, of the two teenagers in the car that won't move, my sense that when they left the house on Ross Lane, their lives, like the lives of their family, ended, too.

"Do you remember being in the car?" I e-mail Jody later, wondering if she, too, has a static image of what was, in fact, occurring in motion.

"Yes," she replies. "That memory is seared in the brain. Like so many others from the minute the light went on. The fear of perhaps being driven somewhere to be killed; the dirty smell of oil and grime in the car, as though the dust itself was invading the senses, anchoring the everyday into the surreal. Confusion, and my mind racing, trying to play out all the possible scenarios, figuring out how to call the police, and a pervading disbelief that it had happened at all."

"So you were in the car," I say. "Then what?" Like many of the questions I ask Jody, I ask it more than once, maybe more than twice. Not because I don't remember her answers or expect that they might change, but because of my compulsion to rehearse the events, in order, with the expectation that this might make them more comprehensible, a story I can accept. Sometimes I wonder if it doesn't seem to Jody that we meet over and over for the same interview.

She shakes her head. All she remembers is that she convinced her brother that the two of them should stop at Kathy Ackerson's, because Kathy might know of a place that would be open after midnight in downtown Medford. Jody hoped that, once inside her friend's house, she could get access to a telephone and call the police before her brother had a chance to stop her. Or if not at Kathy's, then somewhere else. If there was any place open, a diner or the movie theater, she could excuse herself to go to the women's room and call.

But when the two of them pulled out of their driveway in their father's Ranchero, Billy turned right rather than left, which was the way to Kathy's. For the extra mile or so required by the longer, more circuitous route to the Livingstons',* Jody was sure her brother was taking

---

*Kathy's father's surname was Ackerson. Her mother had remarried a man named Bob Livingston.

her to a secluded place where he would, at last, kill her as well.

"He took the long way [to Kathy's house], for reasons he cannot state," Dr. Maletzky reported two months after the murders. In his 1996 affidavit, Billy provided an explanation, albeit twelve years after the fact.

"I told Jody I needed to stop at the store and buy some cigarettes. We got in the truck and started driving towards the store that was down the road from our house. I remember Jody reminding me that Kathy's house was the other way and I told her I wanted to get cigarettes first. Jody told me to wait to get cigarettes until we picked up Kathy. I agreed."

When they arrived at Kathy's, Jody told Billy to wait in the car while she went to get her friend. As she expected, the Livingstons' back door was unlocked, and Jody let herself in and ran through the kitchen and up the stairs to Kathy's room. It was 1:34 in the morning—Kathy would remember the time exactly, having looked at her digital clock when her friend suddenly entered her room, "breathing very heavily," as Kathy said to the private investigator.

Jody told Kathy she and her brother had snuck out of the house and wanted to go out. Did Kathy know of any place that would be open? Kathy didn't, and said she was too sleepy to go out anyway. If they wanted something to do, why didn't Jody bring Billy upstairs and the three of them could play cards for a while? Kathy "went to put on some clothes because [she] was just wearing a night-shirt," and Jody went back downstairs, trying to figure out what to do. She was afraid to tell Kathy what had happened. What if her friend became hysterical and alarmed Billy? He might in turn become violent, injure or kill some or all of the people in the house, which included Kathy's mother, stepfather, younger sister, and two younger brothers.

Jody considered using the phone in the kitchen and, as a precaution, went to the back door to check if Billy had remained in the car. But she found him crouched against the screen door, listening, she believes, to see if she'd told anyone what he had done.

"Yes," Billy says, when I ask him if he was at the door, but it wasn't to eavesdrop. He'd wanted to go inside with Jody in the first place, but she wouldn't let him. She told him to wait outside, which he did, having apparently sunk into a state of dazed passivity. "I lit a cigarette and sat in the truck for a few minutes, listening to the radio. I remember that my forehead was hurting and I got a loud ringing in my ears," intermittent symptoms that had begun months earlier, after he suffered a concussion (from the car accident in Redding). "Then I heard something like a bee in my ear, a loud buzz, and I got spooked, so I went to wait on the porch."

The two went upstairs to Kathy's room. "Billy," Kathy's interview continues, "was perfectly natural and regular, as he always was, just his regular self." He asked did she have any marijuana because he was out, and she told him she didn't, so he bummed a cigarette instead. In contrast to Billy's description of his sister as calm and self-possessed, Kathy thought Jody "was totally freaked out . . . acting weird." In fact, she was shaking so much that Kathy kept pressing her to borrow a sweater, assuming she must be shivering with cold. After Kathy went down to the kitchen to get a few snacks, the three of them "played cards, drank pop, and ate cookies" for about an hour, Kathy said.

"What game did you play?" I ask Jody, an absurd question—what difference could it possibly make?—but I'm trying to picture the scene.

"It was rummy," Jody says. "Gin rummy."

* * *

All the while she was playing, Jody was trying to figure out if she could somehow get to the phone downstairs and call 911. She knew Becky was alive when they left and that she was gravely injured. The longer it took to call an ambulance, she assumed, the less of a chance Becky had. "Don't you want to go get those cigarettes?" she tried, after Billy smoked the last of Kathy's.

It was nearing three on a school morning—2:47 by her friend's digital clock—and they should get some sleep. "When I suggested he leave and pick Kathy and me up in the morning," Jody recalled for her affidavit, "he knew this was a ruse and saw that he had misjudged me as a supporter of his plans and what he had done. He simply went back home. If I did not want the 'freedom' he had won for me, then neither did he."

Jody watched from Kathy's window as Billy got into the Ranchero and, when the taillights had disappeared, became immediately distraught and told Kathy to quick, get her mom and dad, Billy had beaten her parents to death with a baseball bat and he'd probably killed Becky, too. The report was so incredible that at first Kathy didn't believe what her friend was saying, assuming it was some awful practical joke, but because Jody was crying she went to get her mother. As it happened, Renea Livingston was on her way upstairs to tell the girls to settle down before they woke up the rest of the house, "and that's when Kathy told me that we need to call the police," Renea explained to Detective Leon Stupfel, who interviewed her at 5:42 that same morning. "Jody was out of earshot for a minute and I said, 'Kathy, are you sure?' because I thought Jody had a tendency to exaggerate things, and Kathy said, 'I think she's sure.'"

Renea took the girls down to the kitchen. By that

time, she said, Jody "was pretty hysterical ... she had trouble telling me but she did say she thought her mom and dad were dead ... so I thought okay, I'll wake up Bob [her husband and Kathy's stepfather] and we'll call the police. And [Jody] kept saying, 'Hurry, do it right away.' Because she was frightened. So we did, we hurried."

"How many times did you run away?" I ask Billy.

"Three or four, I guess. Three. There was one time that it was just, you know, a joyride. Me and another guy in his dad's car. We didn't go anyplace. We were in town when we got picked up."

"Did you ever run far away?"

"Once I got to Vancouver."

"Canada?"

"Nah." He laughs. "Washington State. Vancouver, Washington."

On the evening of April 8, 1980, Billy, who was then fourteen, was working on his bike in his father's workshop—the small outbuilding adjacent to the one Linda used for storage—when his father came home "really drunk and started yelling at me for leaving tools lying around." Billy apologized. He'd begun putting the tools away when his father cuffed him and asked was he looking for a fight. Rather than attempting to defend himself, Billy kept his head down and continued restoring order to the workshop. He told his father no, he didn't want to fight, and asked him please to stop hitting him. Then, he says, "my father hit me in the face and knocked me to the floor with a bloody nose." Bill told Billy to get up, and when Billy didn't, he began kicking him. "I got up so my father would stop kicking me, but then when I tried to get up he hit me in the side of the head." Because Billy doesn't remember how the incident ended, he assumes he was knocked unconscious for a brief time. Alternately, he might have been literally frightened out of his wits. When he opened his eyes and looked up, his father was gone. Scared to move, Billy remained on the floor of the workshop for another two hours, until midnight, when he crept up to the living room window and saw that his father was asleep on the couch. He came in, washed his face, and went to bed.

Billy says his mother routinely locked herself in the bedroom, purposefully ignoring the strife without, but when I ask Jody about this she can't recall any instance in which Linda was not vigilant with respect to both Bill's drinking and her children's whereabouts and finds it unlikely, almost inconceivable, that their mother would have retired for the night without knowing that all three of her children were where they were supposed to be, in their beds, asleep. Perhaps it's easier for Billy to believe that Linda didn't see certain events than that she did nothing about what she saw. However the conflict played out, whatever Bill did or didn't do, at school the next day Billy told a friend he was running away. The friend, eager to escape the foster home in which he'd been placed, suggested they head up to his real parents' home in Vancouver, Washington, just over the Oregon border. He was sure his parents, who were hippies and dope dealers (perhaps this explains his placement in foster care), would welcome him and Billy.

"We got some money together and bought bus tickets," Billy recalls. "When we got there we called his parents and told them what had happened to me."

The friend's father picked up his son and Billy from the bus station and brought them home, and Billy called Linda to let her know that he was all right but didn't say where he was, allowing his mother to believe that he was still in Medford. When she asked why he hadn't come home from school, Billy said Bill had attacked him and that he wasn't coming back. Linda told Billy she didn't believe him and ended the call under the impression that Billy was at a pay phone in downtown Medford, waiting for Bill to come pick him up.

The next morning, Billy's friend's mother "convinced me that I should call mom and let her know I was staying with friends for a while so that I could figure some things out." Linda apologized for disbelieving what she now knew was true: Bill admitted to her that he'd beaten up their son. She cried, she told Billy she loved him; she begged him to return and promised that things would be different. This time she'd kicked his father out of the house, she said. She'd told Bill she was divorcing him. Billy had little reason to trust in his mother's word. Only two months had passed since Linda's last tearful promise that things were going to change. Wary, he said he loved her, too, but that he needed time to think. At the idea of being thwarted, Linda grew furious and insisted that Billy come home right away. He refused and hung up.

A day later, his friend's whereabouts were traced by the foster care agency, revealing where both boys had gone, and Linda called Billy. If he didn't come home immediately, she threatened, "she would report [his] friend's parents for harboring a runaway and have them arrested." Not doubting his mother for a moment, and aware that he was already indebted to his hosts for their generosity, a rare enough experience that he placed a premium on it, Billy returned to Medford. But, as a police report had been filed, he didn't have to go home. Instead, he was taken into the custody of the Children's Services Division.

After being held overnight at CSD, Billy was referred to a psychologist named Marie Taylor,* who interviewed him, and to whose questions he gave careful answers. Billy told Marie that yes, he was unhappy, but he blamed this on school. His bad grades, his conflicts with other kids, his inability to stay out of trouble: these were what had prompted him to run away, he said. Too, he "couldn't take all the yelling and confusion at home." Although he'd returned willingly to Medford, this was only out of consideration for the people with whom he'd been staying. He still did not want to go home.

Billy was afraid to tell the truth—afraid his parents would find out and retaliate—and as Carol Wood's report had been destroyed, Marie had no way of knowing what "yelling and confusion" really meant, nor why the fourteen-year-old boy in her office not only refused to see his parents but also asked to be placed in foster care, a request so unusual that it should have alerted the agency to the likelihood of severe abuse. Typically, even chronically battered children cling to the parents who torture and rape them. Perhaps Marie hoped that placement in a shelter home "for the purposes of evaluation" would make her new client's situation a little clearer.

Billy's custody was transferred to the Jackson County Youth Shelter, a group home that housed eight adolescents, where he remained from April 15 through May 7. The shelter's mission was to provide temporary room, board, and support to troubled, abused, runaway, and homeless youth. There were strict rules of conduct, a daily schedule that included structured and free time, and all residents were expected to complete domestic chores. During his three weeks in the shelter, Billy was counseled, observed, and disciplined, and the staff's findings were organized into a comprehensive report made to Children's Services.

"Billy appeared to function best under structured situations," the report said. "He had difficulty managing his free time, especially in social situations. This is when he usually got himself into trouble." Upon arrival he was "very quiet and withdrawn," and when he did begin to talk he didn't speak honestly about himself but made up stories. Staff members found it easier to speak with Billy privately, but even then it was "very difficult" to get him to "disclose his feelings." Given his reticence, they paid particular attention to nonverbal cues when summarizing their impressions:

> Billy's most striking feature is his eyes and facial expression. He rarely smiles and he maintains a consistent expression regardless of his mood. His large brown eyes most often reflect a sad, frightened look. He maintains [eye] contact well, even when lying, but there is often a sense of distance, as if one were looking in a mirror. His voice rarely fluctuates in volume, even when he's angry. . . . Billy also criticized himself frequently and on a few occasions mentioned suicide. He has a very low opinion of himself, reflected also in the stories he makes up about himself. . . .
>
> Billy requires a situation where he is loved and a concerted effort is made to reinforce his positive qualities. . . . Both individual and family counseling are strongly recommended—individual, to help Billy find out who he really is, and family, to help bring an understanding and cooperative interaction to his home life. . . .
>
> Billy has shown that he is capable of kind and gentle nature [sic]. We are hopeful that through careful consideration of the above recommendations, Billy will learn to achieve this.

For a boy who would be fifteen the following month, Billy's behavior was notably immature. His pranks included dropping a fly in another child's juice glass, disconnecting a phone while someone was using it, placing a boy's croquet ball in dog feces, and generating conflict by spreading rumors. Some of these complaints he qualifies by explaining that the report failed to include antecedents to his acts. For example, he tells me, he "did not drop the croquet ball in dog shit until after" he'd been antagonized. He attributed his trouble getting along with the boys to their being "abnormal."

"Shy, he had a brief crush on a girl . . . which was not returned . . . and [he] withdrew, obviously very hurt, but refused to talk about it." In a separate transaction he convinced a fellow resident to "make dirty remarks" to a different girl, who slapped him when she discovered that he had been the instigator. The pattern wasn't new; during a trip to California he'd incited a cousin to make unwelcome sexual comments to Jody.

As had been true of his previous delinquencies, cigarettes caused a lot of problems for Billy. "By far, the most difficult restriction for Billy was not being allowed to smoke cigarettes. He was instructed when he first arrived that he was to earn this privilege. Billy found this requirement incomprehensible as he tried everything he could to beg, borrow, or steal a cigarette." The staff expressed frustration with Billy, who was caught smoking in his room, the boys' bathroom, "and even under the house," but no one seems to have considered the problem from the point of view of addiction.

The "most disruptive" of his pranks also followed a pattern that had been set long before—trying to trick other kids into thinking he had drugs. He supplied a "short-term resident with peppermint tea under the guise of marijuana," with the result that he single-handedly ruined a dance held later that evening. The boy smoked the "marijuana" in the boys' bathroom with something other than the desired result. "Accusations [were] made, searches performed, anger, lying, hours wasted, feelings hurt . . . a lot of negative consequences imposed on innocent people." Either Billy was incapable of controlling his impulses or he was intentionally repeating what he knew to be a recipe for punishment, or both.

Three months earlier, on February 15, Billy had been suspended from school for possession of a small amount of dry alfalfa he claimed was marijuana. "When my mom brought me home from school, I tried to tell her that the marijuana was really just some alfalfa that I was using to trick the other kids. . . . My mom told me that I was a 'damn liar.' When my father got home he told me to go out to the barn and wait for him." Out in the barn, keeping company with the tractor wheel to which he'd been tied more times than he could count, Billy decided he "couldn't take it anymore." He got on his bike and rode the familiar two miles to the Jackson County Sheriff's Office, where he asked to speak with the counselor he'd been assigned after Carol Wood was fired. But as it was a Friday evening he was told to return home; the counselor had left for the day and wouldn't be back until Monday. "I told them I couldn't go home because I would be whipped. I was given a choice: to go home or to go to Juvenile lock-up. I chose lock-up."

At fourteen, Billy was smoking pot regularly enough that his claim about the alfalfa may have been an attempt to scam his classmates so he could finance his habit, but Billy had little confidence that anyone might like him in and of himself and had established a pattern of resorting to fakes and props to impress peers.

"He doesn't really have any friends and usually he's more friends with little kids than kids his own age," Jody told Detective Davis when he interviewed her after the murders. Jody's friend Kathy added that at the time of the murders he "got along much better with her two younger brothers, who were then thirteen and fourteen, even though he was sixteen or seventeen." (He was, in fact, eighteen.)

Billy's affidavit rarely alludes to friends; the only one he mentions separate from a generic reference to his peer group is the foster kid with whom he ran away. Outside of school, or juvenile detention, he seems to have been an unusually solitary—lonely—boy, who spent much of his free time by himself. In answer to a letter I send him before we meet, asking what he liked to do when he was a teenager, Billy writes around the topic of friendship, suggesting a life among peers without mentioning any names or even using the word *friend*. The only one Jody can recall is "John, a blond, chubby kid in the fifth or sixth grade."

"I was a member of a dirt bike club," Billy tells me in his letter. "We would get together at a place with lots of dirt trails." He gave up the bike at sixteen, when he got his driver's license, but he still loved bowling, swimming, and taking girls "to the YMCA pool, public pools, and lakes. . . . I also loved going to parties," he adds. "I started selling killer grass at age thirteen, so I was always getting invited to the best parties. . . . It was such a rush. I don't think it can be explained. To have so much social power beginning at an early age."

Though Billy did smoke marijuana, it seems unlikely he was the dealer he describes, who at thirteen was working for local growers, paid "two grocery bags packed with leaf, and a bag of buds" after harvest. If he can't explain the rush of social power that comes with such a position, perhaps this is because he never experienced it. Billy's reminiscing about his career as the kid everyone wanted to know because he had "grass coming out of his ass" doesn't sound any different from his assertion that he "was so good at bowling [he] was thinking about turning pro" or that he had "a ten-speed that [he] took to such distances, it would have broken most men," comments that are clear instances of wishful boasting, the kind of fantasies that have an effect opposite to the one he intends, making him seem pitiable rather than cool.

Speaking with Billy in prison, I return several times to the subject of friendship, trying to elicit stories that will help me understand his isolation. Each of his answers recasts the party scene of his letter, featuring a teenage Billy who is sought out because of the marijuana he's happy to share. When I see—at last—that he can't conceive of spending time with another kid who liked him for himself, without the added enticement of drugs, I stop asking.

"Billy responds to authority in whatever way he can receive the most attention," the shelter report concludes. "He never resists punishment. In fact he accepts discipline . . . too readily. He managed to stay on some form of punishment or restriction for the majority of his stay here."

Billy had, of course, been taught to confuse punishment with love. He'd been told he was stupid and wicked and loved, and he'd been beaten for that bewildering set of provocations all his life. That the shelter report recommended individual counseling to help him "find out who he really is" suggests that his sense of self was not only frail but also disorganized, perhaps arrested at some point in early childhood by the treatment he'd received, perhaps fractured by that treatment.

Linda and Bill may have thought of the cruelties they imposed as discipline, but *discipline* (from the Latin for *instruction*) means to teach by imposing order, external order that is ultimately internalized. Abuse achieves the opposite, ushering in fear and confusion: internal chaos. Abuse impedes learning; it makes a child into an agent of dissonance and destruction. At fourteen, it was the "yelling and confusion" at home to which Billy asked not to be returned. When Billy was nineteen and the judge who sentenced him for murder gave him the opportunity to speak for himself, Billy said he was "confused about it all," and that he couldn't "understand [him]self."

"You've tried to sort it out in your own head and you can't?" the judge asked.

"Yes," Billy answered.

He was, as he had been for years, confused. While Jody read compulsively and had developed a means of insulating herself from her environment by retreating into the well-ordered realm of her imagination, an internal landscape filled with what she took from books, Billy seems to have lacked the means to create internal order for himself. Only later, when he was away from his parents and in a strictly structured setting—prison—would he begin to make sense of his life and himself, begin to construct an autobiography that explained and justified what he had done.

As the report from the shelter home indicated, the fourteen-year-old Billy may not have known who he was, but he did know where he was. Evaluated by the caseworker responsible for making referrals from the shelter, Billy told her he "refused to return home until his parents acknowledged that family problems do exist and are willing to work on them." The generalization, like "yelling and confusion," was not nearly as compelling as the truth he felt he couldn't tell: he was terrified of his father and considered his mother complicit in every beating he received. On whatever occasion Linda hadn't provoked one outright, she'd allowed it to happen, refusing to see what she saw, failing to hear what she heard. Perhaps she did, as she said, love him, but what did it mean, what was it worth?

"Throughout my years growing up," Billy summarizes in his affidavit, "whenever I stood up to my father or whenever I tried to get away, my mother would talk me into coming home, telling me things would change for the better, telling me that she loved me. She would always end up taking my father's side, letting my father do the same things to us kids, and things never did change for the better like she promised."

BILLY "PICKED UP SOME CIGARETTES AT A 7-Eleven store, then went home . . . he could see that Becky was alive. He thought that he would end her life by injecting air or poison into her veins, as he had some hypodermic needles in the house, but decided to go upstairs and wait," Dr. Maletzky wrote in his report. "He turned on several lights, going from room to room, looking at pictures in magazines and wandering about. Finally the police came to the door and, after a short time, he opened it and voluntarily surrendered. . . .

"Mr. Gilley has difficulty describing his feelings during the murders. He said he was frightened and at times he said he was detached, as if it were like a movie and he was watching his hands doing the murder, but he did not say that he felt outside of his own body or that he felt estranged or apart from reality. He described knowing what he was doing, planning it, and recognizing that some others would think it was wrong. Of interest is the fact that he had no plan for the disposal of the bodies and thought instead Jody might help with this. Even after he returned home [from Kathy's] he did not make attempts to hide the bodies. . . . He had no plans at that point for what he was going to do for the next several hours or days, how he would live or support himself, or what was going to happen to Jody, though he had a vague idea that she would run away with her boyfriend as she was talking about this earlier"—a boyfriend Jody never mentions when speaking of the murders. Given Linda's hysteria about sex and the rigid control she maintained over those hours Jody didn't spend in school, it's hard to imagine Jody having had much of a chance to develop a relationship with a boy, let alone a bond serious enough that she might plan on their running away together.

"Did you have a boyfriend at the time?" I ask her, to make sure I'm correct in assuming she did not.

"No," she says, "but I liked a boy." The boy's sister was on the debate team with Jody and they'd "talked a couple of times." That was the extent of her romantic career in tenth grade.

"Overall," Dr. Maletzky summarized, "Mr. Gilley describes the event as almost an inevitable one. . . . He believes that he acted with deliberation, forethought, and justice, at times implying, but not stating, that [his parents] deserved to die. . . . He honestly says he does not believe he should be punished. He does not believe he is dangerous to anyone else."

For his part, Dr. Maletzky found Billy cooperative and apparently sincere. "He shares a sense of responsibility for the murders of his three family members with his mother and father," Dr. Kirkpatrick reported on October 16, 1984.

"I think that all three of us caused it," Billy said to him.

"WE GOT THE CALL AT 3:10 IN THE MORNING,"
testified Oregon state trooper David Scholten, "and it
was four or five minutes after that that I arrived at the
residence." In another five minutes, troopers Rupp and
Springer joined Scholten, and took positions around the
house. Trooper Rupp knocked on the side door, just to
the left of the window over the kitchen sink, the one
through which Jody had watched Billy swinging his bat
at the cardboard box. He could hear movement inside
the house, but no one came to the door. As Billy remembers it now, he wasn't looking at pictures but sleeping.

"I did what Jody told me," he says. "I went home because it was late. It was time for bed." When he saw that
his father was dead, Billy says in his affidavit, he suddenly felt "completely exhausted . . . went to my bedroom and lay down." Awakened by the banging on the
door—if he had fallen asleep, it could not have been for
longer than a few minutes—he went to the upstairs bay
window, opened it, and looked out.

"I turned the spotlight on the person who came to the
window," Scholten said, and using the squad car's PA
system "advised him that I wanted him to come downstairs and out the front door and to keep his hands
where we could see them, which he did."

"They told me to get down on my knees and put my
hands on my head," Billy says. Then Trooper Rupp
searched him, handcuffed him, and asked if there was
anyone in the house who was injured. Billy said no because, he tells me, he thought they were asking if anyone
needed medical attention, which, he implies, could not

have helped Becky. The officers put him in Trooper Scholten's patrol vehicle, and Scholten "advised the defendant of his rights and asked if he understood them, and he said he did."

At 3:48, Detective Richard Davis arrived at the house on Ross Lane and entered the front door with troopers Springer and Rupp, Davis guiding their way with a flashlight. Immediately he saw Bill on the couch to the right of the entrance, and, as he said, "it was quite obvious that the man was dead." Davis "shined the flashlight along the floor toward what is the kitchen area and saw the body of a young girl and approached toward her and [he] could see her chest raise [*sic*] so [he] stopped right there and called for the medical crew." The paramedics came in and began working on Becky, readying her for transport to Providence Hospital, some five miles to the west, while Davis went on to the master bedroom, where Linda was lying, dead, her face covered with a bathrobe, which Davis picked up and then replaced.

The disposition of the bathrobe would become an issue in Billy's appeal, as it is his contention that while he had reverently covered his mother's face, Davis dropped the bathrobe back on her in a haphazard and disrespectful manner, thus tampering with the evidence, as it was *after* he had disturbed the bathrobe that Davis took forensic photographs. Possibly this would make little difference to a juror, but it has (or has developed) real significance for Billy, who conveys indignation about the manner in which the robe was allowed to fall unceremoniously over his mother's face. Not only was Billy's rage directed first against his father, whom he hit many more times than he did his mother and to whom he returned to strike repeatedly even after he knew he had killed him, but the fact that he did not extend to his father this most basic respect the living pay the dead—

that he did not cover Bill's defiled face and shattered head but left it for anyone to see—seems doubly significant in the context of the concern he betrays over Linda's face. In contrast to his treatment of his mother, leaving his father's face uncovered seems to have been an act of purposeful filial profanation.

"I'M CONVINCED THE NIGHT OF HER DEATH was the best night of her short life," the character of Billy says about Becky in "Death Faces." Jody, in the voice of Billy, fantasizes that Becky, flush with the success of having performed her lead part in the class musical so well, "probably dreamed of the praise she'd reap from her teachers and peers in school on Monday, praise she was not destined to receive."

"I must be honest," Billy says in Jody's imagined reconstruction, "I hated [Becky] and no matter what Jody says now, Jody hated her, too. Becky was a big baby and a spoiled brat, siphoning off not just a little extra, but all of the parental love available for their children. Certainly that was Jody's opinion of Becky, especially when forced to clean up after the 'infant' when it was 11."

"Does the Jody character in 'Death Faces' represent your perspective?" I ask Jody. "When she speaks is she voicing your feelings?"

"Yes." Jody nods. "At least as I understood them at that time. Which is now, what, more than ten years ago."

"What about when Billy speaks?"

"That was my attempt to reveal what I thought were his feelings."

"Were you resentful of Becky?"

Jody nods. "I was as alienated from Becky as I was from the rest of the family. She was given preferential treatment, mostly as a function of her age. She would have fallen from favor when she hit adolescence, just as Billy and I did, but she wasn't there yet. She could be a brat. She was experimenting with cigarettes—she and her friend Tina [Kathy Ackerson's half-sister]—I guess I probably felt as if she was becoming what I was trying to escape."

"Death Faces" is an unsettling document. A "creative nonfiction" narrative, it allows Jody to tell the story of her family from her brother's point of view. She can't know his point of view, of course, not from the inside, and she uses Billy to express her own feelings and opinions. The hatred Billy betrays is Jody's own—*no matter what Jody says now,* the imagined voice of Billy cautions—an emotion the adult Jody controls very carefully. In fact, Jody's ability to feel hostility—anger—is something she identifies for me as a casualty of her childhood.

My separate relationships with Jody and Billy are circumscribed by my focus on their past, and this dictates how I experience each of them. I'm not a friend, never a casual observer. Our conversations are limited, largely, to their childhoods. I wonder in what ways this validates, or invalidates, my response to them as individuals? Am I concentrating on the part of their lives that defines them? Or is my experience skewed rather than representative?

Up until the night of April 27, 1984, I find it difficult to think of Jody and Billy, within the context of their family, as entirely independent, whole individuals. It seems to me that while they were growing up together, at the mercy of their destructive parents, they arrived at an adaptive symbiosis. Billy expressed their emotions, their fear and rage, while Jody managed to preserve their ability to reason and function in contexts, such as school, that required measured, controlled behavior. "Of interest," Dr. Maletzky reported of the night of the murders, "is the fact that [Billy] had no plan for disposal of the bodies and thought instead that Jody might help with this."

I trust Jody, as I don't her brother. She holds herself to a standard of honesty that Billy does not. Billy is manipulative; he doesn't always tell the truth; he may not know how. But with me he is emotionally present in a way that Jody is not. I find him readable, *feelable,* as I don't Jody, whose defenses are engaged when we're together and speaking about the past, as they are not when she writes: not in our early e-mail dialogue when she acknowledged a self who was out of reach and unknowable, inspiring her fear and anger, and not in her preface to "Death Faces," written less than ten years after the murders. In her preface Jody admits to having contacted her brother for "the self-serving reason of pumping him for information for future literary use." But she abandoned their correspondence. She was, she wrote, "too afraid of what he might tell me about me."

To what part of Jody might Billy have had access that Jody herself did not? Billy wasn't unknowable or out of reach. On the contrary, as far as Jody was concerned he was far too much of a presence even in prison three thousand miles away, continuing to ask that she write and visit him. Could it be Billy who, at least in Jody's imagination, retained a part of herself that Jody decided she didn't want to see? A wounded, raging self who had been within reach but whom she disowned and abandoned along with her brother?

II

AFTER

I can be and so often am so terribly
normal. And happy and whole.
Which is just so wrong, don't
you think?

JODY (GILLEY) ARLINGTON
in an e-mail to the author,
March 26, 2005

This, this here isn't an interview,
it's a séance you're conducting,
because I've been dead for the
last twenty-one years.

BILLY GILLEY
in a conversation with the author,
December 1, 2005

"I MET JODY WHEN SHE CAME INTO THE LEGAL aid office with Kathy's parents, the Livingstons, for adoption," Thad Guyer tells me. "The secretary's all excited, comes running back from reception to my office. 'You'll never guess who's in the waiting room,' she says. 'It's that girl, the one from the murders.'

"Everyone knows about it. Small town, lots of media. The secretary tells me Jody's there with people who want to adopt her. Now the Livingstons, they're sympathetic, they're well meaning, but ignorant. They're what Jody's leaving behind."

As she was over fourteen, the law stipulated that Jody had some say over who would assume her care, and after Thad had spoken with Renea, Bob, and Jody together, he asked the Livingstons to leave his office for a few minutes and wait in the reception area so he could discuss the matter privately with Jody. Why, he asked her, not two days after her parents were murdered, was she pursuing adoption by the neighbors? From Jody's perspective, the answer was simple.

"I need a place to live," she told him.

"But that doesn't mean the Livingstons should adopt you. You have other options." There were informal arrangements, Thad explained, without any paperwork, and there were different levels of guardianship. Any of these was more easily reconsidered than adoption. Thad suggested Jody wait to make any big decisions until she'd recovered enough to consider her choices calmly. She and Kathy's parents left the legal aid office having established the Livingstons as her legal guardians.

"Not an hour after the meeting, Jody calls me," Thad says. "Will I go with her to the house on Ross Lane so she could get her things? I suggest this is something she should be doing with the Livingstons—people who just that morning she was considering as adoptive parents— because it would give them an opportunity to nurture her. It would offer all of them an occasion to begin to es- tablish their new bond."

"I don't want them to nurture me," Jody told him. "I want to go with you."

After contacting the DA's office to secure permission to enter the crime scene, Thad drove to the Livingstons' home and picked up Jody. With her, he ducked under the yellow police tape cordoning off the property. Curi- ously, while Jody remembers Kathy was with them and that the three of them entered, Thad remembers he alone accompanied Jody into the house, and Kathy told the private investigator that it was only she and Jody. The house, Thad tells me, smelled strongly of blood, a smell he compares to the odor of carnage he encoun- tered in Vietnam.

" 'Put your hand over my eyes,' " he remembers Jody asking him. "She didn't trust herself not to look," he ex- plains. Is his scrupulousness inspired by the fact that, in 1984, Thad was hurtling toward a midlife crisis? His marriage was on the rocks; he was working on his repu- tation as a womanizer. It wasn't long after he became Jody's "personal lawyer and protector," as Betty Glass called him, heavily inflecting the word *personal* to con- vey intimacy, that rumors of his sexual involvement with Jody were flying, quite possibly launched by Betty herself.

"You cover your eyes," Thad says he told Jody, "and I'll lead you. I'll hold your hand."

I try to picture them in the house on Ross Lane, pick- ing their way around blood spatters, a twosome in his mind, a threesome in hers. Upstairs, in what Thad calls Jody's "little attic bedroom," she gathered a "minimal amount of clothes," a few books and record albums, and Bunny, her sister's favorite stuffed animal, which Jody wanted to take to Becky, on life support in the hospital, and which she ended up placing in her casket.

Among the books Jody kept from her childhood bookshelf is V. C. Andrews's *Flowers in the Attic,* a gothic horror story that remains in her collection today, among more literary fare. The story of four children whose mother forces them, after their father's death, to live in her wealthy parents' attic, *Flowers in the Attic* deals with themes of incest, child abuse, and secrecy. Because the children's mother and father were half siblings, their marriage incestuous and their offspring polluted, the children's grandmother won't allow their overt presence in her home. Imprisoned in the attic for years, until one of the two younger siblings, who are twins, is poisoned and dies, Christopher, seventeen, the resourceful pragmatist, and Cathy, fifteen, the tempestuous narrator, consummate what has always been their intense attachment and escape with the remaining twin to an uncertain future.

Jody has kept *Flowers in the Attic,* she tells me, because of a comment her grandmother made after the murders. "What had happened was just like what was in that book," Betty said, and Jody has long intended to reread it to figure out what her grandmother might have meant. In fact, when I read the novel, the parallels between its overwrought plot and Jody's own family history do strike me as stark, but not because of the brother-sister incest. Whatever Billy imagines he shared with his sister, none of my conversations with Jody suggest it was in any way mutual. From what I understand of the Gilleys, it's Linda who seems to have stepped from its pages, especially from the perspective of Betty.

Wasn't Linda a mother whose sordid background pollutes future generations and leads her to sacrifice her children for the sake of appearances? That Betty would insist on the book's eerily forecasting what befell her adopted daughter's family bears witness to her sustained anxiety about Linda's origins, her secret past that couldn't be overcome in spite of Betty's sustained efforts.

Flowers in the Attic casts a spell that's hard to throw off, and I find myself wondering what the teenage Jody thought of this story and even if she might not have kept the battered paperback—which she rescued first from what remained after an electrical fire that destroyed her bedroom and left its cover scorched, and then from the murder scene—as a vessel for what she can neither discard nor allow into her present life: the story of an older brother who rescues the sister he loves from their unredeemably wicked family.

"Why you?" I ask Thad. "Why did you want to be her guardian?"

"I didn't." Thad smiles. It's a playful smile, flirtatious and at least a little disingenuous. "I tried to farm Jody out to the Arnold family. Phil Arnold," he clarifies when I raise my eyebrows in question. "Phil was the civil rights lawyer who brought me out to Oregon in the first place. He was a good friend, married, and he and his wife had three daughters. The Arnolds were nice, they were normal. Too normal, Jody thought. And then there was Connie."

"Connie Skillman?"

Thad nods.

I meet Connie when Jody and I visit Medford. She lives in neighboring Ashland, Oregon, as she did in 1984 when she ran Jackson County's Victims' Assistance Program. Now she designs gardens, an antidote perhaps to work that kept her immersed in the aftermath of violent crime. Terraced flower beds ascend to her front door and she comes barefoot down the path to hug Jody before she offers me her hand. To me, Connie looks the way mothers are supposed to look: calm and capable and prepared to face, or face down, what comes her way. Part of this is her physical presence: a former figure skater, she still projects the grace and strength necessary to rebound quickly from a fall.

"Jody had a hard time deciding," Thad says. "She couldn't decide. We talked and agreed that Connie's family might be very rule-oriented. Connie didn't have any kids left at home, and Jody was afraid she'd be controlled to death."

I nod, but after spending an afternoon speaking with Connie, I wonder if Jody might not have been threatened by her openness, her emotional availability. What would have happened to Jody's tightly managed feelings in the company of a surrogate mother who invited—perhaps even required—the emotional presence of those around her? Jody had never lived in a home where it was safe to feel, and in the months following the murders she was even more determinedly "steeled" against emotion than she had been before. If the Gilleys' disastrous parenting precipitated their own deaths, it also prepared at least one of their children for catastrophic emotional upheaval.

"Okay, then," I say to Thad. "Why you? Why did Jody want you as her guardian?"

He smiles and replaces his drink on the table between us. It's clear we've arrived at a part of this story he likes well enough to perform, and his playfulness shows me the man Jody met twenty years before, the attorney unconventional enough to wear his hair long, dress like a hippie, and hang a big poster of Darth Vader in his office. When Thad describes the private plane he flew in the eighties, a high-performance, fuel-injected Mooney, as "black, like Darth Vader's," I take note that his identification with the *Star Wars* antihero—the "dark father" inseparable from his black mask—has endured for so many years. Perhaps its value is as a disguise, as Thad seems to have come home from Vietnam intent on good works, making a career of social justice and civil rights, serving as a public defender.

"I saw two types of clients in legal aid," Thad says. "There were the ones who found me callous and unfeeling because I didn't soften the picture, I didn't paint it prettier than it was. And there were the others, who appreciated my detachment, the fact that I assessed a situation and gave them honest, reliable information."

I nod. Detachment, analysis, honesty: these would have appealed to Jody.

Jody trusted him immediately, Thad says, and he tells me she understood the message he was consciously telegraphing, that he "perceived her as a winner." Within seconds of their meeting, he tells me, he'd tacitly confirmed what Jody wanted most to believe about herself and what her parents had withheld: she was a person of worth; she had only to apply her will and talents to achieve what she wanted.

From Jody's perspective, Thad's reward for the faith he placed in her was the fulfillment of this judgment, the satisfaction inherent in "republish[ing] the story of Pygmalion in a small Oregon town," as she wrote in "Death Faces." "He sought to live vicariously through her, to empower her and feel her power; to teach her and watch her intellect flash upon others; to groom her and enjoy her beauty."

The day after he helped her establish the Livingstons as her legal guardians, Jody called Thad again. Would he escort her to her parents' and sister's funeral? Already she anticipated being attacked as her brother's collaborator, and she wanted someone with her to discourage assailants and extricate her from potential conflicts. Thad accepted what was a flattering invitation, to be chosen as Jody's bodyguard and given a role in the drama everyone was watching. If, as he says, Jody responded to his embracing her as worthy, it was equally true that Thad found it gratifying when she looked to him as the mentor and father she wanted. At the funeral, Thad stayed close enough to Jody to intimidate anyone who tried to approach her. "She cried over Becky," he remembers. "But not for her parents." Among the mourners and voyeurs were print journalists and camera crews from local TV news stations. The event was a must-see, the culmination of what Thad describes as days of nonstop media attention, and it wasn't only Jody's guilt over having failed to defuse her brother's violence and save her little sister that made her worry she'd be accused. Already, Connie tells me, calls were coming into the DA's office suggesting Jody had been involved in the murders.

"Calls from whom?" I ask.

"People. People who read the paper, saw the news. They figured there was more to it than what had been reported, and that she was part of it. Otherwise, why would Billy have killed one sister but not the other?"

"I REMEMBER BEING SHOCKED WHEN I GOT the indictment," Billy says of learning he was being charged for intentionally killing Becky. Jody had stated clearly to the police that Billy had taken their sister up to her room and asked that she keep Becky upstairs, where she would be safe. Whatever Billy had done to their parents, it was different from what had happened with their little sister.

Arraigned on three murder charges, Billy was appointed a lawyer, Stephen Pickens, who hired a psychiatrist to examine his client and establish whether there was any basis for an insanity plea. As Billy was found mentally competent, Pickens was left with only one possible defense, to argue for reducing the charge leveled against his client, from aggravated murder to manslaughter. For this he needed to gather mitigating evidence, something that would convince a jury that Billy's act was less premeditated than it appeared, reasons to believe that the murders were provoked, in this case by what Billy described as a history of severe abuse. For this, Pickens needed at least one credible witness to testify that his client had been cruelly treated by the parents he killed. The obvious choice was his sister Jody.

But Jody's testimony was critical to the state's case against her brother, and from his privileged vantage as a legal aid attorney, Thad Guyer knew Jody had "at least been considered as a possible co-conspirator" in the killings. Medford was a small town, and Thad knew DA Justin Smith; he'd heard the joke making the courthouse rounds, the one that went, "Did you hear the one about

Billy Gilley? He went to bat for his sister." Determined to protect Jody in whatever way possible, and aware that if she cooperated with the DA's office the state wouldn't pursue her as an accomplice or accessory to murder, Thad allowed the prosecution access to Jody while refusing it to Stephen Pickens, "for fear that blaming Jody might become an aspect of the defense or sentencing."

"She was sixteen years old at the time, and emotionally distraught, and I may have simply told her that she should not discuss the case with anyone without consulting with me first," Thad stated in the affidavit he prepared when subpoenaed by post-conviction counsel, a copy of which I obtain through Billy, not from Thad, who doesn't allude to either Pickens's request or his refusal to grant it when I speak with him.

Even after he'd had "one or more conversations with [Pickens] regarding the case," and understood that Billy's attorney was concerned over "how little he had by way of defense," Thad didn't relent. Nor did he discuss the matter with Jody, who was frightened by the little contact she'd had with Billy since the murders—the letter with the dagger and the puddle of blood— frightened of Billy himself, who was making accusations against her and saying that she'd betrayed him.

Billy's turning on Jody would prove a costly mistake. Thad told Jody not to offer any information that wasn't directly elicited by the DA's questions. The fact remained that Jody and Billy were the only people in the house when their parents and sister were murdered, and while Billy never suggested that Jody helped him kill any of the three, he did say that his sister had understood and tacitly approved his plan. In a videotaped interview made three weeks after the murders by a clinical psychologist, Dr. Abrams, Billy claimed he and Jody "had discussed killing their parents on previous occasions, and that his sister had encouraged him to commit the murders." Jody, he said, "wanted to skip school the next day," and told him she "wouldn't be able to unless I killed them." During Becky's school play Jody "brought up the killings again," Billy said, asking if he "thought they would get enough money afterwards to have a party."

It seems unlikely that a juror would take Billy's word over Jody's. His juvenile record included first-degree arson, first-degree criminal mischief, second-degree theft, reckless endangerment, and disorderly conduct. Aside from his rap sheet, numerous psychological profiles in his Children's Services Division file suggested Billy was impulsive, prone to antisocial behavior, and, on occasion, paranoid. The staff of the youth shelter had found him dishonest, irresponsible, and lacking the self-control necessary for group counseling. Dr. Maletzky, who examined him two months after the murders, considered him a sociopath. Still, Thad judged, the protection granted Jody by her brother's delinquent history wasn't absolute. Also of the opinion that Billy was a sociopath, and therefore belonged in prison, Thad saw only one reasonable course of action: to guard details that might complicate what, for his client's sake, needed to be presented as a clear-cut case.

Other than Jody, two people who would have testified on Billy's behalf were Linda's friend Frances Livingston (no relation to Bob and Renae Livingston) and his grandmother Betty Glass, neither of whom made an attractive character witness. Frances was significantly overweight and had not had much formal education. And Betty, unhinged by the murders, had become a spectacle in downtown Medford, accosting passersby to tell them her grandson was innocent, her cold and conniving granddaughter had planned the murders, and the DA was so incompetent that he "couldn't even pick his nose right." When Billy said he wanted his grandmother to testify, Pickens refused. He didn't trust her to conduct herself in the courtroom any better than she did on the street.

But Billy didn't know what his grandmother was doing out in front of the courthouse, and says Pickens didn't tell him that Jody's lawyer, Thad Guyer, wouldn't allow him access to his sister. According to Billy, when he told Pickens he wanted to testify on his own behalf and explain that he'd never meant to harm Becky, only to kill "my parents, in order to protect myself and my sisters from the physical and psychological abuse," Pickens refused. He couldn't allow him to admit to the purposeful murder of his mother and father, because his plan was to try for the reduced charge of manslaughter. For this, he had to prove Billy had attacked his parents with criminal disregard for their lives, but not the intent to kill. Over and over, Billy's attorney asked him "questions about Jody's testimony to the police . . . statements that contradicted my own statements." Pickens didn't believe him, Billy felt, "because he continued to challenge my credibility by using Jody's statements."

On June 1, 1984, the DA's office interviewed two inmates in the Jackson County Jail about conversations they'd had with Billy. One, Keith Armstrong, said Billy told him that "Jody had collaborated in the killing of the parents and that while in the midst of killing them Becky happened onto the scene and began screaming. When she started to run away he struck her." Billy told Armstrong that his father had been "cruel" and used to take out his frustrations on his children "due to a poor marriage." Linda, Billy said, "was the craziest woman he'd ever known," and a "violent argument" had precipitated the murders. The other inmate, Steve Martin, asked Billy directly why he'd killed his parents. "Because Dad used to beat me with a hose," he answered, and "my mom's crazy and she raised my little sister so that's why I killed both of them." Neither of these reports conflicts with Billy's statements to Pickens or to the psychiatrists who evaluated Billy at Pickens's behest. On June 25, 1984, an Oregon State Penitentiary inmate, Paul Dizick, told the state police officer who interviewed him that a year or so earlier, Billy had "asked him about committing the crime of murder." He'd wanted to know if there were firearms that couldn't be traced by ballistics and where to shoot someone "so as to ensure their death." Mr. Dizick's advice was to use a shotgun and to kill more than one person—three or four—and then to act crazy, so as to set up an insanity plea. When Dizick asked whom he wanted to kill and why, Billy told him he was being kept "prisoner," and "implied that he hated his father."

Toward the end of June, when Billy was evaluated by Dr. Maletzky, it was the doctor's opinion that he had "taken poor care of his appearance," and that he betrayed "a good deal of tension with some facial tics that remit[ted] as the interview continue[d]." Billy told Dr. Maletzky he believed that "if there [were] a God," his parents and sister were in heaven, and possibly "better off now that they were dead." That he should imagine Becky happier and better off for having been dispatched to paradise wasn't so odd, but why would Billy put his parents, whom he felt justified in killing for their crimes against their children, in heaven with her? Twenty-one years later, when I ask him about the possibility of God and heaven, he dismisses both as fantasies.

"Did you ever believe in God?"

"When I was a little kid."

"When did you stop?"

"Probably when my parents died. Then or right after."

"Why then?"

"Because if there was a God then he wouldn't of let any of it happen. But I wasn't . . ." Billy shrugs and looks out through the wire-reinforced glass at the fallen snow, still absolutely white, undisturbed. "I hadn't really believed for a while," he says.

He began to question the existence of an unseen and powerful being, he tells me, when he was a little boy, living on Dyer Road, and learned that Santa Claus, the Easter Bunny, and the Tooth Fairy were not real—and, though he doesn't say this, when he was routinely beaten, frightened of the dark, and made to go to sleep without a night light.

In the months after our conversation I find myself returning to the moment when Billy speaks about God, both because of the childish incongruity of lumping God in among Santa, the Easter Bunny, and the Tooth Fairy, and because of the unanswerable logic of that same incongruity.

Upon her arrival at providence hospital, Becky was comatose. At Billy's trial, the attending neurosurgeon, Mario Campagna, explained her condition as "extremely critical ... premoribund. ... She was breathing a little bit on her own, but that's about all. Her pupils were what we call dilated and fixed, which meant there was no response to light. She couldn't move anything, she couldn't talk, couldn't see." In what Campagna understood as a quixotic attempt to save her life, he "took her to surgery ... and took out most of the right side of the skull. ... We put her on a respirator after the surgery. ... She never did breathe on her own and died on the 29th of April, 1984." One aspect of Becky's diagnosis would prove critical to her sister's psychic survival. Because doctors were sure that her head injuries were so severe that her life couldn't have been saved even had she received immediate attention, they were able to release Jody from speculations as to whether she might have improved Becky's chances of recovery if less time had elapsed between Billy's attack and the arrival of the ambulance crew. That Becky's injuries were necessarily fatal didn't dismiss Jody's guilt, however. Her ethical position couldn't be altered by information she didn't have during the agony of the card game with Kathy and Billy.

"I'm sure the ICU nurse knew that Becky was already dead," Jody wrote in 1995, "but I believed the respirator was proof my little sister would be okay. ... I was convinced by her softly twitching hand that she was alive and going to be okay."

*   *   *

While Becky was in the hospital, Billy behind bars, and Jody living with the neighbors, Bill's and Linda's families arrived from California, crossed the yellow crime scene tape, and began carrying off whatever they wanted from 1452 Ross Lane. There wasn't much of value in the house, except for the comic books, and when police stepped in to stop the plunder, most of what was taken was returned, except for the comic books. Bill's sister, Christina Sanders,* made the funeral arrangements and untangled what remained of her dead brother's finances. Several among Jody's father's and mother's relatives offered Jody a home, but she wasn't prepared to leave behind everything that was familiar for a life in California with people whom her parents had consistently bad-mouthed and taught her to distrust. Taking her 1999 affidavit as an official opportunity to acknowledge those to whom she did turn, Jody wrote that her "greatest comfort came from Ms. Connie Skillman of the District Attorney's Victims' Assistance Office."

Offering help to crime victims was a new idea in Jackson County at the time of the Gilley family murders, and Connie conducted the entire operation from a converted broom closet in the courthouse. Thirty-eight when her father's father was murdered, Connie had found dealing with the criminal justice system to be so fraught with anxiety, frustration, and injustice that she was inspired to single-handedly introduce her hometown to the idea of victims' services.

Connie's grandfather, Milton Janusch, had lived year-round in a cabin he'd built on the outskirts of Medford until 1982, when a young man came to his door and asked to use the toilet. "I made him get down on his

knees and beg for his life and then I shot him in the fucking head," Janusch's killer said after he was arrested. He
threw a coat over the old man, shot him again, and
called friends to come over and party. When they refused, he stepped over the body, made himself a sand-
wich, looked around for where Janusch might have
stashed his liquor, stole his truck and his credit cards,
and went on a three-day spree before he was caught in
Wenatchee, Washington, some five hundred miles north.

"This was a person," Connie says of her grandfather,
"who was very important to me and to my children, especially to my four sons." As Connie was the closest relative in the area, it fell to her to represent her family's
interests to the various agencies that responded to the
murder. Confident and proactive by nature, a woman
who raised five children and who conveys optimism as if
it were an informed choice, the perspective she's decided
to embrace, Connie tells me she was shocked by what
turned out to be an overwhelming, at times impossible
task. That it was her family who had to absorb the cost
of driving up to Wenatchee to retrieve her grandfather's
impounded truck and pay the fees to have it released she
considered unfair. But it was an outrage that she and her
husband were left to clean up the blood and brain matter spattered over his cabin. Dealing with the DA's office
was so stressful, she discovered, that on her first visit her
hands were shaking too much to turn the knob of the
building's front door. Once inside, the only useful information she was able to glean was that the suspect's
mother worked as a secretary in the police department,
a position from which she tried to stymie Connie's attempts to find out, for example, when her son was to be
arraigned.

Already pushed to the limit of her patience, when
Connie arrived at the courthouse for the arraignment
she found herself in an elevator with the parents of her

grandfather's killer, and a captive audience to his mother's characterizing him as "a good boy." When she stepped off the elevator she happened on the "good boy" smiling for the cameras, apparently without remorse. Galvanized by rage, she responded to her own family's plight by turning it into a cause. During what became a year-long apprenticeship, Connie went to nationally recognized victims' advocates for guidance and accessed paperwork from programs throughout Oregon to adapt for Medford's needs. In the end, she made herself so visible and necessary a presence that Justin Smith—the district attorney who would prosecute Billy—included her office in his bid for reelection.

"Information on the case. Recovery of funeral expenses. The opportunity to make a victim impact statement that is presented to the sentencing judge." As she speaks, Connie ticks off the rights of a victim of violent crime on her fingers. "Someone to clean up the blood—at the state's expense. Reparation for other costs related to the crime. Someone to explain to a child what happens in a courtroom. Someone to help you choose what to wear to court. Something as simple as saying, 'You know, you only have one chance to make a first impression. If you're called to the witness stand, you dress like you would for Sunday school.' When my grandfather was murdered there was no one, not one person, who could do even that much."

Two years later, when Jody needed help, Medford had Connie, who came to the house on Ross Lane and went inside.

"What was it like?" I ask her.

"The house?" Connie shudders, and the lovebird on her shoulder, a pet that spends a lot of time out of its cage, ruffles its feathers in response, a tiny, highly colored echo of the movement. "One of those places you just wanted to wipe your feet when you left. Dust, clutter, dirt. *Dirty.*"

Connie's house is clean, and it looks orderly, as if she could locate whatever she needed—a key, a sales receipt, her microwave's owner's manual—within a minute or two.

"I gather Jody's mother wasn't very interested in housework," I say. "It sounds as if the only people who ever straightened up were Jody and Becky."

"And remember," Connie adds, "the family, the extended family, they'd ransacked the place before Jody even had a chance to retrieve her things, what she wanted of them. Which wasn't much." Connie looks toward the ceiling and closes her eyes. "Jody's room—it was an oasis. Magical. Totally different, a world apart from the rest of the house. Tidy. Organized. Books shelved and alphabetized. *Books.*"

"And Jody?" I ask. "How was she?"

"Amazing, under the circumstances. An amazing young woman who had to make important decisions overnight." She brings her left hand up to the lovebird, strokes its rosy throat with her forefinger. "How did she come across? Lost. Not scared, just lost. Shut down. Flat affect. Absolutely flat. Glassy-eyed. She told me they—the law enforcement officers—kept asking her the same questions over and over, as if they didn't believe her. 'What do they want?' she kept asking me. 'What am I supposed to say?' And, you know, people did fault her for . . . well, really, for not displaying emotion."

I nod. My first meeting with Jody followed an e-mail exchange that had been immediately frank and intimate, and perhaps because of this I was struck by how little emotion she betrayed in person. I was a stranger, of course, not a friend or confidante, but my knowledge of the violence in her past, the enormity of the loss she was forced to navigate at sixteen, didn't prepare me for her telling what I understood to be a shocking story without any palpable shift in affect, not even as much as a minute adjustment in the tone of her voice or a fractional incline of her head toward mine. The words Connie uses to describe her at sixteen—"robotic, emotionally shut down"—no longer apply, and Jody is able to describe feelings carefully and articulately, but I never sense I'm observing or experiencing her emotions, only that I'm listening to her report of them. We laughed frequently during that dinner, but it was laughter that recognized absurdity: an intellectual response. When Jody spoke of grief or anger, her voice and her expression remained, as they had been, composed. Our conversation helped me understand how I make people uncomfortable by speaking of my father without dropping the tone of my voice into the register reserved for fatal illness or natural disaster, without pulling my listeners into a secluded corner—in other words, without warning them.

People who cross the threshold between the known world and that place where the impossible does happen discover the problem of how to convey their experience. Some of us don't talk about murders or intergenerational sex within our families. We find words inadequate, or we lose them entirely. Those of us who insist on speaking what's often called unspeakable discover there's no tone reserved for *un*natural disasters, and so we don't use any. We're flat-affect; we report just the facts; this alienates our audience.

"I am as normal and well-adjusted an individual as any whose life reads like the script to a Greek tragedy," remarks Jennifer Saffron, a pen name Jody created for herself in college, in an essay "Jennifer" published in *The Georgetown Journal* during the fall of 1992. When I e-mail her, asking about the pseudonym, Jody replies that "Jenny is slang for a female ass and saffron is yellow and

I was a yella arse for not having the courage to publish it under my own name."

"Boy," I type back. "You are one girl who needs a decoder ring." But, as Jody explained, because she was part of the publication's editorial staff, her submissions had to be anonymous.

"You say your father sacrificed your sister, your mother ambushed your father, you slaughtered your mother, and now you've gone blind and are being chased around the countryside by three blood-soaked women with snakes for hair? Is that all that's bothering you, Orestes?" Jennifer Saffron writes, paraphrasing Aeschylus's *Oresteia* (and confusing Orestes, who does not go blind, with Oedipus, who blinds himself upon discovering he's had intercourse with his mother).

The story of Orestes, who with his sister Electra plotted to kill their mother, Clytemnestra, to avenge her murder of their father, Agamemnon, and all of Orestes' family—the House of Atreus—provides one of the few examples Jody found throughout the history of literature as she cast about for stories that might help her make sense of her own life. But Jennifer Saffron doesn't limit herself to classical allusions. Titled "Here's the Story . . . of a Man Named Milpy," Jody's essay references the theme song of *The Brady Bunch,* a sitcom that fascinated children like Jody and me not only because it was a direct descendant of *Father Knows Best* and other series that presented soothing images of an attainable normalcy but also because the Bradys were a successfully *restored* family, the seamless graft of a widow and her three daughters onto a widower and his three sons. We couldn't aspire to an unblemished past, but we did have fantasies of redemption. United, the two halves of the Brady family transcended their separate griefs and reached a point of collective amnesia, living in a sunny suburbia where there was never a problem that wasn't inherently funny and couldn't be resolved in twenty-two minutes. Watching it at ten or twelve, I understood the program as educational and paid it the kind of close attention that Jody did her Harlequin romances, depending on it to teach me what was amusing and acceptable—what was normal in a family.

The replacement of *Brady* with *Milpy,* the name Jody chose as "Gilley in literary disguise," summons James Thurber's "The Secret Life of Walter Mitty," whose eponymous hero's name has itself become a reference to the use of fantasy as escape from an intolerable reality. "Violent death runs in my family," begins Milpy, whose tone is his most salient feature. Armored by a smart-alecky, sophomoric humor that quashes any possibility of pity, Jody qua Milpy catalogues the tragedies that befell both sides of her family, daring the reader to feel an emotional connection to people portrayed as freaks, and accelerates toward "a Freudian analyst's dream come true: Billy Jr., not scoring high on the son-o-meter, taking a cue from *Friday the 13th,* murdered them and his younger sister in their sleep."

The first blank in the post-sentencing report generated after Billy's trial, the blank that follows the words *SUMMARY OF THE FACTS,* is filled with hurried script, a hybrid of printing and cursive executed with what looks to have been a black felt-tipped marker. "killed mother father & sister," it says. The first time I page through the documents, I stop in the midst of what I'd intended as a quick overview to consider the abbreviated statement, arrested by the casual way the few cataclysmic words had been dashed off. Shouldn't the statement have been written and punctuated carefully and correctly? Shouldn't there be a special font or style of inscription, a writing implement used only for recording murders—something, anything—for words like that? Maybe the bureaucratic equivalent of a branding iron could scorch the information onto the form. I stare at this *SUMMARY OF THE FACTS* for some minutes and return to the Xeroxed document several times in the days that follow. The words *killed mother father & sister* are rendered in the same hand as that which flows out from under a waitress's fingers and onto her pad. Or it's a meter maid's scribble on a parking ticket: functional, forgettable. Apparently, the tone missing from the spoken language of murder, incest, and other unspeakable acts is absent from the written as well. And the lack can't be remedied. To create that tone, that special script, would be to imply that in some small measure we condone abominations, we accept their existence enough to give them a mode of reference.

"But they must have understood," I say to Connie of the people who faulted Jody for her lack of emotion. "They must have known she was in shock. That if her affect was flat, it was flat because she was in shock."

"Still," Connie says.

Still.

Trying to help me see Jody as she was at sixteen, just after the murder of her family, Connie stops talking to pantomime dropping an invisible cloak over her body. Silently, she acts out drawing a zipper from her knees all the way up over the top of her head, hiding herself. This is how defended Jody was, Connie says, how off-limits. Her simple performance stays with me. I think of it during subsequent interviews with Jody, my notebook lying open in my lap, ready to receive whatever she tells me. Later, when I read what Jody's said, I wonder what words I could add to convey the emotional content of what she's described—I try to imagine the part she didn't articulate—and I see it again: a hand drawing a zipper closed from the inside of a cloak, disappearing the girl underneath. But perhaps this is as good as any of the ways we fail to adequately describe the experience of trauma and abuse: it disappears you.

"Alone at home, that's where I grieve, not in public or in conversations with people," Jody writes me, explaining what shouldn't require explanation. But we want— we insist, really—that people, *victims*, emote to guide or confirm our feelings about what they've endured, especially if it falls outside the borders of our own experience. If they don't, we hold them in suspicion.

A MONTH AFTER MY VISIT TO THE SNAKE River Correctional Institution, I receive a letter from Billy, and with it the drawing he promised me of the layout of the house at 1452 Ross Lane. When we spoke about the murders I asked him so many questions about the interior of the house, which I didn't see when I visited Medford, that he said he'd mail me a floor plan to clarify what he couldn't when we met and were not allowed to use pen and paper. At the time of my visit to Medford I'd been disappointed that I hadn't been able to secure permission to enter the house, but Billy's floor plan shows me something more compelling than anything I might have learned from the structure itself: Billy's vision of his home.

The plan is meticulously executed in blue ink on white paper, every line, even one as short as that indicating a single stair tread, measured and drawn with a ruler. Doorways, plumbing fixtures, kitchen appliances: all of these appear as they would in architectural blueprints. Each room is identified, and Billy has furnished the house with beds, tables, and chairs, even a minute television on a corner stand, to which he's added a V for antennae.

On the couch adjacent to the living room's front window he's traced the outline of a tiny man with the annotation "father slept on couch" floating above the spot where he attacked and killed his father. A similar figure of his mother lies, also faceup and featureless, on the bed in which he murdered her. Becky, whom he killed when she was trying to get back to her mother, is placed not where she died but on the bed in her own room, next to an asterisk with the reminder "Becky often slept in Mother's bed." Billy lies on his bed in the smallest of the downstairs rooms, Jody is in her attic bedroom. The five figures are not only androgynous but also stylized. Their perfectly round and featureless heads remind me of plastic toys for preschoolers.

That Billy chose to represent his family as he did might not strike me so strongly had he not included a supplementary map of the outbuildings. On it he's divided the barn into two equal parts. In one is "Billy's Hot Rod," a generic drawing of whatever car Billy was trying to rebuild at any given time. The other side, belonging to his father, is empty save for a huge tractor wheel, its deep tire treads indicated by a ring of zigzags that make it look like an outsize circular saw. "Billy was tied to this tractor wheel for whipping," reads the legend written next to it.

Adjacent to the barn, on the other side of the fence around the Gilleys' property, is a cow. "Neighbor's Cow that Billy made Pet out of," announces its caption. There is also a horse and a goat. These animals, placed around the house and barn, have human eyes, a feature I recognize from other of Billy's drawings. Cats, chickens, horses, pigs, squirrels, deer, dogs, tortoises: Billy draws them all with grotesquely large and human-shaped eyes fringed by extravagantly long lashes.

I know about the use of the tractor wheel, from my conversations with both Jody and Billy, and I'm not surprised to find he's used it as the emblem of his father's territory. I find it stark and sad, but more disturbing to me is the juxtaposition of people who lack organs of sight with animals that have huge, wide, hypervigilant human eyes. In the coming months Billy will send me copies of some of his illustrated children's stories, fairy tales about talking animals and magical relationships between animals and humans—always with an animal in the role of savior—and these stories will support my reading the floor plan of his home as autobiographical.

In the nonfiction narrative of Billy's life, the story of himself that he tells to himself, the only creatures that bore witness to his suffering were mute animals, incapable of conveying what they saw, incapable of effecting his rescue. The humans who did see his anguish might as well have been faceless, blind, and dumb, for all they did to help him.

IN JAIL FOLLOWING THE MURDERS, IN THOSE moments he considered the possibility that his attempt to free himself and his sisters had backfired so completely that he'd killed Becky and incarcerated himself, Billy was despairing. Only his grandmother visited him. Jody didn't respond to his letters. The rest of his extended family withdrew and went back to California after they'd plundered their dead relatives' belongings and taken in the spectacle of the funeral. He had no friends; his lawyer neither liked nor, he sensed, believed him. He had no means to distract himself from rehearsing the miserable narrative of his short life.

In what he acknowledges to me as a feeble attempt at suicide, on September 21, 1984, Billy removed the narrow blade from a disposable safety razor and cut his arm, nicking a vessel that bled dramatically for a short time but didn't require suturing. The gesture produced no result other than his removal from the cell he'd occupied originally to what he calls a "rubber room," where he couldn't hurt himself. Although no one interpreted Billy's cutting himself as anything but a bid for attention or pity—one that instead earned him contempt, further hardened the DA's office against him, and encouraged law enforcement to dismiss him as a coward as well as a sociopath—it did precipitate his third post-arrest psychiatric interview, the one with Dr. David Kirkpatrick, whom Billy still faults for what he considers the indefensibly insensitive remark that he "did not even have the right to kill himself at this time," because he had a "monumental task" before him: repaying his debt to society.

But Dr. Kirkpatrick wasn't unsympathetic in his assessment of Billy's personality. He found him "engaging, intelligent," and not without remorse, a young man "struggling with extreme existential, moral, and redemptive or restitutive conflict."

In Euripides' play *Orestes*—a later work that casts the ancient story in human rather than divine terms—the Argive assembly condemns Orestes and Electra to death by stoning, and Orestes defends their having killed their mother by reminding their accusers of Clytemnestra's infidelity. In consideration of this, the assembly offers the siblings the choice of committing suicide. This was the extent of mortal law to respond to the terrible ambiguity of breaking the most sacred of taboos in righteous defense. In the end, Apollo intervenes to spare their lives.

Without the option of deus ex machina, heightened public consciousness of the physical, sexual, and emotional abuse that unfold in often deceptively normal-seeming homes has slowly changed the way Americans view parricide, which they have generally tended to dismiss as a crime of unalloyed depravity. Despite his juvenile record, enough of Billy's early experiences align with those of the typical "victim-offender" that he and his post-conviction counsel have crafted an appeal that hinges on his original attorney's failure to present him as an abused child. A term applied to battered women and, increasingly, to children who attack and kill their abusers, victim-offenders are considered by today's courts as a distinct category of murderer, one that was a new concept in 1984, introduced a year earlier to the general public when the February 14, 1983, trial of Richard Jahnke commanded the attention of the entire country.

In November 1982, sixteen-year-old Jahnke and his sister, Deborah, seventeen, lay in wait for their father, who had beaten them and their mother for years, and who had sexually abused Deborah. Brother and sister armed themselves with guns from their father's arsenal and strategically placed other firearms throughout their home in Cheyenne, Wyoming. When their parents returned from an evening out, Mr. Jahnke got out of his car and walked toward the garage, giving Richard the opportunity for which he'd waited. Jahnke's attorney, Lee Adler, successfully introduced evidence of long-standing battery, including the fact that his client had reported his father to social services several times to no effect. In the end, Richard, who had meticulously planned his father's death, was found guilty not of first- or even second-degree murder but of manslaughter. After intense media coverage familiarized the public with the antecedents of his crime, "a letter-writing campaign was initiated to influence the trial judge in sentencing" and in less than three weeks collected 4,000 letters and 10,000 signatures on petitions urging leniency. Paul Mones, an expert legal consultant who has devoted his high-profile career to educating the public and the legal system about parricide, and who provided a declaration for Billy's appeal, puts it succinctly. "Courts are finally waking up to the problem. Kids just don't take these actions unless something is very, very wrong."*

With respect to Billy, Mones was approached for a comment on the likelihood of his committing future acts of violence. Not sufficiently familiar with the Gilley murders to address the case directly, Mones offered a generic response: parricide is the "result of a highly specific set of circumstances, that being the dynamic of the parent/child relationship."† Because this dynamic ends

---

*Kathleen M. Heide, *Why Kids Kill Parents: Child Abuse and Adolescent Homicide* (Columbus: Ohio State University Press, 1992), pp. 14, 17.
†From Mones's declaration, dated January 10, 2003.

with the death of the parent(s), parricides do not, generally speaking, pose a threat to others.

In the wake of Jahnke's instantly infamous murder of his father, "the subsequent child-abuse defense attracted a flood of national media attention, from *People* and *Rolling Stone* to *60 Minutes*,"* and helped establish the characteristics that typify parricide. Like Jahnke, Billy was a white male between the ages of sixteen and eighteen with a long-standing history of abuse. He'd reported the abuse to an appropriate authority without result. When he asked to be put into foster care, and later, when he attempted to run away, he was returned to his tormentors. The six months leading up to the murders were marked by increasing familial tension and a renewed sense of the impossibility of his escaping the home. He attacked his parents when they were defenseless; even the words he spoke upon killing them were those uttered by virtually all nonpsychotic children who kill their parents: "We're free." The choice for children like Billy is stark: to remain the passive victim of what appears to them to be a reign of terror that will never end or to take a "most drastic measure to assure the cessation of the abuse."†

An even more useful precedent for Billy's case would have been that of Jerry Ball, who killed his mother, father, and two younger brothers with a baseball bat in January 1983. At sixteen years old, he had endured a lifetime of abuse from both parents, rarely expressing anger until one night his mother "cussed" him and "he started swinging the baseball bat and couldn't stop. Jerry expressed sorrow in the aftermath of his actions that he had killed his six-year-old brother, who had never really

---

*Alan Prendergast, "The Killer and Mrs. Johnson," *Westword*, March 19, 1998.
†Jennifer James, "Turning the Tables: Redefining Self-defense Theory," *American Journal of Psychiatry*, 1985.

done anything to him. 'He hit him to shut him up,' the psychologist said. 'His brother was screaming.' "*

The problem for Billy was—and remains—that under Oregon law "extreme emotional disturbance is a defense only of intentional murder, not of aggravated murder," and the fact that Billy killed his parents as they slept, presenting no imminent threat to him or to Jody, meant that he was necessarily charged with aggravated murder, which in Oregon was also the charge automatically given a multiple murder. "No Oregon case has ever held that a defense of 'battered child syndrome' may be asserted as a basis for self-defense or the defense of another," the Appellant's Reply Brief states. "Oregon law . . . has always required that the threat *be* 'imminent,' "† rather than perceived as imminent due to past trauma.

The brief goes on to argue that although Drs. Stanulis and Levin testified, post-conviction, that Billy suffered from post-traumatic stress disorder and organic brain syndrome and therefore had been mentally incompetent at the time of the murders, the three mental health experts Pickens retained in 1984—Drs. Abrams, Maletzky, and Kirkpatrick—found Billy to be sane. Billy was aware of his actions at the time of the murders, they determined, and had committed them with forethought and intent. Pickens had no reason to suppose there was any basis for a mental defense, a theory that is in Billy's case the product of "hindsight" and therefore inadmissible, as an appeal can rest only on information available at the time of the original trial.

Clearly the law varies from state to state. In West Virginia, the fact that Jerry Ball had bludgeoned his two

*Greggory Morris, *The Kids Next Door: Sons and Daughters Who Kill Their Parents* (New York: William Morrow, 1985), p. 151.
†Appellant's Reply Brief, November 2006.

little brothers to death didn't dissuade Paul Mones from defending him nor did it prevent experts in parricide from testifying on his behalf. Two psychiatrists from Boston's McLean Hospital, Ronald Ebert and Shervert Frazier, who was later appointed director of the National Institute of Mental Health, said, simply, "Jerry was a kid who had suffered severe abuse, which triggered the murders." Like Billy, and like many other parricide offenders, Jerry Ball hit his parents far more times than was required to kill them, a reflection not of an innate thirst for destruction but perhaps of his belief in the omnipotence of his mother and father. Good and loving parents appear powerful to their children *and* they empower them; they help them discover their own strength and effectiveness. Abusive, tyrannical parents not only loom as implacable gods but also strip their children of confidence in their own ability to effect change. Every child has a hard time accepting the death of a parent; a battered child has even less sense that he, vulnerable and unworthy, might have the strength to dispatch his abuser—better to hit him again, and again, just to make sure.

Though it may sound implausible to someone who hasn't been subjected to chronic battery, when Billy tells me that, at eighteen years old, he "didn't really expect his father and mother to stay dead," I don't disbelieve him. Having been told all his life that he could do nothing right, that he was a loser, destined for failure, why would he imagine he'd managed to bring about so profound a transformation in the world as he knew it? What other than his parents' harping on his inevitably ending up in jail might have reassured him that he had in fact made them "stay dead"?

AFTER THE FUNERAL, THAD GUYER TOOK JODY home to the Livingstons, leaving her in a situation that deteriorated within two months. Judging by the investigative report based on Kathy's interview—which took place fifteen years after the murders, during which time she'd had no contact with Jody—Kathy was suspicious of Jody's cerebral nature, unable to understand how she might have developed her intellect at the expense of her emotions to protect herself from an unbearable family life. "Jody is very precise about what she does and calculates every move. . . . Jody's mind is always clicking," she said. In Kathy's opinion, her friend "spent an inordinate amount of time reading and planning the rest of her life." Unused to domestic violence and unable to imagine its effects, Kathy was "creeped out" by Jody's ability to compartmentalize or, if need be, deny her emotions and continue to function. Though she'd witnessed how the Gilleys treated their children and commented on the absence of love in the Gilleys' home, she didn't make the connection between Jody's environment and what was not Jody's essential nature so much as her response to that environment. When the two girls went to the house on Ross Lane—without Thad, in Kathy's version—Kathy found it "very disturbing" that Jody could enter her parents' bedroom, where "there was a comforter on the bed with blood still soaked on it." But Jody wanted Bunny, the toy Becky always took to bed, and knew she'd find it where her sister had been sleeping. A goal-oriented individual, inured to forging past what disturbed or hurt her, she went in the bedroom, walked past the bed where her mother had died, and picked up the rabbit. Another person might have admired what he or she saw as courage and strength of purpose unusual in a sixteen-year-old, but Kathy faulted Jody for what seemed to her a lack of feeling.

The girls' friendship had always been a function of geography rather than temperament, and Thad attributes their inevitable falling-out to Kathy's envy of Jody's receiving a monthly $260 death benefit check, giving Jody the ability to buy things—clothes, music, movie tickets—that Kathy couldn't afford. But it's also true that Kathy, revealed by her conversation with the private detective to be less sophisticated and psychologically acute than Jody, had been pulled into the wake of three brutal and suddenly notorious killings, the kind of crime that was, or had been, unheard of in Medford. Perhaps it was beyond her ability to play host to someone directly connected to the murders. Jody, after all, was doing weird things, walking in her sleep, for example, her empty arms carrying what she believed was a quilt and saying, like Lady Macbeth trying and failing to scrub away the stain of her guilt, "Here, wash this. It's covered in blood." If Kathy remembered being upset by a blood-soaked comforter, it may have been the one she couldn't see. Probably it was easier to focus her fear of what Billy had done, of the sudden realization of what didn't seem possible—murder within a family—onto Jody and assign at least some of the fear she felt to what she called Jody's "creepiness."

Too, as Billy himself reminded Jody and her new guardians, he might be jailed but he still existed. A month after the murders, he placed a collect call to the Livingstons, identifying himself to Kathy, who answered the phone, as "George Osborn" and arguing that yes, she did too know who he was and he wanted to talk to

Jody. "When Jody got off the phone," Kathy said, she "told me that Billy said, 'I can't believe you told them that I did it all and that you told on me. I thought we were going to run away and be free.' " The call was followed by the letter with the bloody dagger, postmarked June 1, 1984:

> Dear Jody I want you to giv grandma mom's weding ring and the clock that belonged to grandpa, it will be beter for you in the long run! And I don't want you to hert grandma any more, and if you tack my car away from me you will be sorry but wont be able to say it!
>
> All my love Billy

Aside from the drawing, the letter's salient feature is its childishness, the spelling, grammar, and phrasing one might expect from a boy of eight rather than eighteen. The note's casual tone and failure to convey any urgency or anxiety about the future reinforces the impression that the writer is very young, very unaware of the gravity of his situation. Billy's suggestion that Jody had hurt their grandmother alludes to the implicit insult of her having chosen the Livingstons as her guardians rather than Betty. By the time Billy went to trial, in November of that year, the rift between Jody and her grandmother had widened to the point that Betty publicly voiced her suspicion that Jody was a "snake in the grass [who] put Billy up to it," as he was by nature a sweet-tempered person, incapable of plotting the murder of his own family, an opinion that stood in direct contrast to that of his paternal grandmother, Essie Mitchell, who said he was "full of hate all the time."

* * *

Jody's relationship with Betty was but one of those she abandoned in her new life, after the murders. If Kathy found that Jody carried too many unpleasant associations, Jody felt the same to be true of Kathy. Soon, Thad tells me, she wasn't staying at the Livingstons' but was spending the night at other friends', whom Thad characterizes as wild, living on the east side, where the rich kids lived. And there was a boyfriend now, on the other side of town, Warren, whom Thad grants a grudging admiration. "Warren was a great break-dancer," he tells me. "He was a lower-income, west-side kid. I went looking for Jody at his place, and when neither of them were there I spoke with his mother, very white trash, a cigarette hanging from her mouth the whole time she was talking."

"But if you weren't interested in becoming Jody's guardian, why were you running around town after her?" I ask him. "Why wasn't she the Livingstons' problem?"

"I'll tell you why." Thad leans forward. "Because the Livingstons couldn't control her, and if they didn't control her, their guardianship would be terminated. Jody would end up in foster care."

So Thad qua Professor Henry Higgins—to update Jody's Pygmalion analogy—emotionally invested in the fortunes of his orphaned Eliza Doolittle, kept chasing after her. And by the time he caught up with her, one afternoon in late June, with her wild east-side friends, "lying in a Stratolounger, wearing a lot of makeup, with her weird hair," he had something to tell Jody. Two months had been enough for the Livingstons. They'd lost patience with her acting out and no longer wanted to be her guardians.

"So," Thad says, "there she is lying there looking up at me, full of attitude. Kathy hates her, she says, because she has money and she won't spend it on Kathy. Who do I think she should live with? I tell her, 'Pick Connie Skillman if you want someone caring. Pick the Arnolds if you want a normal life.' "

"Normal?" Jody drawled in her most sarcastic tone, of which Thad does a convincing imitation. "It's a little late for that, don't you think?"

"Well, where do you want to live?" he asked her.

"I want to live with you."

Thad shakes his head. "Nooo," he says to me, drawing the word out. "Unh-unh. 'That's not going to work,' I tell her. 'I'm in the middle of a divorce.' "

Thad tells me he left Jody in the Stratolounger and went home to talk to his soon-to-be ex-wife, Debbie, who said she was willing to let Jody live with them, in their attic, until Jody decided what to do with herself. "So," Thad says, "Jody moves in. Her behavior is totally erratic. One week she's fine, the next she's reverted back to being a quasi delinquent" (a term that overstates what was really no more than truancy). "I had some control—she was a little more responsive to my attempts at discipline because she knew I had no problem humiliating her by chasing after her."

In September, Thad moved out of his house and into his friend Dan Hake's place, at 1469 Stardust Way, "a nice place with a great hilltop view," on the eastern border of Medford, and Jody moved with him. School started, she broke up with the break-dancing Warren, and Thad tried to establish what he calls "some loose rules." He knew he couldn't prevent Jody from cutting school, as she had on the day before the murders, but he asked her to tell him when she was playing hooky, which she did not do. "Then she stops coming home at night," Thad says. "I don't know where she is. I have to go looking for her." Jody had a new boyfriend, Rob Brooks,* from the wrong side of the tracks in Thad's opinion. He found Jody "hanging out with a lot of dead-end teenagers, no adult supervision, beer, marijuana," which, Jody stresses to me, she never once smoked.

"If you're not home in one hour," Thad told her, "I'm coming back for you."

To avoid embarrassment, Jody returned to Stardust Way, where Thad confronted her. The school had called, he told her. She was a truant, and she was failing her classes.

"What are you going to do about it?" Jody challenged.

"I'm grounding you," Thad told her. "You go to school, you come home—that's it." Thad laughs. "I can't make her, she tells me, because I'm a womanizer."

"You're . . . you're just like a hideous monkey in the forest!" Jody said when he grounded her.

"That's a direct quote," Thad says, clearly still amused by the expression of Jody's outrage. Given the hostility of her response to his girlfriends—and he admits he did see a lot of women in the wake of his divorce—Thad interprets Jody's judgment as jealousy.

"No." Jody shakes her head when I introduce the idea. "The only problem I had with Thad's girlfriends was that they were ridiculously young"—sometimes as young as she—"and that offended my sensibilities."

Too, Jody remembers sexual tension between herself and Thad. Uncomfortable with what felt like his attraction to her, Jody finally spoke to him about it.

"And?" I prompt.

"And he was a gentleman. We talked about it. He stopped."

"Stopped what?" I ask.

"Well, it wasn't as if he were *do*ing anything, so all

there was to stop was his . . . his conveying that he felt that way toward me."

With or without the extra frisson of physical attraction, Jody and Thad were emotionally entangled. Jody abided by the grounding; she went to school and reported to an after-school clerical job Thad gave her at his office. She wanted to go to Georgetown, she told him, the university he'd attended, and which had informed his commitment to civil rights and social justice.

Because he believed Jody could go wherever she wanted if she studied hard, Thad encouraged her ambition, pleased that she showed up for work religiously. The fact that she was a model employee made it all the more surprising to him when the school called to say she hadn't been to class for a week.

Thad confronted her. It was one of the very few times, he tells me, that she cried in front of him. "I've ruined everything, haven't I?" Jody wept.

"Well, you've derailed," he agreed. "But we can get you back on track."

The transformation, he says, was immediate, and marked by a change of costume, always significant in a Cinderella story, or in a Pygmalion story, for that matter. Jody went from her borderline grunge/punk incarnation to a picture-perfect coed. "Skirt and blouse, with a brooch at the neck. No more weird hair or makeup," Thad says. "Very conservatively feminine." She abandoned her "dead-end crowd" for a new group of friends from the right side of the tracks, spending most of her time with Rachelle Cox, a well-groomed good girl with a strict mother. The school counselor professed astonishment at so complete an about-face. Not only was Jody making A's, her attendance record was suddenly perfect.

"One night I come home from work," Thad says, "and Jody's kneeling over the coffee table, and the top of it's covered in Post-its, arranged in a hierarchy. A-list kids on top, and from there all the way down, level by level, to the losers. She's mapped out the social strata of the entire eleventh grade, one name to a Post-it." Jody pointed out her position within the scheme, placing herself significantly below the upper echelon to which she aspired. "She told me which Post-its she knew and considered friends," Thad says, "and which she needed to cultivate in order to get where she wanted—the top." The exercise showed him the intensity of Jody's ambition, her focus, as well as what Kathy judged her unnerving tendency to calculate her every move to ensure a desired outcome. "By the twelfth grade," Thad tells me, "she was there. She was the most popular."

"I was sooooooo not the most popular!" Jody exclaims when I share the story with her. "And I'd totally forgotten about the Post-its. This is such an embarrassing story."

It's a good snapshot of Jody, both because it bears witness to the focus and determination that characterize her approach to any given situation—a mental organization Billy was unable to achieve until he was separated from his parents—and because it explains the unease of a girl like Kathy when exposed to a personality as fiercely goal-directed as Jody's, who never felt the confidence to leave anything to chance. That was a luxury for other girls, carefree girls who might consider their social lives an arena for recreation. Jody's social life was work, as it would be for years to come, when, surrounded by D.C. power brokers, she was immersed in what felt to her like "an alternate universe. It sounds glamorous, but it was hard and painful. . . . No one goes from that kind of background and jumps class without consequence. I didn't trust anyone. I had to learn boundaries and all kinds of socialization that other people had received at home."

In fact, very few people jump class at all, whether or not they come from loving homes. It requires a level of determination that is beyond unusual, extraordinary.

"They were an interruption," Thad says when we talk, moving without transition from the Post-its to the murders. "Billy didn't do a thing for her. Jody was always going to be the success she became. If anything, he made it harder. She had to ignore the stigma of being a murderer's sister, and of being accused of collaborating with a murderer. She didn't have the chance to run the usual gamut of emotions in relation to her parents. She would have cycled back toward them. As an adult, she would have made peace with them."

I nod, but I don't agree with him. Jody's estrangement from her parents was not the typical adolescent's breaking free of familial bonds; it grew out of abuse. And while the murders neither made Jody ambitious nor forged her intent to jump class, they did end the life she had before so that she never had to abandon her family, to choose to live in one world while they remained in the one from which she escaped. Too, the murders gave her access to the help—the people—she needed to realize her goals. She knows this, and it compounds her guilt at having survived. "From any objective viewpoint," she wrote in 1993, "informed by values of 'success,' of 'achievement,' of worldview and aesthetic appreciation, I have benefited from the murders. At present, I don't care to calculate the ways I have not, the things I have lost."

IT WOULD BE HARD TO FIND TWO LESS SIMI-
lar approaches to autobiography than Billy's and
Jody's. But both siblings have used narrative—creating
meaning and continuity through storytelling—to manage the psychic impact of the murders, and both have
written stories of animals to approach a human situation that perhaps defied comprehension if left in the
realm of human beings.

The emotional core of "Death Faces" was published
by itself in *The Georgetown Journal* as "Early Ambitions" by Kara Curry, as Jody continued the practice of
using pseudonyms borrowed from spices so she could
write anonymously about some of the more disturbing
incidents of her childhood, in this case one that inspired
her to sleep with a knife in her bed.

"In the summer of '83," Jody wrote, "my father bid on
a contract to beautify the eucalyptus trees at Stanford
University. A local Californian tree service subcontracted to my father, who really needed the money. Father, my brother, I, and two other workers (Dave and
Jackie) climbed into my dad's rigs and drove down to
Palo Alto for the summer. We were to stay in the home
of the original contractors, who stayed elsewhere."

During the first week of cutting back the eucalyptus, a
limb came down bearing a nest of newborn squirrels.
"The mother was missing. Three hairless and embryonic
baby squirrels landed nearby. One did not survive the
fall. To my horror, my brother threw the dead one in the
chipper."

Despite the predictions of Dave and her father and

even a couple of passersby that the tiny creatures would never survive without their mother, Jody took the remaining two and their nest back to the borrowed house and fed them human infant formula every two hours. "Whenever I put my hand in the nest, they squeaked and moved toward its warmth, they nuzzled my fingers. They were so helpless and young. I wanted to save them." But they didn't live longer than two days in her care, and she blamed herself when they died, wondering if she'd given them spoiled formula.

In the moment, Jody was anguished in the way children are when they fail to save orphaned or injured animals. Already she'd daydreamed about them becoming her pets, animals she'd raised herself. Believing in her ability to save them, she believed, too, in her power to kill them. But Jody's emotionally charged account of the squirrels' fate was written in 1991, eight years after the squirrels died and seven years after her brother murdered her parents and sister, and this passage about a nest of three siblings without a mother to protect them and whose annihilation is authored by forces beyond their control or understanding can't be read as anything other than a miniature prefiguring the larger tragedy that befell her own family.

The proof of this is in the epilogue to the story. The summer following the murders, at the wheel of Thad's Volvo, with him as a passenger, Jody ran over a squirrel, and in the wake of what was an accident she was so overcome with what she calls "grief" that she cried "uncontrollably. I don't think I've ever cried like that before. I couldn't stop the tears. I stopped the car.

"Thad, accustomed to what he affectionately called my 'acrylic veneer,' looked at me incredulously and said, 'You're a softy. Deep down you're just a softy,' as though it were some kind of revelation."

"Early Ambitions" makes no reference to the murders.

The presumptive death of the run-over squirrel echoes the sacrifice of the nest of squirrel pups and, for a reader unaware of the murders, Jody's grief appears to be a response to innocence lost, in that the essay is an account of her father's wolfish behavior during that summer at Stanford. Away from home, Bill could drink openly after a day's work, and as Dave, too, drank a lot, the partnership of the two men was sealed if not founded on their shared addiction. By habit, Jody closed herself in her room each evening and read while the rest of the crew made their way through one beer after another. "After a while," Jody/Kara wrote, "my father came to my room to persuade me to come out and join in with everyone else. Was there something wrong with me that I had to hide in my room? Did I think I was better than everyone else?"

As it happened, Bill didn't get Jody to leave her book and join him and his friends, but he did do something that disconcerted her enough that she took a knife to bed with her. "I made a pact that whoever attacked me, no matter who they were, would be stabbed."

"But what did he do?" I ask Jody.

"I don't know. Something."

"A physical something? Or did he, I don't know, did he proposition you?"

"No. No, that came later."

"But it must have been something pretty menacing for you to have taken a knife to bed."

"I think it was . . . it was maybe just the way he looked at me."

The summer of 1983, when Jody was fifteen, was the point at which she became aware of herself as sexually desirable. She noticed, as she hadn't before, that men looked at her in her shorts, seeing not a child but "the young, beautiful one who could not be disguised by the grime and the company she was keeping." Did this new sense of herself enable her to perceive her father's aggression, as she hadn't before? If suddenly she understood him as a predator, this knowledge alone could have been enough to frighten her, even if he hadn't subjected her to an overt physical advance. Too, Jody reminds me, the fear that lingered in the wake of Billy's molestation resulted in her being particularly sensitive to any perceived sexual threat.

Embedded within "Death Faces," the dead squirrels appear, in contrast to the murders, as a manageable, mournable experience, allowing her to confess feelings of guilt and horror. "On the way home, [after striking the squirrel with her car] I looked for *evidence of what I had done,* but when we reached *the scene of the crime,* there was no evidence of a squirrel, dead or otherwise. . . . *I'll never know if I was an instrument in the death* of that squirrel or not" [emphasis mine].

Typically, Jody uses the word *instrument* when she and I speak of the guilt she feels in relation to her family's destruction; it's a word she always applies to her brother in the context of an unanswered, unanswerable question: Was Billy the instrument of Jody's desire that her parents die?

Evidence. Scene of the crime. Instrument in the death of. These are strong terms for accidentally running over a squirrel—so strong they reveal their true object.

THE COMPLEXITY OF BILLY'S FEELINGS ABOUT his mother permeates not only his conversation and his letters but also the children's stories he writes and illustrates. When he describes Linda, Billy, like Jody, uses the word *depressed*, a conclusion he and his sister have reached independently, as the few letters they exchanged never touched on the topic.

"When I think about how she sat there watching TV," Jody says, "eating her bacon that she wouldn't share and never going out of the house. And the ulcer, that chalky ring of Mylanta around her mouth—now, when I add it all up, I see a woman who was profoundly depressed. But not then. I didn't see it then."

As a child, Billy was very aware of his parents' acrimony and his father's ability to hurt his mother. Still, his sympathy barely has time to register on his face before it's occluded by resentment. I ask him if he still has nightmares and if his parents are present in those dreams, and he nods.

"They don't have to be nightmares, exactly, but the two of them are always hanging over my shoulder. Whatever I'm doing they're always there, with me. I can't get rid of them." Across the table from me, he looks back over his shoulder, and acts out trying to brush something off from where it clings to him. The expression that goes with the gesture, a look of revulsion and horror, is so intense that it startles me, conjuring vampires or wraiths even in the brightly lit institutional setting. It's an image of Billy that will remain with me, the dread these ghosts inspire. The parents he killed are joined to him forever. Murder has made them his as irrevocably as birth delivered him into their arms.

But the stories Billy writes are sunny. They're fey and redemptive and marked—all of them—by unlikely salvation. My favorite, "Katrina and the Seagull," takes place in Puerto Rico, its heroine, Katrina, a nun who hasn't enough money to provide for the orphans in her care. While this much has been borrowed, it would appear, from the 1960s fantasy sitcom *The Flying Nun,* the rest is original. Dying of an unnamed disease that has rendered her barren, Katrina takes the orphans out to search for food in dumpsters, teaching them how supermarkets throw away food that is still good. While rummaging in the garbage, she sees a cat attacking a seagull and quickly takes up a toy she finds in the dumpster and hurls it at the cat, frightening it away. She carries the wounded seagull to the orphanage and nurses the bird back to health. A magic seagull, it casts a spell on her so that she can talk to animals.

The seagull explains that he was born from the union of two clouds; from them come his magic powers, and he asks Katrina what wish she would have him grant her. Bring the orphans a bunch of bananas, she suggests; they love them. The seagull complies, and brings a bag of gold coins as well, but when he delivers the treasure he finds that Katrina has fallen into a coma, the mysterious disease soon to claim her life. The gull flies to his parents, the clouds, and asks them to help save the nun. The clouds tell the gull to inhale them into his breast, fly back to the dying woman, and exhale the cloud-parents into her mouth. He does as they say, and Katrina is saved, reborn as a magic gull. She lays eggs, and is given the offspring she always wanted.

Like other of Billy's stories, "Katrina and the Seagull" casts an animal in the role of hero, empowered by language and other supernatural gifts that allow it to rescue

a human being. And, like the other stories, it reprises a
scene from Billy's childhood, in this case the mother figure providing food for her children from a dumpster.
The character of Katrina recasts Linda as a dying
woman, a barren woman, a chaste woman, and a virtu-
ous and selfless woman—all wishes that, if granted,
would have changed the past radically and saved Billy
from his fate, saved him from orphaning himself and his
sister. Katrina's transformation from woman to bird, a
universal metaphor for a (if not the) holy spirit, rewards
her love for children with fecundity. In Billy's fantasy,
motherhood is earned through generosity and self-
sacrifice.

Having rejected his mother's fundamentalist religion—
in part, he tells me, because of its dogmatic insistence
that animals lack souls and don't go to heaven—and concluded that there is no God, Billy seems to have created a
curious and playful animism, granting consciousness not
only to animals but also to clouds and, in other stories,
plants.

When Billy tells me his hope that his work might
someday be published, and that he spends much of his
time writing and drawing in his prison cell, I suggest to
him that an editor might receive a gritty graphic novel
more readily than a children's book, explaining that the
juvenile market is very crowded and that publishers tend
to buy stories without illustrations and commission the
art separately. Graphic novels are an expanding market,
suddenly hot, I tell him. Couldn't he draw on his prison
experiences or on stories inmates have told him? From
Amazon I order him a couple of books intended to guide
the aspiring graphic novelist. But, no, Billy explains
after he receives the books, he has no interest in writing
for adults, none at all, and as I get to know him better I
understand that realism can't provide the solace he
needs. In January 2006, he sends me a letter describing

his most recent illustrated story, "Ned No-Arms and Buttercup."

"It's about a boy born with no arms and his pet chicken," he writes. "The fun really starts when he discovers he has the power of telekinesis." In the lower right corner of the letter's last page, near his signature, is a drawing of an armless boy using his telekinetic powers, indicated by his staring eyes and delighted smile, to get himself an apple from a basket. That Ned No-Arms's powerlessness and implicit castration is not the result of an accident but innate, an aspect of his essential self, hints at how soon—from birth—Billy's parents managed to strip him of any sense of himself as an effective, useful human being. And yet, Ned is not alone, nor untouched, because tucked into the bib of his overalls is Buttercup, the pet chicken, another symbol of spirituality, albeit somewhat comic. Neither is Ned without sustenance: by virtue of an invisible force granted by fantasy, the apple is coming to him, floating through the air. Had Billy not shared with me a number of biblical drawings of Adam, Eve, and the Garden of Eden—including one with the tree of knowledge from which the apple of sexual knowledge dangles—I might not read Ned's receiving his apple as a restoration of potency despite his having been castrated (by virtue of having no arms). But symbols aren't chosen randomly, without meaning, at least unconscious meaning, and Billy didn't give Ned a slice of pizza, or one of the candy bars he himself likes.

That all of Billy's stories are characterized by alienation and misunderstanding among humans, and that they include animals that talk and are endowed with perceptions and powers that transcend human abilities, suggests he doesn't place much hope in meaningful communication between people. And why would he? Interviewed by Children's Services, evaluated by one mental health professional after another, counseled by social workers in the group home, Billy told many of these people outright that he was suffering at the hands of his parents and that he would prefer foster care to living with them. Even when he was afraid to make a direct accusation, Billy described a family that was profoundly troubled. But no one saved him. The only result of his speaking out was that his parents were shamed; they were enraged and vengeful. Now, more than twenty years after he killed them, he sits alone in his cell, writing and drawing, creating alternate worlds, narratives in which he restores to himself some of what he has lost.

Whenever I felt low, I could simply drive the isolated highways, country roads, and sometimes the interstate listening to music and thinking until I found myself again, or at least found the courage to keep trying. Renewed, I'd tell myself I would eventually find a reason for all that happened. And though I had thought of suicide as a way to stop the pain, anger, and fear, I considered it only because one should always weigh all options before making decisions.

I slowly drove down the hill on the curvy road toward the valley on September 5, 1984. For everyone else it was the first day of high school. For me it was the first day of walking and sitting among my peers since the tragedy that had struck my family in the middle of April, when my life became composed of new friends, new patrons, and many awful memories.

So begins "The First Day of School," an essay Jody wrote in 1995. At twenty-seven years old, a graduate of Georgetown University, she was making a living in New York as a freelance writer. The eleven years and three thousand miles between her and the murders, and the vantage from her carefully reconstructed new life, allowed her to write a sense of order onto what had been a decade of emotional turmoil.

Jody hadn't finished out the tenth grade among her old classmates at Mid-High. She may have been able to "steel herself from deep emotion" but she hadn't had the sangfroid to endure two months of the whispering, pointing, and anonymous notes in her locker suggesting she was as much a murderer as her brother that had characterized her return to school at the end of April. One day was enough to convince her that she wasn't going back to Mid-High, and Victims' Assistance provided a tutor so she could complete the semester in private. Summer was devoted to a crash course in what it was like to be an average upper-middle-class American teen, lessons courtesy of Thad Guyer, who might have come along too late to provide her more than a veneer of normalcy, but knew that rock concerts, driving lessons, and the keys to his car represented powerful distractions, if not solace, for a sixteen-year-old. Accustomed to her parents' selfishness and disregard, Jody found that Thad's offering her his shiny red 1978 Audi 2000 while keeping the much older of his two vehicles for his own use was itself a mystifying expression of love, and in "The First Day of School" she called the car a "surrogate womb" from which, she wrote, she drew "a perhaps unnatural amount of self-esteem."

Read in conjunction with "Death Faces," completed two years earlier, "The First Day of School" reveals the Audi-womb as critical to Jody's psychic survival. "This is the story of my rebirth," "Death Faces" begins, and birth can only follow on a period spent in utero. Before she had the Audi, Jody had been dead, in limbo, waiting to be reborn. The image she uses to evoke this state, "a hollow husk of who and what I was before," invokes growth and change. An empty vessel, it anticipates new life: metamorphosis.

The narrative of Jody's life, the story of herself by herself, reads not as a story of overcoming tragedy but as the death of one girl and the arrival of another. The Jody Gilley she had been perished with the rest of her family and was replaced by Jody Arlington, as she now called herself, who resembled the girl she'd been before, but only up to a point. "Little did I know that I was my own Frankenstein, an experiment that would go awry, then be reforged, over and over again," she wrote in 1995. Like most of us, she misidentifies the doctor as the monster—for it is the doctor who is named Frankenstein; the monster has no name—a useful conflation in this context because Jody was both doctor and monster, both author and narrative.

Arlington was a name she chose in transit, in a car, driving to Los Angeles with Thad, Thad's soon-to-be ex-wife, Debbie, and Jody's friend Jackie. On their way to a Billy Idol concert, in service to what Jody called Thad's "socialization program," they were scanning billboards in hopes of happening upon an acceptable new surname. School would reconvene in a few weeks, and Jody was returning not as a Gilley but as . . . who? "Unsatisfied with them [the billboards] I decided to add the elements of chance and utilitarianism to the process. Students with last names beginning with the first five letters of the alphabet were to register [for classes] first. The next street sign we crossed that started with one of those five letters would be the new last name. Arlington Blvd. was the winner."

Reassemble is the word that comes first to my mind, before *reforge* or *re-create* or *reintegrate*. Once I separated from my father, I undertook the task of salvaging what remained of myself, which, as in my old dream, was not everything. In the dream, my face is shattered, and I gather up the pieces and set out to find a surgeon who can put them back together. When I find the surgeon and unfold the handkerchief in which I've saved the pieces of my face, I see they haven't remained intact. Once living flesh, they've dried and shriveled. "Can you do it?" I ask. "Can you sew them back together?" The doctor says yes, but the scars will be disfiguring. I won't look at all as I used to.

When I wake up, I discover that expressions I'd never analyzed before make sudden, visceral sense: She fell apart. Fell to pieces. Was shattered. Came undone. Unglued. Came apart at the seams.

What I wrote to Jody before we met—that I felt there were parts of myself that my father had yet to relinquish or I had yet to reclaim—was true, and would remain so. Certain aspects of the girl I had been were broken beyond repair; some remained intact, others I jettisoned. My childhood fantasies of my father were gone, my innocence a thing of the past. My already poor relationship with my mother had been damaged even further; after her death, it would take me twenty years to address it adequately. My eagerness to mold myself to others' expectations had gotten me into trouble for the last time: I promised myself this. I saw how remaking myself over and over in the hope of winning my mother's love had been an apprenticeship that served my father's purposes too well.

At twenty, I'd planned never to marry or become a mother. After, I found I'd lost the part of me who saw myself as necessarily alone, the part that served a lie: that I didn't need anyone else. And I married and had children a decade or more before any of my friends did. Initially it seemed baffling and ironic that I'd fallen in love with a man who was so very straight an arrow—who'd never once smoked pot, or even a cigarette, who wouldn't start the car until my seat belt was buckled, who balanced his checkbook, grew his own tomatoes, drank infrequently and in moderation—but it wasn't an accident or a mistake. If I hurried to gather a family around me, it was because some part of me understood that my psychic survival, my remaining reassembled, depended on structure I wasn't capable of creating and preserving alone, for myself.

Like Jody's, my force of will persisted, a gravity-like pull that drew the fragments together again. My former self, lacking any sense of mortality, believed she had time to spare. Her successor, who began to take form at twenty-five or twenty-six, as much as a third, or more, of her life already spent, is always in a hurry, self-disciplined to a fault. There isn't much to recommend trauma, but for those who aren't permanently undone, it has an eerily focusing quality.

Still, the reassembled are aware of fracture lines, of being, like mended teacups, carefully glued together and not at all strong at the broken places. Jody hasn't written the memoir she once planned to write about her family. "My life unravels whenever I decide I'm going to write that book. I am whole because that story doesn't define me. It's a piece of me. But when I sit down to write, it's all that I am, and it devastates me."

Devastate is a loaded word; its definition is to lay waste. Not many of us use it to describe the power our pasts hold over us. Jody has done the necessary work of autobiography already; she's narrated herself toward understanding, sanity. To return and linger in her past for as long and sustained an effort as a book requires would be not only painful but, she fears, dangerous to the equilibrium she consciously guards. The life story that she engages with is the after part of her life, the continuing, living narrative of the reconstructed Jody, not the terminated life of the girl she was before.

"WHAT'S MISSING?" I ASK JODY IN AN E-MAIL dated February 12, 2007. "I was pondering the Bettelheim essay [from *Surviving and Other Essays,* a book I borrowed from Jody] on reintegrating after trauma—trying to see it as it related to you—and, thinking of my own experience, I realized that for me, part of the 'after,' the rebirth, was that when I reassembled myself I didn't have all the pieces I had before: some were lost or sacrificed to the experience of my father, others jettisoned, perhaps new aspects were added. So, in sum, I think of myself as something analogous to a rebuilt engine.

"Can you identify parts of yourself that did not survive the destruction of your family, the losses you said you 'didn't care to contemplate' twelve years ago, when writing the introduction to 'Death Faces'? And if you can, what are they? Are you aware of new aspects of yourself that you cultivated?" Here is her answer:

I, too, view myself as a rebuilt engine. A reconstituted self. What was lost . . . took place in the years leading up to the murders, and the reconstitution took place literally over the course of half a decade or more afterwards. More of a process than caught in time. The murders [were] one more thing in a list, an escalation of dysfunction.

What was jettisoned? My faith in my parents as protectors, or rational, or even capable of genuinely loving me, on the night they didn't believe me about my brother's abuse, and when my mother wouldn't listen to me about the dangers he represented, when they had the chance to send him to MacLaren.

When my mother sat on me and blew smoke in my face, she and Billy laughing at my discomfort, I no longer had any sense that they were my family at all. Or when in absolute truth she said she would kill me if I ever got an abortion. What kind of mother (or god) would think that was okay?

Or what about the police? Children's Services? School? They weren't really getting it either. My family life prepared me for the murders because I had walled myself deep inside . . . developed the same distrust and isolation that [my parents] had towards the outside world, but it was directed at them. I knew they weren't normal. That what was happening wasn't right.

The one thing that I lost was rage. Uncontrolled anger. Physical violence. I have not engaged. I don't even know if I can scream. I mean really scream. Needless to say, rage and self-hatred gets channeled in other ways. But rage at others? Hitting? No way. The self-implosion of the family created a severe sense that there was potentially something wrong with me. That there was no way that I could come from such a horrible background and not be damaged beyond repair. That mental illness wouldn't descend. That I might have the same makings of a killer, abuser, monster—since often that is the case. That I would never have a normal life, be loved, be able to love, etc.

To gird myself against imminent psychological disintegration I studied the stages of development and what was "normal" and wouldn't allow myself to fall far outside those boundaries. What I loved about the holocaust literature was that it demonstrated how we are all capable of anything in the right conditions. . . . In the camps the world was turned upside down: Right is wrong. Wrong is right. Protectors are killers. Killers are protectors. All relationships and all understanding of the world and oneself, and order and justice and divinity—all of it disintegrated. Surviving was part luck, part cunning, and taking food or shoes from the nearly dead. Knowing that the thin veneer of civility that masks human savagery is universal in extreme situations made me feel a lot more normal. I cultivated being normal.

Spending those years studying myself, my family, all the things that led to that night, was not unlike what Bettelheim did in the camps to maintain his own selfhood. Regaining trust in people and institutions was a big cultivation project as well. While 80% of the time people are terrible, I hold out for the 20%.

I lost the opportunity to grow out of adolescence with my parents, so I never gained any perspective on the situation. [How much of it] was me? What were their circumstances at that moment that were causing them to be so terrible? What if things stabilized or she divorced him and got a job, or my views of them then mellowed or their behavior and beliefs did?

Reading this, I remember a dream that Jody recounted for me, a nightmare she had in college. In it, she returned home as an adult and Becky answered the door, "cool and dismissive." Jody asked after her mother and Becky told Jody about "all these great things [their mother] was doing to change and improve her life. . . . She had a new job, she lived in a new house without my dad." The dream disturbed Jody because she'd held on to her vision of an abusive and dysfunctional mother and "imagining a world where she evolved was terrifying." Beyond the adult Jody's "not want[ing] to feel connected [to Linda] or a bond with [her]," there was a further grief implicit in the dream, "the wish [for my mother to be] a real, vibrant, and functioning person capable of shaping her destiny and making sound decisions."

When I learn that Jody has decided she will never have children, I can't stop myself from reacting as a woman who understands motherhood as guarding her sanity and happiness, and I ask if she doesn't imagine that raising her own child could assuage some of the loss she's suffered. Couldn't knowing how to be a good parent from the bad example of her own give meaning to her difficult past? But Jody's brother and her maternal grandmother murdered members of their own families; her paternal grandfather and her father drank and battered; her abusive mother failed her children with catastrophic results. Though the odds of Jody bearing a criminal child are small, some of what allowed Billy to kill—the impulsiveness he shared with his father and grandfather, and perhaps other, undiscovered chemical/neurological deficits—is arguably genetic. In any case, it's the proximity of the idea, rather than the likelihood of carrying a child who could return her to the wasteland she fled, that threatens Jody's psychic equilibrium. As she wrote me before we met, she manages and protects a "carefully arranged reality."

As do I. But this is something I don't recognize in myself until I see it in Jody. Aware of my own fault lines, I avoid being reminded of my father. Among the scores of photographs on view in our home, there are many of my mother, of my grandparents, great-grandparents, my husband and our three children, my mother- and father-in-law, my husband's brother, his uncles, but not one of my father. When a stranger asks about my parents, I say they're both dead, without feeling I'm telling a lie. I've lost the audiotape of his voice, put away the letters he wrote me so carefully that I don't know where they are. And though I sometimes compose letters to my father in my head, I never write them down. Or if I do, I don't mail them—not anymore.

Because I fled from my father without attempting to address any of our differences, I've had to resign myself to what I find uncomfortable: a lack of resolution that leaves me prey to fantasies of reaching an understanding we never had. Usually these are deathbed scenes, in which my father is weak and unmanned, unable to approach me. There's no physical contact; sometimes I speak to him from the door of his room. Over the years I've edited my father's side of the conversation. It used to be that he asked my forgiveness. Later, I settled for an explanation, although I couldn't imagine what it might be. In the end, all I wanted, all I want, is for him to recognize that what he demanded of me was not in my best interest. A modest hope, and yet my father's reply to the one letter I did mail, some years ago, reveals it as ambitious, less than unlikely.

But I do write, I write every day, trying to shape a book, an essay, a review, always in the effort to force coherence from what I find impossible to understand. No matter the story, the setting, the characters, there is nothing I write that doesn't in some measure address what happened between me and my father, that doesn't respond to the chaos he ushered into my life. Writing allows me the illusion of understanding, of control. Although it's a treatment rather than a cure: the illusion lasts only as long as I am immersed in the act of writing.

The murder of one's family, sexual intercourse with a parent—these experiences, and any other that once seemed unthinkable, too awful to come true—have a long half-life. People don't recover from them so much as manage their effects.

Jody removed herself from the geography of her former life—she moved from the West to the East Coast—and, when she discovered this wasn't enough, she banished the artifacts of that life from her physical environment. She did this all at once, she tells me, on a weekend afternoon in 2001, characterizing her mood as having been one in which she was "tipsy on despair."

This is not a casual remark but a phrase she uses deliberately each time we talk about the incident, and I consider the description over and over; the words insinuate themselves into my thoughts, arriving unbidden and always disturbing. I equate *tipsy* with *giddy,* a celebratory state, and find Jody's attaching it to *despair* provoking in its dissonance. But Jody's father's drinking was a catalyst for violent argument, a guarantee that everyone got hurt, either physically, or emotionally, or both.

On those evenings when Jody and I meet for dinner, she impresses me as a woman who treats the occasional glass of wine gingerly, with a respect born of suffering. Like me, and by her own admission, Jody is something of a control freak, and I come to understand that it is this aspect of her personality that has invented the idea of being "tipsy on despair." Her idiosyncratic repetition of the phrase teaches me a key aspect of her psychic survival: Jody treats despair itself as a controlled substance, one that—for her, anyway—invites abuse. As with the infrequent glass of wine, she allows herself so much and no more despair, and depends on a strict internal calculus to manage the grief, anger, and fear that might produce it. It's a defense she's carried forward from her childhood:

When I was a little girl, I had to be impervious to pain. I proved that I was by running barefoot through patches of star thistles. These thistles grew in intermittent patches in the fields surrounding our house. My brother and I would walk across one of the fields to Grandpa Ed's farm. Ed wasn't really our grandfather but our neighbor. He let all the children ride his horses and play in and around his rambling house. He also molested all the little girls and, in exchange for our compliance, bought us Barbies and clothes. We were nine and ten years old though, so I don't think we knew we were prostituting ourselves. No, we did know. This story is not about that experience. This story is about the star thistles.

This is the first paragraph of "Young Love," another memoir published under the pen name Jennifer Saffron in *The Georgetown Journal*. "Young Love" is "not about" Jody's experience of being molested by a neighbor but about armoring herself against pain, specifically the injury she describes in the subsequent paragraph, of having her bare feet "punctured" by thistles to the point that they "left bloody footprints on the flagstones" outside her house—or is it? The glancing reference to sexual abuse is typical of Jody, who often introduces the most damaging aspect of an event in an aside, and is always quick to tease out and identify what she considers her responsibility with respect to any given situation.

"Molested how?" I ask Jody about the true story, after I read the somewhat fictionalized "Young Love."

"Oh, you know, sitting on his lap and he'd, you know, kind of fondle you through your clothes."

"Sort of standard creepy-old-man stuff? Without going any further?"

"Pretty much."

It's an interesting paragraph for all it contains. At twenty-three, with the destruction of her family seven years behind her and the landscape of her childhood far removed, Jody was looking back at her past. "Young Love" is one of several submissions she made to the journal that the editorial board didn't find too dark or depressing to publish. And yet it's hardly a sunny look at girlhood. Observing the child she was at ten years old, this is who Jody saw: a girl who understood pain and the importance of remaining "impervious to" pain; a girl who was testing her ability to deny whatever might impede her progress as she escaped her home; a girl who knew that life required hard bargains and who was ready to extract a cost when she found herself caught in the arms of an abuser. In evoking the vulnerability of a child on the cusp of puberty, forced into sexual contact for which she's not prepared, Jody relies on archetypes from the stories all little girls know by heart: the prick of a thorn or a spindle and the virgin's blood it draws from *Snow White* and *Sleeping Beauty*, the bare foot from *Cinderella*. As the ironic title suggests, the only untruth in the paragraph cited above is the declaration that "Young Love" isn't about what happened in the home of the neighborhood pedophile, who might have fondled her through her clothes but did not attempt any further exploration, not when Jody was ten, anyway.

While the move to Ross Lane had "looked good on paper"—"Too good," Jody says, "because it meant that we couldn't get the assistance we needed"—the Gilleys were bankrupt at the time of their deaths and had been struggling for months, fielding calls from collection agents, relying on food stamps and government-issued cheese bricks and milk powder, eating vegetables they grew for themselves, and keeping chickens, originally to supply meat as well as eggs. But, Billy explains, "the first dead bird my mother had to pluck was the last. She wasn't gonna do that twice."

He laughs at the memory of Linda grappling with a dead chicken, and I wonder, as I do often during our conversations, what it's like for Billy to reminisce about people he murdered, if he's able, somehow, to separate the mother with whom he grew up from the one he killed.

If Jody and I have carefully arranged what we call reality, how much more so must Billy have to manage his perceptions? He tells stories with what seems like genuine ease, laughing spontaneously at what amuses him, recalling happier moments with what appears to be nostalgia. What are missing, generally, are negative emotions—anger, hurt, grief. Initially I'm struck by what I perceive to be his lack of self-pity; later I realize that Billy recounts instances of severe abuse without any emotion whatsoever. Even the murders themselves, when we speak of them, don't inspire so much as a blink or a shift in facial expression or tone of voice. Moreover, when he describes killing his family I have the sense that he's talking about something that happened to him rather than an act he authored. In his affidavit, prepared twelve years after the murders, the account reads as a series of responses to a situation unfolding independent of his intentions. After the initial attack on his father, the scene picks up hectic speed, Billy running from one room to another, cataloguing actions with a flat, anesthetized quality. The sentences are all short, simple, declarative, and identically structured: "I panicked . . . I turned on the light . . . I asked Jody . . . I told Becky . . . I went downstairs . . . I didn't know what to do next . . . I felt the back of her head and I felt blood."

His allusions to crying and screaming have an emotionless feel to them, as if he referred only to their physical manifestations, the tears or the noise but not what elicited them. It's a style of reporting emotion that is not unlike Jody's. Perhaps this is one of the very few things they still share, an adaptation that dates back to early childhood.

ON WEDNESDAY, NOVEMBER 14, 1984, BILLY went on trial for three counts of aggravated murder. Two days later, a jury of six men and six women found him guilty on all counts, even though Jody's testimony indicated clearly that he had not planned to harm Becky. His attorney, Stephen Pickens, had conceived an argument that relied heavily on forensic photographs of a machete resting on the mantel just a few feet from Bill Sr.'s body. It was Pickens's contention that if Billy had wanted to kill his father and mother he would have used the ready and more efficient blade rather than a baseball bat. At best, this was a feeble defense, and while Pickens did note the presence of the machete while cross-examining Jody, he didn't mention it in his summation. He never actually made the argument he said he had planned. When a journalist outside the courtroom asked him why this was, Pickens said he forgot.

"My attorney," Billy says in his affidavit, "did not use the defense that I had talked to him about . . . did not talk about my killing my parents to protect myself and my sisters. . . . The whole time my attorney represented me the only conversation that we had about the machete was one time when he asked whether the machete was mine. I told him it was and that I used it to split kindling."

Part of Stephen Pickens's job, Connie Skillman tells me, was to educate his client. "Billy was a child, too," she says. "He needed guidance. Was his attorney advising him?" Billy knew nothing about jurisprudence, he tells me, but what he'd seen on TV, one or two programs from which he'd mistakenly concluded that an attorney had absolute power to determine what his client could or could not say.

"If I'd known I had the right to testify no matter what my attorney's advice was," he states in his affidavit, "I would have chosen to testify."

Did Billy forget the conversations he had had with his attorney? Is he consciously misrepresenting them. In 1984, Pickens told Medford *Mail Tribune* reporter Mark Howard that his client had chosen "not to take the witness stand in his own defense," and in 1997, when subpoenaed by Billy's post-conviction counsel, he reported that Billy had been "adamant" in refusing to testify on his own behalf. Pickens may have been sloppy in failing to mention the blade upon which his argument teetered, but it would be wrong to judge him dishonest from allegations made by Billy, who has lied in the past, and who has a motive to portray Pickens as incompetent.

The *Mail Tribune,* Medford's local paper, reported that Jackson County's district attorney, Justin Smith, built "an air-tight case," using testimony from Oregon State Police criminalist Brad Telea, detectives Richard Davis and Leon Stupfel, Officer Rupp, troopers Scholten and Springer, medical examiner Larry Lewman, surgeons Robinson and Campagna, and his star witness, Jody Gilley. Among these ten, Pickens cross-examined only Jody and did not call any witnesses for the defense. He had none. According to Billy, Pickens allowed him to believe that his grandmother would testify on his behalf when, in fact, Pickens went to considerable trouble to ensure that she didn't.

"Later [after the trial had concluded] the bailiff talked to me," Betty Glass states in her affidavit, "and said he had orders from Billy's attorney to take me out [of the courtroom] if I opened my mouth to say anything in [*sic*] Billy's behalf." On the face of it, Pickens's defense was so minimal that journalists outside the courthouse asked him why he'd even brought the case to trial if he hadn't intended to defend his client. Pickens answered that the only alternative was for Billy to plead guilty to the charges and that "in a trial he at least had a chance of an acquittal or a reduced charge."*

When called as a witness, Jody did exactly what Thad told her to do. "Literally terrified that everything I said about my abusive redneck household would be heard by my peers through the media and used to persecute me at school," Jody stated in her affidavit that she "listened to the questions, told the truth, gave short answers, and volunteered nothing." Thad's concerns about the possibility of her being implicated in the murders had ignited her own fear, as did the palpably hostile presence of Betty, who she knew was denouncing her publicly as a murderer. "When I testified," she stated, "I was fearful for my own fate, . . . extremely emotionally traumatized, and in denial about what abusers my dead parents had been. I realize now that some of the accounts I gave of our home life, sexual and psychological abuse, and the whole tenor of who the Gilleys were as a family, may have been inaccurate and misleading, at least by omission."

As a witness for the prosecution, Jody heard only those parts of the trial that unfolded when she was on the stand. It wasn't until years later, while reviewing the transcript in order to write "Death Faces," that she "realized how stark some of [her] omissions were when viewed within the context of the rest of the trial testimony."

While she could not "attest to all of Billy's 'motives' in the parental murders [she did] know that saving Becky and [herself] was at least his rationalization, or even his cause." Billy, she said, believed she and Becky "would have been as emotionally abused, their potentials and

*Mark Howard, "Gilley Found Guilty," *Mail Tribune*, November 16, 1984.

self-concepts as destroyed as were his. . . . Billy saw this and said so in the weeks before the murders."

"Well, Mr. Gilley," Judge Karaman said on December 27, 1984, "I heard the trial, I arraigned you, and now this is the time for sentencing, and you have been given an opportunity to tell me in your own words anything you may have on your mind which you would like for me to hear in mitigation of the sentence I might impose. . . . Is there anything you can offer me? I have to sentence you now, and frankly, you've put me in a position where I am sentencing you from a lack of information."

"I'm just confused about it all right now, Your Honor," Billy said. "I still can't understand myself."

"All right," Karaman said. "You've tried to sort it out in your own mind and you still can't?"

"Yes."

"Is that the way you feel?"

"Yes."

"You're not mentally ill. You've been examined by a good number of psychiatrists. The only conclusion I can reach is a very severe personality disorder, antisocial personality. With the type of acting out you did in this case, the best I can do for society is to try to put you away for as long a period of time as the law will allow, and I see no choice."

"Well, I was physically threatened several times," Billy said, "and I had great fear."

"During that day?"

"Yes. Well, it was a couple of days before. It happened several times that week. It was just something that happened often in our family. Counseling—I'll get settled up in the penitentiary and I'll try to get this straightened out."

Much later, for his appeal, Billy testified, "I didn't understand what that opportunity [sentencing] signified for me. I was never told that I would have the opportunity to speak to the judge directly and that I could tell him anything that I wanted about myself or my case. I remember thinking that this was just a formality because, as my attorney told me, all we had to do was show up for court. After the sentencing, after the judge had sentenced me to three consecutive life sentences, I asked my attorney what consecutive and concurrent meant. He told me that he would come and see me and explain it. I never saw him again."

Unaware that he could have prepared comments for the judge, Billy responded simply and honestly to his predicament, as he never would again. He'd been mistreated and threatened and had committed a crime the magnitude of which confused him to the point that he couldn't understand himself.

"Law enforcement officers got stuck on the fact that Billy killed his little sister," Connie Skillman tells me. "That ruined his chances of a lesser sentence. It got around that he'd said he didn't want Becky to grow up and be like his mother and it cemented the idea that he'd acted alone, without Jody's involvement." Connie remembers Billy's demeanor in court struck people as arrogant, a word I find impossible to apply to the man I meet. Like Jody, Billy betrayed no emotion in court, most likely a function of shock, the pressure of scrutiny. Billy's was the face of someone who'd suffered years of abuse, and its blank canvas tempted observers either to assume he had no feelings or to project negative ones onto it.

Jody wasn't present at Billy's sentencing but the presentence investigation Judge Karaman reviewed included her "victim's statement," in which she responded to a series of questions. Asked to describe the nature of the "incident" in which she had been involved, she said,

"My entire family was viciously murdered by my brother." Her psychological injuries were

> many and almost indescribable. It's very difficult to explain how it feels when the only family you have regardless of the family problems is torn from you leaving you cold, empty and uncertain about the basic foundations and meanings about life and the world. If you can imagine the emptiness, lonliness [*sic*] and remoarse [*sic*] one would have after this incident you would have to triple your estimation in order to put the feelings into perspective and there are so many different feelings to contend with. There are also the feelings of fear, a fear of after me [*sic*]—something about which I consistently have nightmares about. The final fears pertain to the future . . . will I ever understand? What's going to happen to me? What could I have done and more importantly will I gradually become mentally instable? All of these thoughts constantly haunt me.

Among Jody's nightmares, which she dismisses today as "paint-by-number dreams," one stands out. Despite the passage of twenty years, she remembers it clearly. In it she sees a dark, shadowy figure dragging off a girl. She tries to stop the predator but it stabs her repeatedly in the hands and escapes with the child. There's no blood in this dream, nor any pain, but she feels acutely afraid and wakes distressed by her failure to prevent the abduction. It's tempting to respond to what seems obvious symbolism and assume the shadowy figure is Billy, the girl Becky, the stabbed hands Jody's inability to protect her sister, her feelings upon awakening fear and grief that derived from her having failed to keep Becky out of harm's way. But beneath the paint-by-number surface is a more compelling drama in which the dark figure, the child, the hands, and the abduction are all aspects of

Jody and the dream an unconscious narrative of her helplessly relinquishing whatever her hands represent— volition? potency?—to an occult presence, a figure whose face she cannot see, a self she doesn't know, with the result that a child self, perhaps an innocent self, is lost. Although the event is dire, fatal to some part of her, she is wounded without being able to bleed or to feel.

The shadowy figure in this dream that recurred into Jody's early twenties conjures the "unknowable" self who was the target of "all [her] anger, confusion, and fear." The violence Billy did to his parents and Becky is finite: these people are dead. The violence he did to Jody and himself is something they carry, and with which they are forced to commune, at least on an unconscious level. Because Jody and Billy shared a hatred of their abusive parents, because he named her as his motive for murder, because their deaths freed her and provided her opportunities she might never have had otherwise, because Jody accepted the terrible gift for which her brother still pays, she bears this dark figure within her. And what alternative does she have, what means of refusing the gift other than to destroy herself, if not in body then in spirit?

Question ten on the Victim's Impact Statement form asked "what being the victim of a crime meant" to Jody, who answered that "being the victim of a crime means nothing compared to being a victim of this particular crime." Her brother, she judged "dangerous as well as vengefull [sic] and he is a threat." The "only acceptable thing to do" with Billy, she said in answer to what thoughts she had about his sentence, was "a phenominal [sic] amount of imprisonment." If there had been a symbiosis between Jody and her brother, she was declaring it over. She wanted reassurance that it was a thing of the past, and that it would never return.

"WHEN I FIRST ARRIVED IN PRISON, I WANTED nothing more than to be dead." So begins the prison narrative Billy alternately calls his memoirs or, sometimes, his personal profile. "I was young and attractive. The chicken hawks swooped on me from day one. They told me I could put shit on their dick or blood on their blade."

Ironically, the price for escaping his father was immersion in another environment in which male-on-male predation was the rule, violence the means of displaying potency. Unlike Bill, who hid his brutality from much of the world, Billy's new attackers were eager to flaunt their ability to get away with anything up to and including murder, and although his account of his experiences as an inmate is self-aggrandizing, it also attempts to compensate for his vulnerability.

"If I didn't let him put his black dick in my pretty white ass, then he was going to put his shank in my ribs," Billy writes of the first inmate to assault him. "I started pushing my body into his shank until a flower of blood bloomed on my shirt then spit in his face and screamed 'Stick it in!' over and over again. Unfortunately he refused. I just got a reputation as a crazy with a death wish, who can fight." Although he avoided homosexual rape, Billy describes the result of the stabbing, of his attacker's "sticking it in," as "a flower of blood," sexualizing the blade's entrance into his body by evoking the conventional deflowering of a girl. He ends the account submissively, in a tone of defeat. "I would rather they had killed me," he writes.

In answer to my questions about what he alleges was

Bill's sexual abuse of his sisters, Billy tells me that their father displayed sexual aggression toward him as well, claiming that Bill, intoxicated, had once attempted to rape him outright when the two were camping alone, a statement that echoed what he told Dr. Kirkpatrick in 1984. The account, which lacks texture or detail, is one he gives almost as an aside to reports of his father's inappropriate attention to Jody, and it's hard to imagine that a genuinely incestuous advance from a boy's father wouldn't have imprinted itself distinctly and vividly in his mind. Sadly, it comes across as less paranoid than wishful, damning Bill even as it demonstrates Billy's value as an object of attention, unnatural and damaging attention but perhaps from the perspective of a needy child a step up from neglect. Maybe what Billy says happened did happen; maybe he imagined it happened; maybe, as time passed, what began as a fantasy born out of his emotional abandonment and fear of his father seemed more like a memory than a made-up event.

"What was it like when you and your father were alone together—when the two of you were on the road?" I ask Billy, returning to the topic on the last day of my visit. He's telling me about some of the bigger jobs he did with his father—brush clearing and pruning that had been subcontracted by distant parks or preserves— and I find myself curious about how the family dynamics might have changed when the group was fractured. "Was your father less abusive when the two of you were away from home? More?"

"He ignored me," Billy says. "Indifferent, that's what he was. Like I wasn't sitting there in the truck next to him. Away from my mom, away from her nagging and picking at him and stopping him doing what he wanted, he had less aggravations to take out. So he didn't attack me. But it wasn't like he suddenly decided he liked me. He was indifferent, that's all." Billy says the word for a third time, "Indifferent." The expression on his face is one of disgust, and the resignation in his voice suggests that indifference might have been a more thorough psychic annihilation than battery.

Linda always insisted that Bill take their son with him when he traveled because she relied on his violence to keep Billy in line, but she had the added—and, as it turned out, naïve—hope that Billy's presence might prevent Bill from straying. "He had a couple mistresses," Billy tells me. "There was two outta wedlock kids from before any of us, before he was married. A boy in California—he was six years older than me—and a girl right there in Medford. She's the one who called the house before . . . in the month or so before they died."

"What about the boy? Did you ever meet him?"

"Nope. He died when he was nineteen, in a car wreck."

"Did you know his name, or anything about him?"

Billy shakes his head. "Just that he was six years older."

It wasn't only "mistresses" that his father entertained, Billy says. Bill picked up women in bars—"booze chasers," Billy calls them—who had sex with his father in the back of the truck for the price of a few drinks. If Bill considered the morality, or the immorality, of what was not an isolated incident but a habit of adultery, probably he excused it by telling himself that Linda's frigidity had driven him to seek the comfort of other women. As for Billy, whether out of indifference or hostility, Bill didn't bother to hide his infidelities from his son any more than he did the stack of pornography he kept under the truck's front seat.

Soon after he arrived at the Oregon State Penitentiary in Salem, Billy was "recruted [sic] by a martial artist named 'Weed' to help him run a martial arts school on the yard" as the resident expert in "finger strike techniques"—that is, the art of forcefully poking an opponent in the eyes or throat rather than punching him. "This parental-like role gave me a reason to live," Billy wrote, echoing his characterization of his boyhood martial arts teachers as benign father figures, a series of relationships that Jody thinks were likely transitory and impersonal. If her judgment is accurate, perhaps Billy's early years in prison and his association with Weed were the unconscious inspiration for what became an empowering myth, a way for Billy to see himself as less vulnerable to the violent males all around him.

After the impromptu martial arts school was discovered and shut down by prison authorities, Billy began working in the prison furniture factory, where for two years he assembled desks and chairs for government offices while secretly operating a "black-market hobby ring," training his "fellow cons to make . . . jewelry, delux [sic] picture frames, and drinking mugs, then pay[ing] them to produce the product for me. I once had eight men working for me. It was my over-ambition that got me noticed and fired."

Although he didn't disclose this in his memoirs, somewhat sanitized for his intended readers, among them Jody, the focus of his black market workshop was the clandestine manufacture of shanks from pieces of scrap metal or purloined factory tools. Billy bound one end of the makeshift blades in scrap leather and sold them to other inmates, who buried them in the prison yard (lest they be confiscated by the "screws"), guaranteeing a demand that could never be satisfied as the yard was routinely swept with metal detectors. And there were other illicit enterprises.

In May 1986, Billy was put in disciplinary segregation for twenty-five days for the possession of "pruno," or, more accurately, what was about to turn into pruno, an alcoholic beverage almost exclusive to prison culture made from oranges, fruit cocktail, sugar, ketchup, and water, mixed and fermented in a plastic bag (the container of choice as it can be hidden in a towel). In 1989, he spent 137 days in segregation for writing a short story about two female convicts who escape from jail—perhaps an allusion, conscious or unconscious, to his two sisters, whom he freed from the prison of their home. Although the officials believed the story was fiction, they judged it to contain information on how to escape. Three months after he got out, he went back for another seventy days, again for making pruno, the foul taste of which—"like vomit" is the usual description—as well as its tendency to make imbibers ill, bears witness to prisoners' determination to dull their senses.

The end of his employment in the furniture factory is what Billy remembers as the impetus he needed "to go back to school and get his GED," adding that for him this "practically meant learning to read and write," as his barely literate early letters from jail demonstrate. When I ask how he compensated for the learning disabilities that defeated his teachers, he tells me he taught himself to read with "two brains," a split consciousness that allowed one "brain" to read while the other observed the act of reading and caught mistakes. Gradually, with a great deal of effort, he was able to understand textbooks, and his immersion in language improved his spelling and his ability to communicate on paper. The difference between the letters he wrote Jody at eighteen and those he writes today is marked, and not only because they're much more literate. His childhood more than twenty years behind him, Billy thinks clearly; his natural mental state doesn't appear to be one of confusion. Late in 2006 he sends me a petition he wrote to prison authorities, protesting their disciplining him for the unfair charge of "racketeering"—selling the legal expertise he's acquired to fellow prisoners. My first thought as I read it is that his dead parents would be astonished by its organization and persuasive, if devious, logic.

Once he'd completed his GED training and earned his high school equivalency certificate, Billy was convinced by fellow classmates to try a few junior college classes. If nothing else, it was a way to fill some hours. Away from home, from people who called him stupid and said he would fail at whatever he tried, Billy discovered he wasn't a poor student. He liked his teachers, he tells me, and earned an associate's degree in 1993. He intended to go on and complete a bachelor's, but before he could satisfy its requirements, the program's funding was cut. Aside from three semesters of English composition and a handful of art and design classes, most of his course-work focused on sociology and psychology, including abnormal behavior and anger management, with a couple of forays into religion and ethics.

Because of the hiatus in Billy's secondary school education, he and Jody were college students at roughly the same time. Separated by the width of a continent, by his incarceration, and presumably by a significant gap in quality between Georgetown's Jesuit tradition and the tuition offered by a provincial western community college, still there were overlaps between what Jody and her brother sought from their respective educations. Both needed a frame of reference to understand what had happened in their family, what Billy had done and why, and what it might mean. Billy, who perceived his mother and father as having created an inhuman trap that elicited his violent response, did not regret killing them, except in that he'd landed himself in prison and—to the limited extent that he could acknowledge it—sacrificed his little sister, an act he first explained to himself by reducing Becky to a part of Linda, not a per-

son in her own right, and later revised as an entirely accidental occurrence. As he did not consider himself
guilty or a danger to other people, he was searching for
justification, a means of validating the action he'd taken
against his persecutors. Jody, who also needed to come
to terms with who her parents were and what they had
done to their children, was still struggling with the problem she and Connie Skillman identified in the immediate
aftermath of the murders: her guilt at having been freed
at the expense of the rest of her family.

By conscious design, Jody aligned her psychic quest of
understanding the murders and reintegrating herself with
the crowning demand of graduation from Georgetown,
the school she'd chosen as an emblem of transcending
her past. But she didn't feel she could write a thesis about
the murder of her family without the perspective of her
brother, with whom she'd had no contact since the conclusion of his trial in late 1984. After a silence of seven
years, she wrote Billy a tentative first letter from the relative safety of the East Coast and the psychic armature
represented by Georgetown, describing her studies and
offering the diplomatic opinion that people could, with
time and effort, change. In this initial letter, she explained
her failure to communicate with him by saying she assumed he hated her, a trick of projection in that the truth
was closer to her hating him. It was a careful communication, a little stiff and formal for an exchange between
siblings. She signed it, "Your sister, Jody."

"Let me start by saying that I never hated you," Billy
answered, "in fact I love you very much. I was mad at
you for a while but now I understand what it must have
been like for you. I don't blame you for anything. . . . For
about three years I've been studying college psychology."
From the vantage of his raised consciousness, he assured
her that while he "used to feel hate for mom and dad,"
he now understood their suffering enough to feel "love

and sorrow" for them. I read the letter long before I see Billy's expression when he shrugs the clinging specters of his parents off his shoulders, but even without my having witnessed that look of abhorrence, the claim strikes me as unconvincing and must have thrown the rest of the letter into doubt, discouraging Jody from any hope she might receive genuine information that hadn't been filtered through her brother's perspective, which was very different from her own. Jody tells me she has found Billy's many communications to her as false as were her few letters to him. If his rationales were "delusional," her words had been "cold, calculated . . . exuding approximations of real desires for a visit, a long-overdue reckoning with the past."

"I hope you are doing well," Billy tried again. "Lately, I've been going to college full time, so I've been staying pretty busy." This second letter was shorter, his longhand effortful. Without a single mistake, it appears to have been first written and then copied out perfectly. "Remember I miss you and love you very much," he closed. "Sincerely yours, Billy. P.S. please write soon."

"There are many questions I would like to ask you," Jody wrote back. "I would like to know your opinions about our life at home before what happened." After a brief description of her studies at Georgetown—"history mostly"—she returned to the topic of the murders, again obliquely.

"Grandma Mitchell is very sad and she really wants to know from you why you did it. She asks me about you all the time. She says she doesn't remember anyone hurting you and she asks me all the time why?

"What do you want me to tell her?"

BILLY WON'T TALK ABOUT BECKY, NOT REALLY. She's a hole in the conversation, in all our conversations. Whenever I steer us back to her, he avoids the fact of her murder so nimbly that I am not sure how he does it: a sleight of speech rather than of hand, not conscious. I don't think he could be so deft if he were trying consciously to avoid the topic. One minute we're talking about Becky, or I think we are, and the next Billy is reminiscing about a dog his family once owned, a dachshund he calls Sugar, who somehow insinuates herself into our dialogue at the point where Becky vanishes. Or I think we're talking about Becky when, without transition, we're talking about martial arts, or graphic novels, or his mother's interest in horror movies.

Driving back from the prison to the town of Ontario, traffic moving slowly along the snow-choked highway, I'm trying to understand how this happens when I remember what an eye surgeon once told me. Laser repairs to the retina can leave holes in restored vision, blank areas that don't trouble a patient because his mind fills them in reflexively. Within a week of the surgery, the patient is no longer aware of any lacunae in his field of vision; he can't find them even if he looks for them. Soon he forgets there's something he isn't seeing. I wonder if Billy's avoiding responsibility for his sister's death doesn't represent a similar capacity. A psychic rather than physical reflex, it would—like the eye-brain adaptation—result from his need to create coherence, a picture he can accept, with the side effect of impairing his moral vision.

Because it's not that Billy refuses outright to talk about Becky; that would be less unsettling. Nor is it that he won't describe the circumstances of her death. But he can't answer my question of what it's like to live with the understanding that he killed his little sister, or of how that immense fact, qualitatively different from the murder of his abusive parents, affects him, both in the moment and over the years. Becky is a hole in our conversations because she's a hole in his vision. Before he can consider this blank place his mind has filled it in. One day it's a little dog. The next, when I return us to the same landscape, something else will stumble or be pushed into the hole, another animal most likely. Billy talks about animals a lot, perhaps because he knows I have a dog and three cats and assumes pet ownership is an interest we share. Perhaps because, in the context of the murders he committed, he wants to be perceived as a man who loves animals, removing himself from the group of killers whose heartlessness is confirmed by a history of cruelty to animals.

Frustrated by my failure to engage Billy in a conversation about the sister he killed, I write to him in October 2006, almost a year after my visit, asking directly, as I haven't before in a letter, if he ever thinks about Becky. "I want to know whether or not she pops into your head, and if she does, in what way?"

The letter I receive in answer explains that Billy writes for children because of Becky. Always "good at making up stories on the spot," he alludes to having told his little sister bedtime stories. "I only wish Becky were still alive so she could hear my new stories," he writes. "She would have enjoyed them."

Aside from his having sidestepped the cause of her death—"I only wish I hadn't killed Becky" would be a more honest wish—were she alive, Becky would be thirty-two and long past bedtime stories. Billy's suggestion that his dead sister inspires his children's books strikes me as too conveniently sentimental, a veil drawn before a blank place, a way to fill in one of those holes in his vision.

But I've seen Billy's stories, their careful illustrations and neatly lettered text. I know he invests a great deal of himself in them for some child—not Becky, I suspect, but the little boy he once was, the one who was afraid at bedtime and who would be comforted by stories suggesting that when humans failed him, animals would not. It may be that Billy's refusal to write for adults is part of a larger refusal, a way of resisting the court's verdict of guilt imposed on a child, a badly mistreated child whom it mistook for a man. I wonder if this isn't the context in which to receive Billy's assertion that I haven't interviewed him but conducted a séance with someone who has been dead for more than twenty years. If Billy's life stopped in 1984, then he never got to grow up and become a man.

In December, Billy's Christmas card arrives. It's homemade, as was the one he sent in 2005, a drawing of Santa Claus in his workshop, a reindeer licking his cheek. Santa, who judges whether children are good or bad and rewards them accordingly. Santa, whose fall from truth to fiction caused the seven-year-old Billy to question the existence of any God at all.

On the floor, at Santa's black-booted feet, sits a peculiarly alert and vigilant-looking baby, with rod-straight posture and unnaturally large and staring eyes, wearing a banner that proclaims the year 2007. Atypical as this baby appears—unlike a Gerber or a Pampers baby, unlike any generic or idealized vision of babyhood—I can't see him as the baby new year. After filing Billy's greeting card in the binder in which I keep our correspondence, I flip back to an earlier communication from Billy that includes one of his prison compositions. "Our Wonderful Baby" is its title. "You're the incarnation of the love between your mother and father," it declares. "We will need several lives to unfold all the love we have for you."

The longer I consider Billy's card, the more it strikes me as a wishful self-portrait, one that looks toward rebirth, eyes wide open. Or it looks backward, perhaps, to a time younger than memory, his future like that of any other child, unknown.

BY THE SUMMER OF 1992, JODY, WHO HAD earned all the credits Georgetown required to grant her a bachelor's degree, had yet to turn in her thesis. "Death Faces," the project she'd designed as a means of putting herself back together was itself in pieces, and would remain so until she managed to put another few thousand miles and an ocean between her and her hometown. Having met Serge, a man she describes as "blond, foreign, and an aristocrat," terms that remind me of a Harlequin romance hero, she followed him to Spain, and from December 1992 through November 1994 shared an apartment in Madrid with friends. She got a job writing for *Guidepost* and *Lookout,* both English-language magazines for English-speaking people living abroad, and despite conflicts with Serge's parents, whose disapproval ultimately destroyed their relationship, she would remember her two years in Europe as the happiest she'd yet experienced, the point at which she felt she'd arrived at "normalcy."

"It was completely liberating," she tells me. "Richard Wright spoke of the corpse of slavery being around his neck, and that when he moved to Paris it was cast off. There's something about being in a different culture where no one knows you. Suddenly I wasn't the girl whose family was murdered, I was Jody, a college graduate and budding writer, finding my way. And I learned that with each year that passed, I wasn't judged for my family or my childhood, but by what I did every day and the quality of my relationships and breadth of experiences."

Less burdened by her history than ever before, Jody felt she had the required distance to face the task she'd set herself: writing the story of what she called her re-birth, which she would title with a reference to something she'd seen in the religious art all around her: "that brief look in the eyes and the lines of the mouth when the victim . . . accepts death as a portal to Heaven or Hell." In that the focus of "Death Faces" was the murder of her family, the death faces she was determined to see were those only one person could conceivably have seen— Billy. The only way she could confront, assimilate, and hopefully move past the murders was to use her brother's eyes, to become Billy, at least on the page, and take responsibility for the murders her brother committed.

"You've made the caracture [*sic*] Billy very despicable and seedy," Billy wrote to Jody after reading "Death Faces," which is, in fact, a sympathetic rendering of her brother, justifying his crimes as a response to the "atrocities" he suffered. By the time he received a copy of the thesis, which he told Jody his lawyer had been "hiding" from him "to protect [his] feelings," Billy had been at work for years on his own family history, undertaken for legal rather than psychic purposes.

"Dear Person," Billy wrote to Jackson County's Children's Services Division on November 15, 1991, requesting his case files. "I am presently attempting to conduct a psychological evaluation of my family's past," he explained in a painstakingly crafted, handwritten letter. His formal schooling over, he'd embarked on a curriculum of his own devising, one that allowed him to revisit the murders as part of a larger history of child abuse and its impact on human personality. Armed with the knowledge that the murders he committed shared a pattern of antecedents with other parricide cases, by the time he prepared his affidavit, in 1996, he knew which aspects of his childhood to underscore and how to present them to his advantage.

Free from the calculation that shapes a story told for legal use, "Death Faces" is a creative work in which

Jody took risks that she did not when providing an official account of the past. Identifying the murders as the event that "triggered" her rebirth, Jody could voice a fear that they represented a consummation between her and her brother: a bloody consummation of hatred rather than of love, but a generative force nonetheless. To own her new life, she had to own the act that gave it to her, taking her place not just beside her brother—that wasn't enough—but *inside* her brother, slipping for a moment into his silhouette, trying on his history, his burdens, his fears. His violence. Or maybe it had been their violence, an emotion she'd entrusted to him.

For Jody, so invested in control, the idea of exploring the most disastrous outcome of uncontrolled rage must have been—I was going to say horrible, but perhaps it was irresistible—necessary. A way to both own and disown what she felt. A way to explore on the page what she couldn't allow into her life. Hidden behind the mask of Billy, in defense of his murders and her anger, Jody could reveal her anxiety about being judged herself, and express compassion for her brother, as she hadn't been able to do in the courtroom. Her defense is impassioned, and righteous:

"We [not Billy and Jody but Billy and others who commit parricide] killed our parents because it was the only way for us to live with any dignity, the sole method to escape atrocities which society refused to recognize, measure or remedy, and most of all, to find the singular route open to us to achieve personal autonomy, relevant sanity and 'justice' worthy of the name. . . . To fail to try to understand me, or to have compassion for me, is to close yourself to the most unknowable chambers in the souls of your own children." To fail to try to understand would be to close herself to the possibility of ever finding the part of her that was out of reach and unknowable.

Curiously, given his generally harsh portrayal of Billy and his opinion that Jody was too eager to accept blame that wasn't hers, it was Thad Guyer who suggested Jody narrate the story from her brother's point of view. "Jody called me from Spain, panicking," he tells me. "She couldn't finish her thesis, she didn't know what to do, how to do it. So I flew to Madrid." It wasn't that Jody didn't have enough material, but her copious notes lacked coherence. The story of the murders was still fractured, its parts unassembled and out of sequence, "unprocessed," a psychotherapist might say.

Thad had always insisted that Jody separate herself from the brother he considers an irredeemable sociopath. Unwilling to see Jody's anger at her parents as anything more significant than an adolescent phase, he doesn't believe her mother and father were deserving of hatred—at least this is how he characterizes them to me when we meet. But on another occasion, when alluding to the murders in a communication to Jody, to my surprise he calls them "probably . . . an act of brotherly love." Might Thad have understood and intended the psychic impact of Jody assuming Billy's guilt? Did he imagine it might demonstrate her innocence to her in a way that nothing else could? Whether or not it was a calculated suggestion, Thad told Jody he thought she'd have to circumvent her narrative problem by using Billy's point of view. "I don't think you're capable of telling this from first person," he said.

Which was true. She didn't know her point of view. But she couldn't tell the story from Billy's point of view either, not really, so "Death Faces" became the disturbing account that it is, one in which the narrator is neither Billy nor Jody but a being who existed, if it ever existed, for only as long as a car ride and a game of cards, brother and sister sprung together from the trap of their miserable childhood and yet to separate into accuser and accused.

An impossible creature who existed in the fracture of time, between before and after.

EARLY IN 2007, JODY E-MAILS ME. SHE'LL BE IN New York on the weekend of February 23 for the Armory Show, the annual contemporary art fair, and wonders if we might want to take the opportunity to get together. In the ensuing exchange we stray onto the topic of the annual New York City Tattoo Convention, held in May in the Roseland Ballroom, and from the Tattoo Convention we arrive at Jody's own tattoo, which I've never seen.

"It's the Batman symbol, on my hip," she tells me, "completely hidden by a bikini."

"Batman?" I type quickly, hoping that Jody remains online, eager to see if my guess is correct. "Because of his backstory?"

She replies with one word: "Yep."

Unlike all the other superheroes, Batman has no supernatural gifts. He is the mask of Bruce Wayne, who witnessed the murder of his parents when he was a boy. Both trauma and—more significantly—transformation, the psychic violence of the experience inspired him to cultivate intellectual and physical prowess and, with his original identity disguised, use his abilities to fight crime.

For Jody, one answer to her family's destruction has been to make sure that loss isn't waste. Georgetown, the university she chose because it was Thad's alma mater, the destination that represented both her ambition and her psychic recovery, is an institution that stresses the importance of working to achieve social justice. A Jesuit school, its graduates are charged to use their personal resources for the greater good of society. In the university's own words, "Our students are encouraged not only to study but also to reflect, and through an understanding of the world, to prepare for lives of leadership and service."

After the murders—not immediately, but as a college graduate who had recovered enough to analyze what had happened to her—Jody applied her intimate perspective on family violence to whatever causes it might benefit. She spoke about the roots and effects of violence at a federation of American Clubs in Europe, spoke publicly about a past that she had never willingly shared before, incorporating what she'd learned working for a crisis help line in Madrid. Back home, in the United States, she wrote a column on human rights abuses for Equality Now. She became the chief of staff for President Clinton's National Campaign Against Youth Violence and is on the board of Fight Crime: Invest in Kids and Witness Justice's Survivors Taking Action network. In the wake of national media attention to a parricide in rural Ohio on May 29, 2005, she wrote a piece for the Sunday *Outlook* section of *The Washington Post*, examining the consequences for the one survivor of eighteen-year-old Scott Moody's killing spree, his fifteen-year-old sister, Stacy, whom he shot but didn't kill. Here is an excerpt from what she wrote:

> I knew that only a handful of people, myself among them, could shed light on some of the daunting challenges [Stacy] may face if she survives her physical wounds. The psychic wounds take much longer to heal and require a lot of arduous work. But first, she must survive the day-to-day. She'll have to overcome depression and despair, complete and utter alienation—and guilt. Personal and profound, the trademark tattoo of the sole survivor, that guilt will

sometimes be overwhelming. Why didn't she see what he was planning? What could she have said or done to prevent it? She will spend years looking into the abyss, ever searching for the answer. I know, because that's what I did. . . . Often survivors are told to behave as normally as possible, to do what we would normally do. But there is no normal anymore. There is only before and after.

In answer to the "trademark tattoo" of guilt that only she can see, Jody has branded herself with a different, an opposite and counteracting, trademark tattoo.

Batman uses all his resources, his mental acuity and physical training, his wealth and his inventiveness, and above all his strength of will, to fight crime and avenge its victims. His reborn self is the fulfillment of the human capacity for goodness.

"The Jesuits taught me well that giving back is . . . a path to peace in times of turmoil," Jody writes to me in an e-mail dated September 16, 2007. A few days later we meet after having not seen each other for some time, months during which I've been immersed in a past she has, remarkably, left behind. She hasn't forgotten it or escaped its fallout, but she has left it behind. She isn't the girl in the car that won't move, trapped at the scene of her family's murder. Instead she's married to an artist, enjoying work, friends, travel. She's something no one could have predicted: a happy, productive human being.

"There was a time when I felt like the soldier in *All's Quiet on the Western Front*," Jody tells me, "the one whose feet have been blown off and he doesn't realize that he is running on stumps to get away. That was me for fifteen years. It hasn't been for many years since."

FOR A LONG TIME I UNDERSTAND MY PURSUIT OF the Gilleys' tragedy as driven by my identification with the two older of the family's children: with Jody, in whom I saw an outline of my better self, intelligent and capable, with the integrity and force of will to survive the wreck of her family; then with Billy, whom I allowed to represent the wounded and murderously angry child that I was, a child who masked her internal derangement with good grades and obedience. If I recognize a symbiosis between the two siblings, I also see their reflection of my own split self.

To identify with Jody or Billy is easy for me. It takes longer to understand that I find myself in Becky as well. Her silence is useful here. Becky is dead; she can't, like Jody and Billy, assert her own personality and show me the ways we differ. Confined to the dimensions, only two, of a photograph or a Xeroxed homework assignment, she offers me a surface that her living siblings don't, upon which my projections go unchallenged.

A child who refuses to accept his parents' cruelty and who takes revenge.

A child who escapes into books and academic achievement.

An innocent child sacrificed in the family destruction that the angry child demands.

I've lived as all three of these children. In my unconscious life, timeless, not linear, I remain these three selves. For the part of me I identify with Jody, the self I think of as the high-functioning survivor, the story of the Gilleys is less a tragedy than a blood-soaked fairy tale. In the end, the cruel parents have been dispatched. In the end, though the innocent child had to die, the murderous one was locked away forever and the one with the talent to survive was given her chance.

ACKNOWLEDGMENTS

The author wishes to thank Jody Arlington, Alisyn Camerota, Rachelle Cox, Billy Gilley, Thad Guyer, Chris Quigley, Connie Skillman, and Valerie Smith for their willingness to be interviewed for *While They Slept*. Jody, in particular, endured what I consider was a series of "forced marches" through her past. It is testimony to her commitment to this project that by the time the book was completed, she no longer considered the term a hyperbole.

Thanks to Dylan Brock for his research assistance; to Janet Gibbs for all she has taught me; to Joan Gould and Gila Sand for reading; to my husband, Colin Harrison, and to our children, Sarah, Walker, and Julia, for their patience with untimely dinners, unfolded laundry, and forgotten errands. Thank you, too, Julia, for the hundreds of quiet hours of drawing and reading on the floor of my study.

I'm grateful, as always, to Kate Medina, for her thoughtful (tenacious!) editing, and to Amanda Urban, for her guidance and support. Thanks also to Beth Pearson, Abigail Plesser, Robin Rolewicz, Jennifer Smith, and Evan Stone.

A NOTE FROM JODY
ARLINGTON

Several organizations that help victims and prevent violence are mentioned in *While They Slept*. Had any such resource been able to connect with my family, the deaths of my parents and sister might have been prevented. A portion of the proceeds of this book will go toward these groups, which do great work and are worthy of your support. I have included Head Start, because it is where I learned to read, among my most cherished early memories.

CHILDREN'S DEFENSE FUND
25 E Street NW
Washington, DC 20001
800-233-1200
www.childrensdefense.org

FIGHT CRIME: INVEST IN KIDS
1212 New York Avenue NW, Suite 300
Washington, DC 20005
202-776-0027
www.fightcrime.org

NATIONAL CRIME PREVENTION COUNCIL (NCPC)
2345 Crystal Drive, Fifth Floor
Arlington, VA 22202
202-466-6272
www.ncpc.org

NATIONAL HEAD START ASSOCIATION (NHSA)
1651 Prince Street
Alexandria, VA 22314
703-739-0875
www.nhsa.org

NATIONAL ORGANIZATION FOR VICTIM ASSISTANCE (NOVA)
Courthouse Square
510 King Street, Suite 424
Alexandria, VA 22314
703-535-NOVA
www.trynova.org

RAPE, ABUSE & INCEST NATIONAL NETWORK (RAINN)
2000 L Street NW, Suite 406
Washington, DC 20036
800-656-HOPE
www.rainn.org

SASHA BRUCE YOUTHWORK
741 Eighth Street SE
Washington, DC 20003
202-547-7777
www.sashabruce.org

WITNESS JUSTICE
PO Box 475
Frederick, MD 21705-0475
800-4WJ-HELP
www.witnessjustice.org